# PRESIDENT ADEN ABDULLA

## HIS LIFE & LEGACY

x Shukri Fiican

With my best wishes

Mohamed

London 19/07/2025

# PRESIDENT ADEN ABDULLA HIS LIFE & LEGACY

MOHAMED ISSA TRUNJI

Looh Press
2023

**LOOH PRESS.**

First Edition, First Print May 2023


**PRINTED & DISTRIBUTED BY**
Looh Press Ltd.
56 Lethbridge Close
Leicester, England. UK
www.LoohPress.com
LoohPress@gmail.com
A catalogue record of this title is available from the British Library.

***Cover design & typeset by***: Looh Press
***Printed & bounded by***: TJ Books. Cornwall, England.

**ISBN:**
978-1-912411-61-0 (Paperback)
978-1-912411-62-7 (Hardback)

# Contents

# PUBLISHERS NOTE

Dear readers,

It is our pleasure to introduce readers to an extraordinary biography that will capture the imagination of history enthusiasts. This is the groundbreaking book "President Aden Abdulla: His Life & Legacy" by Mohamed Issa Trunji. This meticulously researched book offers a comprehensive and fascinating insight into the personal and political life of the legendary figure who played a pivotal role in Somalia's emergence as an independent African nation. As the reader progresses throughout the biography, he is exposed to Abdulla's unwavering commitment to the independence of Somalia and his efforts to establish a progressive political system in his native land. The book takes readers through Somalia's tumultuous history, including the colonial era and the struggle for independence.

First of its kind, what sets this biography apart from others is the rich and diverse sources the author draws from. These include Aden Abdulla's personal diary and official government communications that provide a rare glimpse into the man, and his politics and social milieu. These materials, which have never before been fully considered in a published work, offer a fascinating and unique insight into Somalia's character and political upheaval during his presidency. The diary was written in Italian, a language Abdulla was fluent in. It detailed his innermost thoughts and feelings on political matters and personal struggles. The diary is a rich and valuable resource for historians. It provides readers with a rare and intimate view of the man at the centre of Somalia's political landscape. Writing this biography was not without its challenges. The most significant hurdle was translating and interpreting Italian diary notes. The diary deciphering was a time-consuming process, something the author details in his description. It is a significant contribution to the study of the independence struggle in the African continent and we are sure it will prove of immense value to scholars, historians, students and general readers alike.

Sincerely,
Mohammed Abdullah Artan
Founder & Directing Manager of Looh Press
May, 2023

# AUTHOR'S INTRODUCTION

Of all the memories of my youth in Belet Uen, none is more vivid in my memory than the image of Aden Abdulla in his small shop in the town, busy with a typewriter on his desk. It was one of the rare occasions on which I accompanied my mother to the town's commercial district. To reach the centre of the town from the family home, on the outskirts, we crossed a narrow wooden bridge popularly known as *Buundo Liiqliiqato* [Swinging Bridge] which hung over the Shabelle River, linking the town's eastern and western quarters.

That day, presumably in 1951, for some reason, I slipped away from my mother's side and ended up in front of a small shop, one of many on a street corner. To my utter surprise, my eyes fell upon a light-skinned man, wearing eye glasses, busy typing away with a typewriter which sat on a table in front of him. After overcoming the initial hesitation, I ventured into the shop, anxious for a glimpse of the man and what he was doing with the machine. Although I knew nothing about him—not even his name—the image of the man and the gadget he had in front of him would leave a lasting impression on me and only later would I come to know about him through his three children, who became my peers at the government-run local primary school in the town.

Decades later, after this chance encounter, the man would become one of the most memorable politicians of his generation, distinguished not only by the height of the offices he held, President of both the Legislative Assembly and later the new-born Republic, but also by the nature of his conduct while in office, staying clear of the excesses and pitfalls to which many of his colleagues fell victim.

My own first direct contact with him would come later, in 1968, by which time he had become, by virtue of having been President of the Republic, the 124th Member of Parliament, in addition to its 123 elected members, after losing the presidential contest a year earlier. At that time I was an employee attached to the Office of the Presidency [*Ufficio di Presidenza*] of the Somali National Assembly (or the Parliament), where I was one of the interpreters tasked with interpreting the speeches of the deputies, delivered on the Assembly floor in Somali, into Italian, verbatim, so that the minutes of the proceedings could be kept because an official orthography for the Somali language had not yet been adopted.

The former President expressed delight when I recited some passages of a speech he delivered at a state banquet hosted by the Mayor of Rome for him during a state visit in Italy five years earlier, where he had astonished his Italian hosts by giving an extemporaneous after dinner speech in faultless Italian (while they relied on notes), a fact which had been picked up and widely reported in the Italian media. My second unplanned contact with him occurred in early 1980s in the Mogadiscio office of his elder son, Engineer Abdulkadir. That was a brief encounter, in the course of which he enquired about the people he knew in earlier days in Belet Uen. That would be the last time I saw him.

Although he had but five years of formal education, owing to the dismal education opportunities at the time, he rose to become one of the most literate Somalis by the early 1940s. His familiarity with the Italian language was matched by few in the colony and this, coupled with his wide reading in world affairs, soon established him as one of the most politically aware members of his generation. This brought him to the attention of others, winning him recommendations for the different offices he held, often at the insistence of others and not his own.

He was one of a handful of leading political figures who, despite their limited academic credentials and political experience, succeeded in bringing the country to independence and unity in 1960. Today, the east African state is torn asunder by internal conflicts destroying a state that existed for but three decades. At no point since 1991, when the military regime was overthrown by rebels, has Somalia had a government worthy of the name.

As leader of the Somali Youth League, from 1954 to 1959, he emerged as an able administrator who sought and championed the cause of the centre ground, striving to unite the party's desperate factions – factions many believed were tearing the party apart. He became known for his encyclopaedic knowledge of the parliamentary rules and procedure which permitted him to perform his duties successfully, including in his tenure as President of the Legislative Assembly in the late 1950s. With independence in 1960, he was elected provisional Head of State, winning a six-year term in the presidential election held in the following year. Although many of his peers shared his humble beginnings, the story of his rise to the highest office in the land is a remarkable and notable one, particularly in the way he met and overcame episodes of adversity and hardship of different natures from his earliest days.

The second President of the Somali Republic, Abdirashid Ali Sharmarke, in a radio address to the nation on 1 July 1967, referred to his predecessor as the Father of the Nation. Although the Parliament too conferred the title of the Father of the Nation upon him, he never courted or delighted in titles. When he made a mistake, he apologised. In reading his speeches, one is struck by his honesty about his own personal and political shortcomings. The public never had a chance to fully appreciate his extraordinary leadership qualities until many years after he left office. His stature grew with the passage of time and most of today's generation finds it incomprehensible that Somali leaders of such high calibre existed in recent history.

As Head of the State, he crystallized the power of the presidency as a part of the government's three branches, able to exercise authority when necessary, but also able to accept the balance of power inherent in the parliamentary system. Two essential qualities distinguished him from the rest of his fellow party members: firstly, he was above the feuding factions within the ruling party and, secondly, he scorned the corrupt practice of buying votes, such as in the two presidential elections he contested in 1961 and again six years later. On a number of occasions, he alienated many leading political figures with whom he might otherwise worked closely. He did not go for easy populism. For him decency, politeness and respect for others, even if someone disagreed with him, were fundamental values.

The meticulous journal he kept during his years in office are much more than just the personal reflections of a political leader but serves as a rich chronicle of a period of modern Somali history. He produced an entry for each day, usually a page in length, clear and handwritten with few portions crossed out. It details activities including meetings, briefings, press conferences, telephone calls, never neglecting an entry (even when he was on a mission abroad). The diaries, handwritten in Italian language, are kept in the custody of his family. Devoid of vanity and self-congratulation in the diaries, there is a note of despair throughout his writing about the political behaviour displayed by some of his close colleagues with whom he often clashed over government business.

In June 1967, after seven years in office, he turned over the government to his successor and returned to Shalambod, determined to live his last years as a simple gentleman farmer. His friends had expected him to lead them into the 1974 presidential election, seeking a second full term after maintaining his phenomenal personal popularity for seven years. But President Aden decided he couldn't see through another term, feeling that he had "used all the gas in the tank", and it was time to go.

In general terms, Somalia enjoyed a remarkable political stability during his tenure; but his achievements had been squandered by an old weakness at the heart of the Somali politics. Yet Somalia possessed a longstanding tradition of electoral politics and consensus-seeking that has facilitated his vision of a community moving into the modern world in harmony and respect of human rights. The boy who was orphaned at the age of ten, who later joined the liberation movement of his country, died at hospital in Nairobi, Kenya, surrendered by his family members. His death at the age of 98 years robed Somalia of one of its most distinctive public servants in more than thirty years. President Aden, the last of the founding fathers of modern Somalia, was buried in Mogadiscio in a state funeral. News of his death, on June 6, 2007, was met with an outpouring of tributes from around the world.

Given the recent appearance of biographies about or by Somali political leaders, one might ask why another such account. This seeks to differentiate it in a number of ways. Firstly, it is not an exercise in hagiography. Since the subject's long life coincided with almost the entire twentieth century—a turbulent period in his nation's history—the account will be used to illustrate the different stages or episodes in that era. Since the emerging literature of life memoirs, however welcome, represents a light sprinkling, there is still much more that could be said in this field. Indeed, close attention will be paid to the personalities, temperaments, places and scenarios the subject encountered throughout his life, helping to reconstruct a recent but an seemingly distant past, which can sometimes seem inconceivable. Tracing the protagonist's early peripatetic years, which he spent in menial jobs in Huddur, Baidoa, Mogadiscio and Jenale, an attempt will be made to depict the condition prevailing in those places at the time, which, apart from the national capital, have hitherto received little treatment. These descriptions will be based on personal recollections as well as sources (mainly in Italian and Somali), where available.

Section one of the book is organised chronologically, tracing the subject's life. Part one covers his early experiences, including joining the colonial administration in Mogadiscio in the late 1920s. Part two examines Aden Abdulla's entry into politics in the 1940s, particularly his involvement with the leading political movement at the time, the Somali Youth League (SYL), the evolution of the political institutions including the Legislative Assembly created in 1956, and the role he played in its evolution as its elected President. Part three, considers his tenure as the President of the Republic over the seven year period, 1960-67. Part four looks at Aden Abdulla's lukewarm attitude for re-election versus his competitor's vibrant election campaign. It looks also in his refusal to buy votes in exchange for vote, and the peaceful and smooth manner he passed over the power to his democratically elected successor.

Part five looks the time he vacated the presidential palace and adopted the life a gentleman farmer and his involvement with the Parliament over next two years as member of Parliament elected by right as former President of the Republic. Part six discusses the time he spent under detention, with the military takeover of power of October 1969 as well as the nature of his activities over the next few decades. Part seven traces his later life, from the time he vacated the presidential palace and adopted the life of a gentleman farmer. It will also explore the manner in which he returned to the public eye—firstly, involuntarily, through his arrest with former colleagues from politics with the military takeover of power in October 1969 as well as his later involvement in efforts to save Somalia from the brink in 1990, particularly by mediating between the government (then on its last legs) and the opposition.

Owing to the fact that most recent history remains unattested to by records—most of them either lost or destroyed in the civil war or it having evaded documentation in the first place—this study makes use of relevant extant material. This including government documents, newspapers (both domestic and international), transcripts of radio broadcasts and audio-visual material, in order to build a rounded image not only of the subject, his contemporaries but also the period.

This study is also informed by the President's personal diary, which he maintained in the critical years of 1957-69, when he served as President of the Legislative Assembly and later President of the Republic. It is in the entries of the earlier years that Aden Abdulla vividly recounts the experiences of his youth, starting from the time he travelled with his father from Belet Uen to Huddur and from there Baidoa. There is no clear indication in the accounts what prompted him to keep a journal or indeed whether he had a particular audience in mind. It is clear that in his wide reading, he was familiar with political leaders in Africa and Asia, like Mahatma Gandhi, whose habit of producing meticulous and prodigious records provides an intimate insight into his public and personal struggles.

Having served in the domestic staff of a number of, admittedly junior, Italian colonial administrators, it is possible that he observed their practice of keeping such records or sending and receiving reports from their home country. Similarly, there was also a tradition of Italians and other Europeans who traversed the Somali country, often acting as scouts ahead of colonial incursion, who kept records of their observation of life in the area, some of which were subsequently edited and published.

Despite the mystery around their genesis, Aden Abdulla's tomes nevertheless cover all aspects of his time in office, focusing on official business with brief snippets on items of personal concern. Amounting to about a page of handwritten sheet produced each day, the carefully-crafted logs cover practically all his interactions, from meetings, briefings, press conferences, telephone calls (never neglecting event to produce an entry while on an official mission abroad) as well as his forthright take on the disagreements within the party, constitutional matters as well as events of national and international concern.

Taken together, the detailed accounts—whether they cover the colonial period or the post-independence one—provide a nuanced picture of a century, understanding of which still tends to easy simplification and caricature.The diaries, and thus the narrative, begins in Aden Abdulle's earliest days—after his birth in a village outside Belet Uen, the loss of his mother soon after and the departure of his father to join the Dervish movement of Sayyidka. Returning to find all of the family's wealth, primarily livestock, liquidated in the repeated advances made by the forces of Sultan Ali Yousuf, the ruler of Obbia, against the civilian population in El Qurun and the surrounding areas, Aden Abdulla's father was faced with a dilemma: either to remain in the area or go in search of better fortune and stability elsewhere.

Opting for the latter, father and son soon found hospitality among pastoralists, unaffiliated to them by clan, who hired the father as a herdsman, challenging notions of hard, untraversable borders which existing accounts suggest separated Somali clans before and even after the advent of colonialism. In the recollections of the colonial period too, despite the infamy of the fascist regime for its cruelty and brutality, one finds examples of a few good administrators in its ranks, marked by their relative sympathy and mildness with the colonial subjects.

Distinguished by their frankness and level of detail, the subsequent accounts of the 1950s—a crucial period in the development of Somali political culture when the former colony of Italian Somaliland was under a UN-mandated, Italian tutelary administration, *L'Amministrazione fiduciaria italiana della Somalia*—provide a compelling portrait of the challenges encountered by the country and the administering authority, which had ten years to prepare for independence in 1960. Taken with the description in the diaries of the immediate post-independence years from the vantage point of the President of the Republic, this study seeks to reassess the some of the prevailing impressions of that period and specifically its leaders.

Instead of casting judgement on the personalities of the time, this study suggests a new way of interpreting the different political persuasions and orientations prevalent at the time. Rather than defining different leaders on a spectrum based on their perceived ethicalness, uprightness and nationalist spirit—as both popular perceptions and even the literature tend to do—this study will propose that different vying camps and their members can be better understood on the basis of their ideas, methodology and leadership style. Using the analytical lens of leadership style theories to understand the Somali politics of the day offers novel perspectives, raising the politics of the period to a contest of ideas rather than simply personalities and highlighting the complexity of the relationships and the circumstances which affected them.

Two temperaments in particular were prominent. On the one hand were those who assumed what could be called an *idealist* disposition. Such leaders believed in the power of ideas, clinging firmly to a few strongly held ones and focused their time on communicating a vision and trying to inspire others with their beliefs. Others possessed what might be characterised as a *pragmatist* outlook—although they too held to certain values and principles, they nevertheless paid greater attention to the environment and situation in which they were operating. Keenly aware of the immediate challenges in their path, they therefore thought deeply about how to achieve their objectives within the prevailing circumstances.

This framework can not only be used to illuminate the politics of the post-independence period (the 1960s) but also the preceding decades, stretching back to the late 1940s, when a contest emerged—ahead of the visit of the Four Power Commission to Mogadiscio in 1948 to canvass the views of the people in the former colony—between different visions of the future. Seen in this way, the aspirations expressed by different political parties and their leaders will be anchored in relation to the wider context, challenging previous interpretations which simply ascribed them to populist sentiment (in the case of the Somali Youth League delegation) or opportunism (in the case of the Conferenza and related organisations).

Equipped with such a long view, the analysis will proceed to consider how Aden Abdulla and his generation of leaders were concurrently facing problems on a number of fronts: social and economic (the shortfall in human capital accompanied by a perennial budget deficit which made rectifying the former through development projects a challenge) as well as political and cultural (the fact political institutions had not yet become established.

In this way, this study also reassesses the celebrated moment in 1967 when Aden Abdulla, defeated in the presidential election of that year, in due democratic regard for the public will, vacated his seat for his successor. Although rightly celebrated as the first such example on the continent, rather than seeing this event simply as a matter of the President's willpower, an attempt will be made to draw out its wider significance, illustrating how the President's electoral defeat had been a foregone conclusion, something which had its root in systemic problems like corruption of which he was aware. Thus, rather than being an unexpected result to which the President acquiesced on the spur of the moment was an outcome to which he had resigned himself to days and weeks in advance, not least by his unwillingness to play politics.

The narrative of Section one is complemented by a series of essays in Section two. These benefit both from the author's familiarity with the political climate of the period under study—having worked as an interpreter in the National Assembly in the five years from 1964—but also his training as a lawyer, helping to bring fresh light to some of the misconceptions that unfortunately taint understanding of that era, overshadowed as they are by the constitutionally cataclysmic events of the last few decades.

Using a close reading of the President's diary to reconstruct the nature of government in the 1960s, the first essay will illustrate how that time continues to be misconceived, not only by successive politicians in Somalia and the general public who—despite evoking the period, often dubbed the "democratic or civilian decade" in Somali circles—behave, opine or argue in disregard of it. Highlighting that misunderstanding of that period is a consequence of the political events of the intervening changeful years, the essay will suggest that this fact continues to affect, even hinder, reconstruction efforts in contemporary Somalia.

Building on the discussion of leadership styles and seeing the President as an example of a pragmatist leader, the second essay will examine a number of policy areas, notably the "missing territories" dilemma, Somalia's place within the African and Arab regional spheres and the country's involvement with multilateral organisations. Proceeding in this way, an attempt will be made to isolate a set of principles he maintained throughout his political career but more importantly, how he managed to keep to these in the changing tides of several decades where wider factors were at play.

I should like to express my thanks and gratitude to Eng. Abdulkadir Aden for making available the personal Diaries of his father, President Aden Abdulla.

I should like also acknowledge my indebtedness to Haroon Q. Mohamoud for editing an early draft of my manuscript and for providing other source material.

Mohamed Issa Trunji
May 2023
London, UK.

# SECTION 1

## PART 1

# SECTION ONE, PART ONE

# ITALIAN PENETRATION INTO SOMALIA

At the turn of the twentieth century, the Somali-inhabited expanse on the Horn of Africa into which Aden Abdulle and his generation were born stood largely undisturbed by the modern era. Unsure of itself and proceeding hesitantly, more in an attempt to keep up with its European rivals, Italy had only begun to take a serious interest in the vast swathes of land in southern Somali left untouched by the British and French who took their 'cuts' further north. At the time, although much of the Horn was under the sway of the Sultan of Zanzibar, who laid claim to extensive holdings along the east African coast, on the ground, power rested with authorities such as the sultanates.

From the late nineteenth century, the sultans began leasing coastal areas to the European colonial powers, including giving the British right to areas referred to as Jubaland, Benadir and Migurtinia. The British East Africa Company, which leased these territories from Zanzibar, transferred its holdings in the Benadir to the Italian Government in 1893. The lease was for 50 years and was transferable to commercial companies if the Italian Government so desired. In 1905, the British Government arranged that the Sultan of Zanzibar give Italy outright possession of the ports.

Further north, the Italian government had already secured alliance with the Sultan Yusuf Ali of Obbia, one of the major local rulers. He had earnt his sobriquet "Kenadid" (Insubordinate, literally "one who refuses to be reined") for challenging the authority of his cousin Boqor Osman Mohamud of the Migiurtinia Sultanate, before setting up a conquest state in Obbia. In 1888, Sultan Kenadiid signed a treaty which made his domain a protectorate of Kingdom of Italy. A year later, Boqor Osman too signed a protectorate treaty with Italy. Both rulers used their friendship with Italy to press their long-standing conflicts with the Sultan of Zanzibar and with each other. In 1892, the Italian government leased the Benadir ports of Merca, Mogadiscio, Brava and Warsheikh from the Sultan of Zanzibar, who ceded them for one down payment of 40,000 rupees plus an annual payment of 160,000 rupees.[1] The Italians were mostly interested in the ports and guarding the sea lanes through the Gulf of Aden to Suez Canal and not terribly concerned with the inland areas.

The Italian occupation can be roughly divided into three distinct period. In the first, the country was administered through chartered companies and the Italian Government had leased the area to them: the Filonardi Company, known as Royal Italian East Africa Company, from 1893–96, and the Società Anonima Commerciale Italiana del Benadir, commonly known as Società del Benadir, from 1896–1905. Besides exercising control over the ports of the Benadir coastline (Mogadiscio, Merca, Brava and Warscek), they also managed customs, taxes and mining rights. In compliance with the convention signed with the Italian government on 15 April 1896, the company had to fly the Italian flag, pay the Sultan rent, administer the subsidies to the Sultans of Migiurtinia and Obbia and apply the General Acts of Berlin and Brussels regarding slavery, alcohol and arms trading.[2] However, none of these two companies was able to make Italian Somaliland economically viable proposition. The Filonardi Company ended in financial failure, as a result of which it was unable to fulfill its obligations. In 1905 the Italian government and the Benadir Company eventually dissolved their relationship because of the company's failure to abolish slavery under the General Acts of Berlin and Brussels.

As a result of the company's failure, the second phase of colonialism began, when the Italian Government placed the colony under its direct management in 1905.[3] However, the extension of Italian influence beyond the coast of Benadir was painstakingly slow because of a lack of enthusiasm for overseas adventures on the part of Italy's parliament. Although there was some immigration by Italians to the area, this country never could absorb any sizeable number of settlers. There were only a few dozen resident Italians, all military personnel or working as civil servants and technicians.

Developments in Italy would come to have a direct bearing on the affairs of the colony, giving rise to the third and final chapter of the colonial era. In 1922, a Fascist regime came to power, power overthrowing the democratic system of government. One year after the March on Rome staged in October that year, Cesare Maria De Vecchi di Val Cismon, one of the quadrumvirs—the four appointed by Mussolini to lead it—was appointed as Governor of the colony. During his five years tenure, De Vecchi pursued a new policy designed to amalgamate all southern Somaliland, including the Sultanates of Obbia and Migiurtinia, into a single new geographical entity, called Somalia Italiana establishing the political and legislative organization of the country. In 1924, Britain ceded Jubaland and the port of Khisimaio to Italy since the latter felt that it had not received its fair share of the spoils of World War I.

Before 1927, Somalia was a conglomeration of tribal communities without central authority. The new Governor promoted the emigration, from Italy, of a few hundred settlers into the colony who produced mainly cotton until 1931, when this was replaced by bananas because of the drop in prices caused by economic depression. The banana crop was sold at subsidized prices to the State, who directly managed commercialization through an agency, the Regia Azienda Monopolio Banane (RAMB) "Royal Monopoly Banana Enterprise", created in 1935.

## El Qurun, 1908

The singular path that united Belet Uen with the village of El Qurun, about 15 kilometres to the northwest, alternated between high and low ground. The village itself was in the uplands, where the plateau slowly declined towards the Uebi Shebeli. From such heights, one could watch the surrounding areas below, inhabited by the Shaveli farmers. There were no roads, only footpaths that linked the pastures where livestock grazed. Much like the highlands of the wider region, the climate, moderately warm by day and cool by night, proved congenial for man and beast alike, in contrast to the warm lowlands.

The name of the place [Bitter Wells], spelt *El Gorum* or *El Goran* in Italian, appears to come from its plentiful supply of water, which, although brackish, may have been favoured by livestock, making it a prominent watering place.[4] Although the area was semi-arid, indicated by the gypsum deposits,[5] the land was capable of producing two annual harvests of *durra*, sorghum.

The locals, an assortment of Somali tribesmen, largely followed the way of their ancestors, a combination of animal husbandry and farming forming the primary means of economic production there. During the rainy season, which ran from April to June, and from October to November, the area provided plenty of water and grazing lands for livestock. Under the barter system, for their produce, villagers exchanged their products for food and other basic necessities available in major centers, the nearest of which was Belet Uen. Societal relations, land disputes and serious crimes were regulated in accordance with the customary law (*Heer)* and Islamic Laws. Today, after more than a century, owing to repeated mass exodus of its inhabitants to safer places within Hiran region or even to far afield as Baidoa, El Qurun has lost much of its past splendour.

Aden Abdulla was born in El Qurun to Abdulla Osman and Awrala Yousuf Dulaad.. His grandfather Osman had the nickname "Dacar". His date of birth, sometime in 1908 and 1909 is unclear, as no official birth records of natives were kept in Somalia at the time. The father, Abdulla Osman, a traditional and religious figure, yearned to have a son who could succeed him in the leadership of his clan family. The father enjoyed the status of a respected figure in his community and it is likely that his status was enhanced by his association with the Dervish movement. He was given the name Aden, a name which in Somalia was traditionally only bestowed on someone whom it was hoped would be hold a position of leadership and esteem within the society.

Abdulla had previously lost children who had been delivered as stillbirth or had succumbed to the diseases that threatened the delicate children of El Qurun. Infant mortality at the time was common in the Somali Horn but also globally, before declining markedly across the last century owing partly due to the advance of medical knowledge and improved living conditions. Indeed, one of the formulae for seeking divine protection against any scourge in the Somali language uttered almost subconsciously even by those advanced in age, continues to be, "Ilaahoow naga kori" [Oh God, let us flourish beyond its reach].

The birth took place only when the first heavy rains began in the valleys, a happy sign, in a country where the rain is always welcome. His parents both hailed from the same Udejen [Udajen] clan of the Hauia clan-family [*Sono nato a El Gurun (Belet Uen) tra il 1908 e il 1909 da Abdulla Osman Dacar e Aurala Dulcad, entrambi del Gruppo etnico somalo Udegen, rer Raghe, altrimenti Issa Mundullod Hirab*].[6] They divorced soon after his birth [*che ero in tenerissima età*] and just one month after his birth when his mother, Aurala Yousuf Dulad ("Xiirey", Udejen) died, the custody of the child was assumed by the paternal grandmother, Hawa Xerow.

When Aden Abdulla was born, Somalia was a vast limitless territory without any recognized central authority or marked borders. Prior to colonization, the Somali people existed as a culture living in a virtually stateless society. Although there was no institutionalized system of government, people had been subject to traditional authority of the clan elders. The Italian control was limited to the narrow strip of Benadir coast, between Warsheikh, to the north, and Brava to the south with the ultimate goal of establishing a colony that would be economically profitable and whose agricultural potential would attract Italian settlers.

Just before the baby's birth, his father joined the Dervish movement, led by the "Mad Mullah" who was then fighting against the British in Somaliland, though it remains unclear whether he had voluntarily joined the movement or he had been coerced into joining it as was often the case. When the father returned to El Qurun, probably around the time the Mullah's movement had been defeated by the British, he found the unexpected: the family had lost all its properties, particularly livestock, as a result of the repeated advances made by the forces of Sultan Ali Yousuf, against the civilian population of the area. It was a difficult time for Abdulla; he was caught between many worries, burdened too by the difficult choice of settling upon a safer place to which to migrate. He had the choice either to move to Belet Uen or migrate to far distant and unfamiliar areas. He opted for the latter as it seemed to offer better chances of security than Belet Uen then in the grip of the ruthless Dervish forces. The deteriorating security situation triggered a large-scale movement of communities from rural Hiiraan, in a southwesternly direction, towards areas already under Italian control.

Set some 330 km from Mogadiscio, Belet Uen [Big Town], an oasis whose iconic lovely and tall shady palm trees provided much-needed relief from the semi-desert climate,[7] grew out of an ancient settlement. Legends, from at least the fourteenth century, speak of a figure known as Gacalwaa (Lone Warrior), a leader of the Makanne, the Bantu group which originally inhabited the area. Of the two perennial rivers in Somalia, the Jubba and the Shabelle, it is the latter which meanders through the city like a serpent and supplies the water for irrigation. Rainfall has historically been concentrated in between April and May and again later in the year between October and November. These plentiful showers hit Belet Uen's fertile alluvial plains, formed of loamy and dark clay left behind by the flowing floodwater in the valley.

At the turn of the twentieth century, the entire zone was known as Hiiraan [Harvest],[8] which it acquired on account of the fertility of its fields and generosity of its farming folk, who welcomed pastoralists from the surrounding areas to reap the benefits of the season of plenty. The name itself is derived from *Hiiraamaysi* (the act of garnering crops); crops left behind in the field for the second harvest, for instance, are known as *hiiraami*, which is found in the command *Beerta soo hiiraamiya*. The word evolved from being the name of the village, which still bears it, on the outskirts of Belet Uen, which was the most productive stretch and inhabited by the Makanne, noted for their munificence. Hiiraan eventually became the name of the administrative region constituted in 1954 under the Italian Trusteeship Administration.

Sitting close to the headwaters of the Uebi Shebeli [Leopard River], which originate in the plateau in the west, Belet Uen receives the waters at their strongest, which calm further downstream as they advance into Somalia proper. Besides that, its tactical position prompted the interest of the Italians—gradually expanding their presence in the south—by taking the area for a major settlement. Receiving news of Italian designs and keen to hobble them, a contingent of Dervish forces travelled there from their principal seat in Taleeh in the north. Eager also to establish a footing in the central country, they initially set up camp in the uplands, about nine kilometres in the north-easterly direction from Belet Uen, known as Qawlat, where their local commander was Khalif Sheikh Abdulle, the Sayyid's brother and close advisor.[9]

From their temporary seat, the delegation tried to woo the locals into supporting them. They proved, however, unwilling to hand over power of their settlement and submit to the command of the Dervish invading forces. The Dervishes ended up attacking Belet Uen, managing to overcome the local forces. After they took control in 1913, Haji Mohamoud Moallim, known as "Cagadhiig" [Bloodied Feet] was appointed the commander of the garrison.[10] This period, 1910 to 1914, was an important period of expansion for the movement; two forts at Jiidali and Miashi [in the Warsangeli country] as well as Wardere and Qoraxay in the Ogaden were also realised, bringing to completion their domination in the hinterlands of the Somali peninsula.[11] The establishment of these bases followed that of their principal settlement from around 1909-10, Taleeh in the north, which superseded Eyl (or Illig), a coastal fishing village in the northeastern Nugaal area, which served that purpose in 1905-9.[12]

Around the same time, the Italian colonial government, whose penetration across the country began to reach further inward from the coastal areas in the east, settled in Mahaddei Uen, near Jowhar, before coming also to Bulo Burti, a settlement separated by Belet Uen by a one hundred and fourteen kilometre stretch. The locals found themselves caught between the two sides in the military and broader struggle between the Sayyid's and the Italian camps, both of which dealt with them punitively, claiming in each case that the residents in the areas under the respective control were partisans of the opposing camp. That said, the Dervishes did count some initial supporters among the local population, including one well-known leader Indhaceel Raage Daamey, who later had his differences with them.

At the time of the Dervishes' arrival, Belet Uen was already well fortified, with its town walls, made of stone, circling its entire extent with only one gate in its northern side known as Irida Amiin (Sanctuary Gate). The fabled walls were introduced by the Makanne community during their control of the area originally known as "Bela Weyne" [Endless Woe], owing to the frequent bloody clashes that happened between unspecified rival groups in the vicinity. Water was close by too, helpfully making unnecessary long treks for potable water in what was a now tense environment, where violence and attacks were never distant realities. The newly-arrived men took as their base an area within the town walls known as "Lamagala" [or Impenetrable], scenic high ground with a panoramic view over the river's loops across the town, building a fort—or Qalcadda Aamin—near the gate and another building in the area later known as Saldhig [Headquarters].

Young Aden was 10 years old when his family set forth and left Hiiraan. On the journey, father and son found hospitality among pastoralists belonging to the Ogaden Awlyahan, Rer Ali clan family who took the father on as a herdsman. At the beginning, their life among the nomadic clans offered some stability until suddenly, one day, while herding camels, the father was attacked by a hungry lion, leaving him maimed. Despite the horror of the attack, most damage was sustained to one mutilated knee; although its condition stabilised, the joint was left ankylosed (literally, crooked), bent upwards towards the thigh, making any movement contingent on the use of a stick on both sides and putting any physical labour out of question. In the regular moving from place to place, in search for watering points, the injured father was being left behind, but the nomads took care of him and continued providing him with nutrition and transportation. The task to carry daily a full Somali milk container, or *dhiil*, going back and forth between the ever-changing nomadic encampments and where the father was left, fell to the young boy.

The generosity of this people, otherwise unconnected to the family by the kinship ties which proved so reliable in such circumstances, left a lasting memory in the boy's mind, leading him to attempt, repeatedly in later life, to trace the whereabouts of the family who had taken them in, but with no success. Soon after his father's conditions had improved, and he was in a state to walk with sticks, they departed for Huddur, an area under effective Italian control. After a long journey, they finally arrived there, then a small settlement of grass huts with few houses in stone.

This was the first time the boy saw white people, including Arabs and Europeans, wearing strange uniform he had never seen before. He marveled at the sight of buildings made of brick and stone. In Huddur, he made friendship and spent time with group of boys of his age whose parents were either member of the local police units or engaged in petty trading. Its name suggests that Huddur—either after the word for a settlement (centre) or in reference to its white sand soil[13]—had been a nucleus for some time. Known as Hoddur Hadama or Belet Hadama, after one of the resident Mirifle clans, it was an oasis and a site where livestock were watered. An ancient treaty ensured communal access to the wells and work for digging or maintaining a new well was conducted collectively.

In 1908, a demarcation line was drawn between the Somali territories, in accordance with an Italo-Ethiopian treaty of that year, to be administered by the two, the left bank falling to the former. As Giacomo De Martino recalled, when he was appointed Governor of Somalia in 1910, the Italians' authority was effectively limited to the region between the Shabelle River and the sea, apart from a long, slim terraneous strip along the Jubba from Jumbo to Lugh.[14] Penetration into the Upper Shabelle, the vast territory now under their nominal control, became a priority for the Italians and they occupied Huddur in 1914, where a *Residenza* (the seat of District Commissioner) and a garrison was established.[15]

In order to reinforce its presence and strengthen its grip, the colonial authorities focused, for about the next eight years, on consolidating its occupation by recruiting local askaris, building defences and propping up a rudimentary administrative architecture.[16] Already stretched and unable to rely on reinforcements, the Italians sought conscious to forestall the possibility of clashes with the Ethiopians, leading to the fortification of the areas under their control. Since any attack would either have to take the riverbed of the Shabelle, target Lugh or Baidoa, two military sections were constituted, building on the existing garrisons, at Baidoa and Mahaddei Uen.

The extent of the former was defined to the north by the Lugh-Huddur line (which ran up to halfway between Huddur and Tigieglo) to the west of the Jubba in the Lugh-Bardera section and to the east by the Huddur-Tigieglo-Unale Uen stretch while the latter was defined to the north by the Bulo Burti-Tigieglo line, enclosed from the east by the Shabelle River from Bulo Burti to Balad, to the south by the Balad-to-Unale Uen line and finally to the west by the Uanle Uen-Hoddur passage. The task of the troops, with the help of local militias, was to defend their base, remain alert, prevent enemy advance and keep the local population behind the defensive lines.[17] The *Gogle*—perhaps so called by the Italians after the forces, in pre-colonial times, under the authority of chiefs and headmen—besides their role as irregular troops, also acted as district police, sometimes being deployed as in the hinterland to maintain order.[18]

The family spent some months in Huddur, before one of Aden Abdulle's paternal uncles, Habeb Osman, took the injured father on camelback to Baidoa. By the end of the decade, after the consolidation of the colony, it was divided into eight regions, including the *Commissariati Regionali* of Uebi Shebeli, headquartered at Mahaddei Uen, with District Commissioner offices in Balad, Bulo Burti, Itala (Cadale), Mahaddei and Villaggio Duca degli Abruzzi (Jowhar) and, the one of Juba, headquartered in Kisismaio, with residences in Afmedo, Bardera, Kisimaio, Jelib, Gobuin and Margherita (Jamaama). Huddur became the principal seat of the Frontier Region (or *Regione del Confine*), which had residences in Belet Uen, Dolo and Lugh. The other regions were Centro, headquartered at Merca, with residences in Afgoi Uanle, Audegle, Baidoa, Brava, Bur Acaba, Dinsor and Merca; Commissariato of Obbia, headquartered at Obbia, comprised of the districts of El Bur, Galcaio and Harardéra; Commissariato del Nogal, headquartered at Éil, with the districts of Béila and Cállis. Commissariato of Migiurtinia, headquartered at Alúla, with residences at Bargal, Bender Cassim, Candala and Hafun. Mogadiscio, constituted a Commissariato of its own, with one Residenza based in the capital.[19]

## Hoddur & Baidoa: Entering The World of Work

Unlike Hoddur, Baidoa, about 255 km from Mogadiscio, was a major centre with a larger population and offering employment opportunities. In their relocation, the family traded the environs of one river (the Scebeli) for that of the other perennial one in Somali territory, the Giuba (also known as Ganane). Located at the edge of the Magniafulka, the main central upland, before its occupation in 1913 by the Italians, it had not been a place of major settlement, the closest one being Gooyaale, a village to the south. It is easy to see what made the area so inviting. Apart from its plenty pastureland, the area's character was defined by its *Il,* or springs.[20] In the upland limestone landscape, set about 460 metres above sea level, honey-combed with caves and underground springs, it was one spring in particular, perhaps because of it formed at the intersection of two rocks which made it look like an squint, became synonymous with the area as Iscia Baidoa [the Eye of Baidoa]. The label may also be an indication of its importance to life in the natives, Isha having different meanings in the Somali language including hope, a source, etc.

Oral traditions suggest that the water source was discovered incidentally by a caravan of nomads passing by, who happened to see a *weer cad* hyena lapping up the water from the fount. News of it is likely to have reached the Italians soon after their arrival in the environs, since in the same year of their settlement there, the colonial administration dug a canal to catch the water which gushed between the limestone crevice. It was revamped for the free use of the officials and the well-off but the ordinary people were asked to pay for access or to seek water elsewhere.[21]

By the time of the family's arrival in Baidoa in c.1921, the area was under effective colonial control, the capital of the Alto Giuba [Upper Jiuba] region. In the years after the Italian arrival, it was undergoing considerable growth, soon emerging as an agricultural and commercial centre. Although the mercantile classes resident there were from different communities, most of the local population belonged to the Reewin, a clan family whose name, in their Af-Maay Somali tongue, means exactly th "The Big (i.e. Original) Family"—implying that they may have been the earliest settlers in modern Somalia (in contrast to the pronunciation Rahanweyn, "The Large Throng", common among non-locals, which instead suggests they were formed of an amalgamation of different clans, originally from the north, who settled there and through the passage of time became admixed with the earlier inhabitants).[22]

A fort was built after the occupation in 1913, which was surrounded by a wall measuring three metres high and enclosed the *uffici della Residenza* [Residence's offices] and various elements of the administration including the radiotelegraphy station, the infirmary, the operating room and pharmacy. Baidoa's gentle, genial climate and no doubt its other endearing features led it to be described, in one 1929 Italian guidebook as the Switzerland of Somalia.

The father, being unfit to perform any activities which required physical fitness because of his disability, had established a Koranic School, an informal school where children are given basic knowledge of the Koran.

Aden meanwhile struck out on his own, making a living by doing menial jobs. In fact, within days of his arrival to Baidoa, he started bustling around the military garrisons performing tasks such as preparing tea, coffee, or fetching drinking water from the spring for the "Askars". There were two military garrisons: Molinari for the century and Bongiovanni for the Artillery. The military camps were named after two Italian military officers, killed on December 19, 1907 while defending Lugh Ferrandi, a town in the southwestern Ghedo province of Somalia, from invading Ethiopian bands. He also worked as a dishwasher and waiter in *makaayado*, Somali-owned restaurants serving traditional food. It was during this period that, as a result of working longer hours in the restaurant, the young boy developed scabies that was successfully treated.

The boy became familiar with the names of the top Italian officials present in the city. The District Commissioner at the time was a certain Dr. Cavalli, with big drooping moustaches. Also based in Baidoa at the time was the Italian explorer, Captain Ugo Ferrandi, noticeable for his prosthetic leg. Ferrandi earned the reputation of heroically defending the trading and strategic location of Lugh against the increasing encroachment by Ethiopian armed bands in 1895. Public opinion looked upon the Italian incomers favourably. Perhaps because they were few in number, or because they had been sent to Somalia after a rigorous selection process, the Italians were seen as humane, not given to the extreme cruelty associated with those administrators sent to the colony in the fascist era, so much so that the local population called them "Ashraf", an Arabic word meaning noble, typically reserved as an honorific title for descendants of the Prophet Muhammad. Every Friday, for instance, the District Commissioner used to distribute alms to the poor people gathered in front of his office.

At the beginning of 1923, the boy took the big leap when he went to Mogadiscio, for the first time. He accompanied his employer, Tenant (Lieutenant) Steffan, together with his Somali partner, Fadima Hussein, in a long trip to Mogadiscio, the capital. Given the scarcity, or rather the absence of public transport at the time, the trip was made entirely on foot. Fadima was a strong and affectionate woman with whom Aden quickly bonded. This was particularly important for the lifelong emotional wellbeing of a child who lost his biological mother at a tender age. In the capital, she also arranged for his circumcision rituals according to the Islamic tradition at the house of a certain Aghid Yahia, an Eritrean serving in the Italian colonial forces, a rite of passage which is typically performed in Somali culture during childhood, anywhere from about the age of six to ten, in contrast to Arab or Jewish practice where it is carried out on the seventh or eighth day after birth respectively.

When Tenant Luigi Steffan left for Italy, on home leave, Fadima and young Aden returned to Baidoa. However, the boy, much to his chagrin, was not allowed to go with her to Bardera, her place of origin. Fearful of being separated from his only child, his father wanted him to remain under his care. Nevertheless, the return to Baidoa marked the first turning point in his life: his first introduction to school and to the teacher, Mr Tusso. Young Aden enrolled in afternoon class together with other boys of his age. The school, among the first public schools in Baidoa, encouraged his appetite for learning, which would remain with him for the rest of his life. *Ragioniere* (Accountant) Giuseppe Tusso, combined his teaching functions with that of accountant to the town's District Commissioner (hence Ragioniere). Aden remembers the teacher, by then in his early thirties, as a tall man, blond, with spectacles and goatee.

But the boy, although excelling in his studies, was faced with a predicament, being without the means or regular income which would permit him to continue his schooling. He did not shy away from sharing his worries with the schoolteacher, who appreciated his predicament and took him as a cook helper in his house, allowing him to earn some money in order to continue on at school. The young boy could take from the teacher's wallet, ten *bese* every day (singular, *besa*), the smallest unit of Italian currency in the colony then in circulation, bronze coins denominated in one, two or four *bese*. This amount of money was more than enough to buy food. The teacher, who called him "a clever lad," was early to recognize his abilities. Teacher Tusso was, in fact, the man, who first showed him that trust, which later many people would have in him and Aden is quick to credit others who helped him like Mr. Tusso in a formative period of his life. "He was very, very generous to me in my early years in Baidoa, a man I have never forgotten and will never forget".[23]

The young Aden took the required courses, focusing on Italian language in order to achieve educational qualifications required to enter in the colonial government's civil service as interpreter or clerk, positions regarded as the best profession that a Somali could obtain at the time. In the same year, young Aden visited Mogadiscio for the second time; this time in the company of Mr. Tusso who was temporarily stationed in Mogadiscio. The journey to the capital was long and difficult as the caravan took the longer route, from Baidoa, passing through Dinsor, Audegle, and Afgoi before arriving at the capital, instead of the direct route through Bur Akaba and Afgoi. Aden occasionally made the trek on horseback. During the journey, to the displeasure of everyone, the accountant's leopard, kept in a cage mounted on camel's back, mysteriously vanished when the caravan camped overnight.

In Awdegle [Patriarch of the Dighil, one of the clans of the Rahanweyn], the unexpected happened: he came across a Somali man, well dressed on horseback with stick in hand. He stared at the man totally flabbergasted; it was the first time he saw a native displaying such a position of authority. The stranger was Farah Ali Omar, a mature man, of about 25 years, serving as interpreter for the District Commissioner in Awdegle. It so happened that the boy and this man about five years his senior would work, after many years, in the same office at Shalambod as clerks and interpreters in the service of the colonial authority. Aden Abdulla and Farah had later become close friends, as both joined the Somali Youth League Party in early 1940s. Haji Farah Ali would be involved in politics in the subsequent decades, not only as a deputy but also asa minister. In the first internal, Somali-led government, introduced in 1956, Haji Farah Ali Omar would serve as Minister for Economic Affairs and a decade later, as Deputy Prime Minister, Minister for Foreign Affairs and Minister of Finance in the first Egal government (1967-69).

Although new to the "city", Aden still managed to get by, working here and there. He earned a daily wage of one and a half rupees mainly for leading the horse, until all of a sudden relations with his employer turned sour, after he reprimanded Aden for the disappearance of postcards with images of women which the employer kept in his house. Dismayed for being admonished without ground, he quit and was immediately employed as a domestic helper by another Italian officer, Tenant Rossi, a Neapolitan, who had a mistress, Hawa Abdi. The officer went to Villaggio Duca degli Abruzzi and Bulo Burti as part of the military expedition to capture the cleric-leader, Sheikh Hassan Barsane of the Galjecel. A jealous man, Rossi kept the woman and the boy locked in the house during his absence but made sure that they had all the supplies they would need, with meat and milk supplied through a window basket, tied to a rope. During Aden's presence in Mogadiscio, there was much talk about a big ship anchored at the port on board of which, it was rumoured, carried the new Governor of Somalia, Cesare Maria De Vecchi di Val Cismon who would soon reshape the administration and the map of the colony.

## Jenale: Clashes with Settlers

When Rossi's tour of duty came to an end and he returned to Italy, Hawa and Aden were hired by their former employer, Tenant Steffan, who had come back to Somalia after a period of time spent in Italy. He took them to Doon Dheere, near Jenale, where he assumed the command of a unit of native soldiers stationed there to supervise the construction work for the 200 kilometre long irrigation canal, stretching from Jenale Dam up to the foot of the dunes and from there up to the vicinity of the Golwein farming area.

Aden, now a young man, proceeded to Jenale in c.1924. His experiences there would prove memorable, falling a year or so since the start of the fascist regime. It was there for instance that in his encounters with the Italian settlers that he came across the harsh realities of the racialist thinking of the colonial administration. Earlier in the century, up to 1908, Jenale was a small village, in the Shebeli Valley, just inland from Merca populated by native farmers working in traditional farming. As the colonial occupation stretched across the valley however, government officials grappled with the idea of how best to develop their new domain.

In 1911, the Governor of the colony, Giacomo De Martino, declared all uncultivated riverine land property of the state. From 1907 and 1909, the government leased 46 hectares of irrigable land along the Jiuba and Shebeli valleys to 15 private concessioners. These expatriate pioneers had scant success. Most failed because of inadequate capitalization and the inability to attract workers.[24] Dr Romolo Onor, an agronomist for the colonial government, launched an experimental farm at Jenale in 1912 [Azienda Agricola Sperimentale del Governo della Somalia], where ex-slaves and other settled populations were available as labour. Born in 1880 in San Donà di Piave, Veneto, he served as Director of Agricultural Services in the colony, whose initial technical and economic surveys on the discipline served as the basis of later initiatives. After his death in Jenale in 1918, when the company he founded was at risk of privatisation, it received the direct intervention of the colonial administration.

Although concessions were assigned to Italian settlers, the ensuing work built closely on the precedent set by the Experimental Agricultural Company, particularly its planning, supported by government funds in the purchase, processing and marketing of the products. Effective colonization of the Jenale area began many years later, in 1925, constituting a complex of small and medium-sized farms. An informal association among the farmers only arose in 1928. Like the ventures earlier in the century, they were hardly viable initiatives and their survival was assured solely from customs protections and the state monopoly on bananas. A number of possible explanations for this recurring failure can be suggested.

Colonial sources points to the shortage of manpower, suggesting that the local population was sparse, given—in the absence of an official census—as between 600,000 and 1,000,000. The Somalis were generally reluctant to work for the European companies, in no small part driven by the fact that commercial agriculture supplanted traditional forms of subsistence farming linked to locals' means of livelihood, their societal structure and their very sense of honour.

The scarcity of rural labour therefore remained a major obstacle to colonial agricultural development, until the Fascist regime (1925-1935) marshalled the resources and coercive power to mobilize it through forced labour. Ironically, the directives for the commercialisation of the farmland were at odds with a central policy objective of the administration which was to achieve food self-sufficiency in the colony. In order to meet this latter demand, quotas of cereal crops were allocated to the indigenous people.

Until 1934, the plantations extended only on the left bank of the Shebelle River, between it and the sea and in that year, they spread also to the other bank.

This development occurred in response to the demands of the export market. The agricultural projects were faced with the persistent flooding, prompted by the rising level of the river, masked by the marshes and ponds downstream from Gaivero'. The fields were threatened with submersion and it was often not possible to bring new patches, otherwise suitable for banana plantations, under cultivation due to the risk of flooding activity. To protect the fields, it was decided to create an outlet for the river out into the sea, just downstream from the areas under cultivation. Managed by Engineer Gaetano De Angelis, work for a large dam to regulate the water flow of the Shabeli River, started in 1924, was completed two years later.

Between 1925 and 1926 Aden served as a domestic helper (*booy* in Somali) in the estates of different settlers, the most well-known among them were: Papetti, Battelameri, Marchese, Patina, Cav. Squarcina, Pavolini, Chiamberlando and Carlo Vecco, all owners of banana plantations at Kaytoy, Jenale and Lamma Garas agricultural areas. The last mentioned would become the Mayor of Mogadiscio during the early years of the Italian Trusteeship Administration [L'Amministrazione fiduciaria italiana della Somalia, or AFIS for short] in the 1950s. Young Aden was earning his own living but he was craving to go back to school. Colleagues recall how Aden would travel for miles, all the way up to Mogadiscio, to buy or borrow books and other reading material. He undoubtedly read history books and probably other popular books available at the time.

As reading material and writing implements was in short supply in the Dhooboy wilderness, he occasionally scrawled on walls of buildings to practice writing. One day, Mr. Pavolini, one of the settlers, caught him writing something on the wall and screamed obscene language. At the end, owing of differences with some white settlers, Aden and a friend and colleague of him, Mohamed Issa Farah, quit the service for the settlers. A criminal case was then framed against the two boys and they were arrested for alleged theft of money on the grounds that the living standard of the two boys was higher than their income would have permitted them. To the surprise of the Italian authorities, young Aden displayed during the trial an extraordinary ability to discard the false accusations against him and his friend presenting his defence arguments extemporaneously which resulted in their release after 15 days of detention. But the court ruling had angered the District Commissioner of Merca, Dottor De Rege who slapped Aden hard across the face for speaking so assertively "in his self-defence [*perché, secondo lui, avevo la lingua lunga nella mia autodifesa, data la mia età*].

The young man's experiences in Jenale were particularly bitter since most of the settlers deeply held fascist ideas. Most of them were old fascist militants, *Fascisti*, from Turin who had followed their fellow Piedmontese, the new governor of Somalia, Cesare Maria De Vecchi, sent to Africa by Mussolini because he was guilty of brutal political violence at home. Besides these entanglements with the Italians, in the same year Aden sustained a loss, receiving news of his father's death in Baidoa, some months after the fact. Though devastated by the sad news, he remained patient in the face of an event over which he had no control. He did not feel impelled to travel to Baidoa as the burial had taken place immediately after the death. Instead he organized a reading of the Qur'an for his deceased father.

In 1926, after several months during which time Aden ran errands for Italian navy officers, he was employed as a waiter in a restaurant in Afgoi, owned by the Cecchi family, a large Italian household with eight children. Aden enjoyed socializing with the children who, unlike the adults, spoke grammatically correct Italian with the natives. However, this seemingly comfortable time, was cut short as his employer accused him of having close relations with his fifteen-year-old daughter, Alfa. As a matter of fact, the relationship between Aden and Alfa was entirely platonic. But, even such harmless relationship between two innocent people, but belonging to two different sides of the race divide, was frowned upon in those days. The authority took the decision to immediately remove him from Afgoi. Unexpectedly the Commander of the Carabinieri in Afgoi, Brigadier Ziccardi, gave him a sealed envelope to be delivered to the police commander in Wanla Weyn and warned him not to return to Afgoi.

Aden suspected something untoward and after overcoming his initial hesitations, he unsealed the envelope, discovering that the letter was in fact about a deportation order instructing the police in Wanle Weyn to keep him busy in that town, or send him even further. But, since there were no employment opportunities in Wanle Weyn to keep the young man busy, he was allowed to proceed to Baidoa. In Baidoa, Aden was employed by Father Gustavo Montanari, a Catholic Missionary from Turin, as a cook. The priest and the young man often discussed religious matters, and Aden criticized the priest's faith despite being insufficiently knowledgeable in his own to hold his ground in theological argumentation. After a few months, Aden left the service of the priest to that of the District Commissioner of Baidoa, Mr. Domenico Anda.

This period coincided with the visit in Somalia by the Crown Prince Umberto of the Royal House of Savoy, who travelled the length and breadth of the colony. The event has attracted large gathering attended by a cheering crowd which converged before the government offices. The job to present a bouquet of flowers to the visiting Prince fell to young Aden. Who could foretell that that delicate boy would achieve great things, and after 36 years would become President of Independent Somalia!

## Mogadiscio: Aden Abdulla moves to the capital to forge a new life

Without knowing what the future had in store for him, Aden Abdulla departed the rural areas for Mogadiscio, in search of employment opportunities and further education; perhaps noticing or hearing about the expansion of the capital city through the intervention of the colonial government, he was convinced that it would offer chances of better employment than the casual jobs he held hitherto.

In 1928, a contest for nurses was announced, the first of such a training programme ever organized in Somalia. However, on his first attempt, owing to his age, he was not allowed to sit the entry examination. The following year, now 20, he successfully passed the entrance requirements, becoming the first among 20 candidates in the final exam, with a salary of 250 Lira per month.

In those days, the nurses were unarmed military-like organized corps with shorts and shirt color kaki and a red "fez", a flat-topped conical red hat with a black tassel on top as uniform. He was assigned to the ward reserved for whites at De Martino Hospital in Mogadiscio under the direct supervision, firstly of Captain Giovanni Guido, and later, Tenant (Lieutenant) Chiellini. The principal military Doctor of the Hospital was Major Siro Fadda, assisted by Sig. Ferruccio Cotta who was also in charge of the training course. The latter was kind to the Somali nurses and Aden was his favourite student. Exposed to the strong salty wind blowing from the Indian Ocean during the frequent night shift, Aden developed hay fever that later developed into bronchial asthma, which would trouble him over the next 26 years. Those involved in running the hospital-based training for nurses included nuns. One of them, in 1928, was Superiora Adalgise, who became, at the time of independence in 1960, the Mother Superior in Belet Uen.

In the 1930s, De Martino, named after the early century governor in the colony and nowadays commonly referred to as *Isbitaal* Martini, was one of a few health establishments in the capital. De Martino was born in 1849 in London, where his father, Giacomo Ambrogio, was the Minister (Ambassador) of the Kingdom of the Two Sicilies. After holding the post of governor in Somalia from 1910 to 1916, De Martino moved onto the same post in Eritrea (1916-1919) and finally, Cirenaica, where he died in office in Benghazi in 1921. The hospital had a capacity of 120 beds and treated both soldiers and civilians. Besides it, there was the Di Gorgio infirmary in Hamar Jab Jab, reserved for treatment of black troops, but with only forty beds. Finally, there was also a *lazzaretto* or isolation hospital about two kilometres from the city centre.[25]

Aden's desire to continue his education did not end with the nursing classes. The employment, with the relative security of a good salary which it provided, allowed him to satisfy his greatest aspiration: to resume studying. Over the two years from 1929, he attended evening classes, passing the third, fourth and fifth grades with distinction. But here he had to stop: "For the Somalis there are no other possibilities to study," he was told. In fact, the legislation then in force in the colony limited the education level of the natives up to elementary level which ended with the *Classe Quinta* or simply *Quinta* (fifth class). During the colonial period, Somalis were generally assumed to need only a basic facility in literacy and numeracy and the ability to communicate in the language of the colonialists. Too much education, it was felt, could result in raising expectations which, in turn, might lead to incipient protests, and this was the last thing the colonial regime wanted.

Aden Abdulla, instead, educated himself through reading books. He was fascinated by them and spent nearly every minute of his spare time with his nose in a book he jumped into reading, whatever it was, just to learn. Books were scarce and he would go out of his way to borrow books or newspapers he had not yet read. Despite the restrictions imposed on native movements, he travelled, more than once, from Shalambod (known as Vittorio d'Africa in Italian), where he was based, to Mogadiscio with the aim to get books and other reading material. Through intensive reading of printed materials he developed an interest in subjects such as social justice and politics without, of course, publicly manifesting his views as, at the time, no political parties or freedom of expression existed in the Italian colony other than those Fascist groups to which only Italians belonged. All that reading paid off especially when it came to the history. Aden Abdulla taught himself enough to develop the skills and understanding that would help him later in his career.

In recognition of his extra dedication, commitment and hard work, in 1929, he was appointed head of the Somali nursing staff at the hospital and promoted to second-class nurse in 1931. During the brief tenure as chief of nursing personnel in Mogadiscio, he learned clerical works and the related administrative tasks, like typing and bookkeeping. In July 1933, he was given the possibility to opt between a promotion to first-class scale nurse or transfer to clerical services. He opted for the latter position as typist for it carried with it an attractive salary. In the same year, having favorably impressed the governor with his intellectual abilities he was promoted to Class 4 as typist, and transferred to the office of the Deputy District Commissioner of Lower Webi Shebeli in Shalambood.

One issue which troubled Aden was the low wages the nurses were earning. They were virtually equated, in terms of remuneration, to the domestic helpers performing a variety of household services like domestic helpers and cooks for individual colonial officers or their families. Before taking up the clerical post, he raised this matter, on more than one occasion, with the Director of the Health department, Dr. Giulio Bachelli, with the aim of getting the salary level raised or allowing the nurses to go into private practice, outside the working hours, and give then permission to administer injections at home to patients, subject, of course, to medical prescription. His position had given him an opportunity to acquaint himself with some of the grievances of the nurses who had been looking forward to better salaries. This was also the time when Mogadiscio was undergoing a noticeable transformation from small provincial center to a modern city which attracted new immigrants and businessmen ahead of the Abyssinian campaign. Aden suspected that Dr. Bachelli's earlier offer for promotion was a clever move, to silence him, not to continue lobbying around the wages of the native nursing staff.

In 1934, in concomitance with the military build-up ahead of the Abyssinia campaign, the colonial authorities introduced a new rule requiring the natives to salute any Italians they came across, in the style of the ancient Romans. The Roman salute is a gesture, in which the arm is held out forward straight with palm down, and fingers touching. Failure to comply with this requirement would entail the risk of being flogged, a practice the Somalis hated the most.

At this particular time, when Aden's mind was focused on issues related to his new job and the improvement of the Somali nurse's employment conditions, his uncle, in keeping with the custom of the time, was busy arranging an early marriage for him, in this case with Medina Hassan, a young girl from the same clan. However, the marriage proved an unhappy, short-lived one and the couple soon separated.

He met once more Haji Farah Ali but this time in Shalambod who, as interpreter-typist in the District Commissioner's office, was at the peak of his career, being the highest rank a Somali could attain at the time. The District Commissioner, at the time, was Dr. Francesco Cossu, a skilled official though animated by racist attitude towards the natives. Aden's stay in Shalambod did not last long as he was, at his behest, moved to Mogadiscio to work in the General Accounting Department.

By this time, his eye fell upon Asha Elmi Mataan, a pretty seventeen-year-old girl in Mogadiscio. As time passed, his interest in Asha grew and blossomed into love. She agreed to his proposal for marriage, subject to her father's blessing. In comparison with his past short-lived, arranged marriage experience, this time the idea to get married came from him, without the involvement of any of his relatives.

He sent a letter to his future father-in-law through two friends, Mohamed Awale Liban and Farah "Galti", the first a clerk in the government service, the second, employed as a house boy for the District Commissioner of Galcaio, Signor Roberto Asinari di San Marzano. Mohamed Awale would later become

Aden Abdulla's Chief de Cabinet during his presidency, 1960-1967. The future father-in-law made no objection; however, he wanted to meet him personally, which meant that he had to travel to Galcaio, a town situated at more than 700 kilometres north of Mogadiscio. As he started down the path towards matrimony, he decided to travel all the way to that town, to seek the future father-in-law's blessing. The travel plan had further been complicated by the government's decision to requisition all the means of transport, ahead of the Italian invasion of Ethiopia in 1935.

The trip was thus made by sea from Mogadiscio to the coastal town of Obbia. After disembarking at Obbia, he proceeded the journey to Galcaio by land. This journey by sea lasted for 36 hours, from 18 to 20 October 1935. When he finally met his future father-in law and asked for Asha's hand in marriage, the bride's father displayed a high expectation: he asked for 20 camels in bride-wealth, a request Aden half-jokingly responded to by observing that, "There was not enough space in my small suitcase to carry camels". He was however carrying 1,500 Lire. In the absence of camels, the most common means of conveying the token at the time, he promised that he will make all efforts to honour and take good care of his daughter, a promise he kept, marrying only the once—in contrast to the widespread practice of polygymy at the time—until his wife predeceased him.

At the end, with the mediation of the friends, the suitor gave the 1,500 Lire he was carrying as well as 500 Lire received in loan from a Moallim Aden Abdurahman, from his own clan family, who was teaching in a Koranic School in Galcaio. The couple's wedding ceremony was celebrated on 23 October 1934 and immediately afterwards, the newlyweds moved to Mogadiscio.

In the meantime, a new development emerged: upon returning to Mogadiscio from Galcaio, he learned that he would again be transferred to Shalambod as replacement for Haji Farah Ali who, owing to his knowledge of Arabic, was seconded to the Political Department in Mogadishu as personal interpreter for General Rodolfo Graziani (later Field Marshal), appointed Governor of Somalia, ahead of the Italo-Abyssinian war of 1935.

The couple had their first child, Abdulkadir, in 1937. After a gap of two years, they welcomed Mohamed, followed by Fadima, Osman, Omar, Said, Aaliya and Aboukar. Apart from the two eldest children, all the children were born in Belet Uen, their father's political power base. Public service was something Aden's children maintained, counting among themselves three medical doctors, a pharmacist and a dentist. Donna Asha died in 1974 after a period of illness.

## Shalambod: Aden Abdulla challenges Fascist rule

A seminal moment in Aden Abdulla's life occurred in 1935 during a bus trip from Mogadiscio to Shalambod when he quarrelled with a white bus driver over where the vehicle would stop. At the time, the Compagnia Italiana Trasporti Africa Orientale, but widely known by its acronym CITAO, was a public transport company, operating bus services across Somalia and in the days of *Africa Orientale Italiana,* Ethiopia and Eritrea too. The transport company usually reserved seats at the front of its buses for Europeans, relegating non-Europeans to the crammed seats at the back. Aden Abdulla was granted by his direct supervisor in Shalambod permission to go to Mogadiscio to buy books and other reading material notwithstanding the regulations in force requiring such permission to be sanctioned, *a priori*, by the higher authorities in the capital. On his return trip, when the bus was nearing the native quarter of Shalambod, about one kilometre from the one reserved for the Europeans, Aden Abdulla knocked repeatedly at the entrance door between the two compartments to signal the driver to let him alight but the driver ignored the signal. At the bus terminal, all passengers quietly disembarked and dispersed. However, for Aden Abdulla, there were questions to be answered. After disembarking with his heavy luggage he let his annoyance be known to the driver but in polite manner. "What it would cost you to stop the bus in Shalambod and allow us to alight instead of making us to walk for one kilometre with our heavy luggage?" "Well" said the driver, "You were the one making too much noise banging on the door! Listen to me," he continued, "Vittorio d'Africa (Shalambod) is here and not the place where you wanted to alight". He warned Aden Abdulla of severe consequences if he again caused trouble in the future.

The tone between the two became litigious. Since the driver kept repeating the words "*Hai capito*?" [Do you understand?]. Aden Abdulla said that he understood what he was saying but he understood also that, as a passenger, who paid his ticket, was entitled to get a decent service adding that he will think about using CITAO's service in the future. After this angry exchange, Aden Abdulla started moving towards his house, but the driver came after him letting out a stream of invectives and threatening to break his nose. Aden Abdulla paid back in spades.

At this point the bus driver, together with other three or four Europeans took Aden and another Somali passenger, a certain Ibrahim Lughei, by force, first to a nearby bar or restaurant and then to a police station where they remained in detention. They were eventually released after it was discovered that Aden Abdulla was a government employee. Ibrahim Lughey's only fault was to be in the wrong place at the wrong time. In the ensuing confusion Aden lost his bag and, above all, the valuable contents: the books and other reading material.

The violence displayed by the white men was undeniably disgraceful and gratuitous. It was in stark contrast with the polite and good manner displayed by Aden Abdulla. His act of rebellion awoke in him a determination to devote himself to fighting the "deep disease of colour prejudice." He vowed that day to "try, if possible, to root out the disease and suffer hardships in the process". The next morning, he prepared and submitted to the District Commissioner of Shalambod, Sig. Parrotta a long letter detailing the circumstances surrounding the quarrel with the Italian bus-driver.

While the DC was still reading the petition, phone calls came in succession from the Office of the Fascist Party, the Captain of Police, and the Judicial Officer of the region, all demanding a heavy penalty for the young Somali who dared to criticise CITAO, a government-owned public transport agency and its founders, which included, among others, the Minister of the Colonies, Sig. Terruzzi. Mr. Parrotta, a kind and decent person, did whatever he could to protect the young Somali from being incriminated although there was no a case to answer. Aden vigorously resisted the pressure put upon him to apologize to the Italian bus driver. From that day forward, this small, unassuming young man, would show his ability to stand by what he believed was right. But, the stress and the humiliation he went through, have taken their toll on his health worsening his hay fever and bronchial asthma.

## Aden Abdulla risked internal confinement

A couple of day after the incident, with a medical certificate and an application for transfer to another duty station in hand, Aden Abdulla went to see Dr. Francesco Cossu, the Regional Commissioner of Webi Shabeli, in his residence in Merca. He thought that a change of surroundings would do well for his health. Signor Cossu was kind enough to receive him without prior arrangement. Aden took his case to Cossu and not to Parrotta, his direct supervisor because he knew that the latter would have not approved his application. After the usual exchange of pleasantries, the discussion soon turned bitter.

Cossu started the conversation by saying that he had wanted to see Aden for some time about the recent incident he was involved in. Aden began to complain about the verbal and physical abuse he was subjected to by the driver and some of his white friends in Shalambod, stating: "As a free man in his own country, I could not tolerate any abuse by a driver running a public transport service paid for by the commuters", adding that he did not intend to offer any apology to anyone. This strong statement caught Cossu by surprise; it sounded to him like a bomb, words he was not expecting to hear from a native chap.

A fuming Cossu asked: "What did you say? Parrotta must have misinformed; he made me believe that you had apologized and repented for what you had done. If this is what you believe, you cannot stay in this place. Do you know that I suspended a deportation order proposed by the authorities against you to the interior of the country with an obligation to reside in Migiurtinia for daring to challenge a white man and expressing criticism on a government-run transport agency? Migiurtinia, in the northeast, was considered barren and desolate and exile there was considered one of the worst punishments. Aden, overwhelmed by humiliation and anger, could not hold back tears.

Cossu, desperately trying to find a justification for the racist policies in a bid to soothing the young man's anger, simply pointed him to a prejudice in the Somali culture of the pastoralists, saying that, he, (Cossu) would never allow a member of the Reer Magno, a Somali coastal community who lived along the Benadir shoreline whose main employment was as fishermen, to say he and Aden Abdulla were equals. Aden Abdulla pushed back politely, saying, Signor Commissario, you may believe that I am superior to a Rer Magno but I am convinced that if I offend any member of this community, and he reacts by hitting me, the law would deem me to be in the wrong.

Cossu, evidently annoyed, responded in a blunt fashion. "I don't like you. It is better that you go away somewhere else [*cambiare aria*]. You cannot stay in the same place as me. Do you know that I cannot say to Caroselli [the Governor of the colony] that he and I are equal?" Aden Abdulla, trying to help him see the situation rationally, responded: "Forgive me [*Mi voglia scusare Signor Commissario*] but the comparison does not hold. Caroselli is your direct supervisor, and in the public service, each of you has his own role, but as human being and Italian citizens, you are equal. Allow me to add that the comparison would have been valid if the person whom I quarrelled with were a staff working for the Residence of Vittorio d'Africa like Signor Bartolozzi. The driver of the bus works for an organization providing service to the passengers who pay the service. Therefore, he should have respect for me as a customer who paid for the service" [*Quell'uomo della corriera é un addetto ad un servizio a disposizione dei clienti pagatori, e doveva essere lui ad avere riguardo per me, che avevo pagato i suoi servizi*].

Cossu, now flying into a rage, cried out: "Listen, the earlier you and the four or five others like you realise that God did not make the five fingers in the human body the same, the better". As he said this, Cossu put his right hand, held out flat, in Aden's face, concluding, "A white man and a black man will never be equal. And now I reiterate what I said earlier: you cannot stay where I am". Aden Abdulla, taking the application for transfer as well as a medical certificate out from his pocket told Cossu that he came to see him just to apply for transfer for medical reasons. After taking quick look at the application, and visibly annoyed, the Regional Commissioner told Aden to take it to his supervisor in Shalambood.

Once more, Aden Abdulla had shown great political maturity by disputing Sig. Cossu's theory of racial superiority. The following day, he submitted the application to the District Commissioner who, although he reprimanded Aden for bypassing him, advised him to just forget about the transfer, fearing that Mr Cossu might interpret the move as a spiteful trick on him. The physical and verbal abuse he was subjected to, exacerbated by the cover-up of the authorities, outraged Aden, further solidifying his resolve to fight for the dignity of his people. Aden often antagonised his Italian superiors but he was wise enough to do so conscientiously within certain boundaries, pushing as far as he could but not allowing his opponents to fault him on a point of law and have cause to penalise him. In any sense, he had learned to use Italian law against Italians. He despised the arrogance of the Italian officials and the discrimination against Somalis.

## The innocent three and the informer

Soon after coming back from Galcaio, Aden Abdulla received shocking news involving three Somalis, namely: Ahmed Mohamed "Gas", Osman

Hussein "Bartolo" and Mohamed Aflaw, arrested in Shalambod for allegedly disseminating enemy propaganda. The arrest was prompted by a report delivered to the police authorities by one Warsama Omar Dad "Turtacchi" which held that the three men were allegedly spreading rumours that Italy would be defeated in the ongoing Italo-Abyssinia War and Ethiopia would invade Somalia, warning people to convert their money into gold. Warsama was, at the time, employee of an Italian businessman operating in Shalambod. Under the Fascist Penal Code, spreading false and alarming news affecting public security, if proved, carried severe penalty. The District Commissioner of Shalambod at the time was Dr Cesare Del Prato, an honest man, well disposed to the natives. A team from the military tribunal came to Shalambod to probe into the alleged case.

Aden Abdulla, who was deeply sceptical about the credibility of the accusations against his three friends, conducted his own investigations with the aim to find out the truth. He immediately approached Warsama Omar telling him that the three mutual friends risked the death penalty until he confessed that his allegations were groundless. Warsama instantly conceded that the report he gave to the Police was baseless and that he did so for revenge of an insult. Aden Abdulla persuaded the informant to tell the truth in the presence of two mutual friends, Dirie Kheire "Dirie Halac" and Warsama Ahmed, both in the service of the government in Shalambod. Before disclosing the informant's retraction of his earlier statement to the police, Aden approached Cesare Del Prato to inquire about the outcome of the police investigations in connection with the case. Del Prato, a forthcoming and courteous man, revealed that the three accused were likely to face severe punishment and that the military judges resisted his views as well as those of the Regional Commissioner, Barile in defence of the suspects. The situation had further been complicated by the fact that the judges had accused the defendant's counsel of anti-national activities for accepting their case.

It was at this point that Aden shared with Del Prato the crucial evidence in his possession i.e. the declaration the informant made in the presence of two witnesses in which he conceded that his action was revenge against Ahmed Gas who had tried to seduce his wife. The two witnesses were ready to testify before the tribunal. Del Prato instead advised Aden to convince the informant to make the statement before him because he was worried about the prospect of the tribunal indicting the witnesses for perjury.

Aden succeeded in convincing the informer to declare the truth before the

District Commissioner who immediately cabled the statement made before him to the military tribunal in Mogadiscio. In the face of this new irrefutable evidence, the case was dropped and the three men were consequently released. The informant however was sentenced to three months for incriminating innocent people. Years later, during the British military occupation of Somalia, Warsama lost his property and, as a result, he had gone out of his mind. In 1956, Aden Abdulla was instrumental in helping Warsama secure a job at the National Assembly.

## Reflection on the Italian presence in Somalia

In the pages of his diaries, Aden Abdulla gives an in-depth account of Italy's failure as well as its very modest achievements in Somalia, before and during the fascist regime. In the early colonial period, before the *ventennio*, Italy did little worth mentioning in Somalia, but natives were generally treated with some degree of dignity. The situation, however, changed radically with the advent of fascism in 1923 and the arrival of De Vecchi as Governor of Somalia. The new Governor immediately set about reorganising the rather messy pre-Fascist system whereby Italian Somalia had been divided into two protectorates and one semi-colony.

Only in the 1920s was a programme of agricultural development started although this was not well-received by Somalis since most of the activity relied on the policy of forced labour to the benefit of few hundred colonists who arrived from Italy in the area of the Shabelle river. One thing that had deeply disturbed Aden Abdulla at the time was the treatment reserved to the natives serving in the banana plantations owned by Italian settlers in the agricultural area of Jenale. Between 1930 and 1941, almost all the population along the Scebeli River, from Afgoi to Hawai, as well as the Elay from Bur Akaba and Dafet were virtually enslaved and forced to work in the white farms with pitiful wages, two Liras per day and one kilogram of maize for the male labourers and half of this amount for the females. Able-bodied people were forcibly taken from their villages. Among these people there were some relatively well-off and themselves employers.

When, after some time, the head of a family became unfit for work, as a result of exhaustion due to being overworked, poor nutrition or illness caused by the climatic conditions, he was returned to his village of origin without compensations or other end of service benefits. The traditional chiefs were obliged to provide replacement for the invalid workers. There were cases in which some labourers, due to the unbearable conditions in the plantations, fled. If recaptured, the runaway labourers were subjected to stiff punishment consisting mostly of public flogging performed by the Dubad [from the Somali *Duub cad* for "white wrap", after their signature headgear], an irregular band part of the Italian colonial armed forces.

Around 1937-38, Ethiopians political prisoners and members of the Rer Shebeli were added to the existing labour force. The Sheveli were recruited on the basis of an understanding made between the Sultan of the Sheveli, Olol Dinle, and the Italian authorities. After a few months in the plantations, the Sheveli labourers staged a protest and fled in masse returning to their place of origin, the vital stretch of Webi Shebeli basin that runs from Fer-Fer to Callafo.

The rebellion was triggered by two main factors. Firstly, the unbearable working conditions they were being subjected to and secondly, the expiration of the three months, the contractual time set in the agreement with Sultan Olol Dinle. Their aversion to work in the plantations was evidently not be noticed by the settlers who, in the face of the new developments, accepted to renounce the Sheveli's service lest they influence other workers. All attempts to recapture the escapees ended in failure. In fact, as most of them served in the irregular Italian military band, the "Dubat", in many cases, they managed to overpower the soldiers sent to pursue them, skilfully snatching their rifles from them.

This embarrassing development forced, Francesco Saverio Caroselli, the Governor of the time, to issue an order suspending the pursuit of the run-away Sheveli. The Ethiopians, on the other hand being unfamiliar with the local language and more crucially, the local terrain, could not follow the strategy devised by the Sheveli. The cruel environment in Jenale agricultural colony reminded Aden the story of the slave labour in the Caribbean in the eighteenth century he read in the works of Arthur Canon Doyle and Rafael Sabatini. However, the events reported above, did not mean to portrait Italians as bad type of human. In fact, while some of them represented the dark side of Italy, they had, and have, many virtues, including a highly sense of friendship and respect towards the native population.

On the other hand, Italy had realized in Somalia important plans in the economic fields which independent Somalia has driven benefit from. This included the creation of the "Comprensorio Agricolo di Genale" (Agricultural

Estate of Jenale) with the construction of 200 km long irrigation canal. The principal canal, originating from the Jenale Dam, ran up to the dunes, and from there, making a sharp bend, southward up to Goobweyne agricultural area.

At the outbreak of the war, there were several industrial enterprises, mainly in the transport and building sectors, as well as light industrial companies processing local produce. The Italians introduced public utilities and amenities to the towns, built roads, introduced medical and veterinary services and set an example of modern methods of farming. They also established some relatively modest public services organizations for the supply of clean drinking water, and provided health and education services. In comparison with the little attention paid and poor investments made by Britain in British Somaliland, which was only a negligible periphery of an overextended empire across two continents (Africa and Asia), the Italians had expended much more energy on their Somalia.[26]

On the political front, between 1912 and 1923, Italy has pursued a policy designed to extend Somalia's borders beyond the points agreed with Ethiopia, under 1908 treaty. Under this treaty, Italy agreed with Ethiopia the future frontier between Italian Somalia and Ethiopia should run at 180 miles from the Somali coast, a point which corresponds to Bulo Burti.[27] In 1927, for the first time in its history, Somalia was united into a single community, with a vast territory stretching from the Juba River to the approach of the Gulf of Aden, communities formerly divided by geographical barriers. More significantly, in 1940, Italy created a *de facto* Greater Somalia by combining the administration of Ogaden and the British Protectorate of Somaliland within the colony of 'Somalia Italiana', thus providing the opportunity for a large segment of Somali population, previously divided between three different foreign powers, to come under the control of one power, that of Italy. However, all this positive results, had been frustrated by Britain when it reversed the situation in favour of Ethiopia after the Second World War, transferring Haud and Ogaden to Ethiopia, before unilaterally tracing a new frontier, the so-called 'provisional administration line', shortly before Italy took over the administration of the Trust Territory in 1950.[28]

The transfer was viewed by the Somalis as a betrayal of the protectorate treaties that Britain had signed with Somali paramount chiefs in 1884-1886 regarding their territorial integrity and protection. The Somalis have in fact challenged both the agreements of 1897 and that of 1954 between Britain and Ethiopia, and maintained that their 1884 agreement with Her Majesty's government overrode these, urging the case be submitted to the International Court of Justice (ICJ) for an advisory advice on the legal validity of the Anglo-Ethiopian treaties. The United Nations Charter did not give representative of British Somaliland any right to petition to the United Nations, on grounds that the British Somaliland was neither a member of the United Nations nor a Trusteeship Territory. The British action sowed the first seeds of future Anglo-Somali problems, since the treaty with Ethiopia was signed without the knowledge of the Somalis. Yet to do the British justice, the Somalis did receive encouragement to, first set up cultural clubs and then, to organize themselves in political organization, a fact that Aden Abdulla eloquently used to embarrass Giuseppe Brusasca, the Italian Under Secretary for Foreign Affairs during his maiden visit in Somalia in 1950, stating: "The British gave us freedom of expression, freedom to establish political parties, freedom to work for the future of our country, right the Italians denied to the people".[29]. The activities of the parties were regulated under a BMA proclamation, the primary purpose of which was to exercise adequate control over these associations.[30]

## British military occupation and its adverse economic impact

From the economic point of view, Somalia was plunged into such economic hardship as never had been experienced as pre-war time. During the years immediately after the war, which coincides with the British military occupation, much attention had been directed to the maintenance of the territory's security situation, leaving other aspects of the population's life unattended. Agriculture, long touted as the cornerstone of Somalia's guarantee for food security, had not been developed to any real extent.

At the outbreak of the war, there were a number of industrial enterprises, mainly in the transport and building sectors, as well as high industrial companies processing local produce. The adverse effect of the British military occupation was the dramatic fall in economic production in former Italian Somaliland as a result of ruinous measures taken by the British military authorities. These measures included, among others, the dismantling of electric generating plants, lighters and cables, and the removal from the elaborate salt works at Dante (Hafun) for military use and deployment in other theatres of war. The salt deposits of Hafun were producing more than 200,000 tons annually, most of which was exported to the Far East.[31] The industrial plants demolished or closed down were the Majayahan and Kandala mining quarries.[32]

Other infrastructure removed included the 70 miles of narrow gauge railway track linking Mogadiscio, Afgoi and Villaggio Duca degli Abruzzi, the Afgoi Bridge on the Webi Shabelle River, the oil storage plant and oil seed crushing plant in Mogadiscio. Predictably, these drastic measures produced a devastating impact on the Territory's economy and its populations, especially those who, directly or indirectly, were beneficiaries of this most vital means of production and the service industry it supported. Britain was also, at that time, spending only $500,000 per year on Somalia, covering not much more than the cost of the military forces assigned to that country, the salaries of the British Government officials who worked there, and the general government services.[33] The British administration had been operating as caretaker, largely eschewing investments in accordance with provision governing the occupied territories contemplated in the Hague Convention of 1907.

This policy, however, did not endear the authorities to the local population as the deteriorated economic condition hit hard at both the Italian community and the Somalis.

Drawing a comparison between the degree of development achieved in the territories inhabited by Somalis, I.M. Lewis wrote: "...Whatever their motives, and notwithstanding the impress of Fascism, decidedly more of benefit to Somalis had been created in Somalia than in British Somaliland, French Somaliland, or, above all, in the northern province of Kenya which for long was destined to remain a stagnant back-water.[34] At the time of independence from Britain, the entire national budget of the former Protectorate stood at ShSo 23 Million, compared to the ShSo 87 Million budget of former trust territory of Somalia.[35]

# SECTION 1
# PART 2

# SECTION ONE, PART TWO

# ENTRY INTO FULL-TIME POLITICS

In the wake of the defeat of the Fascist regime, the Somalis were unexpectedly ushered into a new era of political consciousness as they had never experienced in the past. They had actively witnessed and taken part in the devastating war between two European colonial powers, Italy and Britain. Like many other Africans involved in a war which was not theirs, the Somalis derived from exposure to the conflict's dynamics dramatic and lasting psychological effects, a sort of eye-opener which left them developing awareness that the white man was far from being invincible.

These events brought them also even more in contact with other populations fighting for independence. Empowered by this new outlook, Somalis started forming national political organizations with the realization that a return to the *status quo ante* was impossible. Somalis' nationalism did not emerge as a reaction to colonial situation; it made its appearance after the collapse of Italian rule. Political movements and any associations having nationalistic connotations or aspirations were banned during the long Italian colonial administration. No political parties existed in Somalia other than the

Fascist Party to which only Italians were associated.

The impact of a national idea on a people in the throes of violent social changes brought about by war produced the first stirrings of a Somali awakening and a Somali national movement aimed at the creation of an independent State. Following the entry of the Italians into the European war in 1940, the British mounted an extensive propaganda and military campaign in Somalia, Ethiopia and Eritrea. By 1941, the entire area had been seized by the British.

The first modern Somali political movement was the Somali Youth Club (SYC)—the precursor of the Somali Youth League (SYL)—established in Mogadiscio in 1943. The creation of this movement was a major stepping stone towards Somali independence. In the beginning, the SYC was primarily actively engaged in promoting social and welfare education and health programs, targeting particularly the less privileged segments among its affiliates. However, it would be wrong to believe that the promotion of the social welfare of members of the Club could entirely be divorced from political matters. To help improve the new club, the British allowed the better educated police and civil servants to join, thus relaxing Britain's traditional policy of separating the civil service from political parties "because the new movement was progressive, co-operated with the government, and was anti-Italian".[36]

In 1941, with the British military occupation, an important turning point began for Aden Abdulla's life. With the end of his employment with the colonial service, he moved to Belet Uen, a major town in central Somalia. Occupied by the Italians in 1923, Belet Uen was incorporated into the Italian Somaliland becoming soon an important administrative and military centre. The city had experienced population surge attracted by employment opportunities and other interests. The retail trading business was dominated by the Arab communities, most of them recruited from Yemen, Aden and Hejaz by the Italian colonial authorities as mercenaries. In the rural areas pastoral communities continued herding their livestock and farming along the river banks.

Among the first to feel the wind of change that was blowing, Aden expressed sympathy to the "Somali Youth Club", which later became "Somali Youth League" political party. The Youth Club fascinated Aden Abdulla, and he became convinced that the first step for the Somalis to revive their freedom was to adhere to this new movement. He took up the leadership of the newly formed Somali Youth Club (SYC) branch of Belet Uen which should have allowed him finally to display all those qualities so far contained by rules and life systems that held little or no account of the intrinsic qualities of the man. In fact he formally enrolled himself as member of the Club in 1944; his membership card bears n. 130.[37] In Belet Uen, he made several new friends including Sheikh Ali Jimcale and Abdullahi Issa, the latter who would later be chosen to represent the Somali Youth League party (SYL) at the United Nations during the crucial time when the future of Somalia was being debated at the United Nations in Lake Success.[38]

Through the powerful British propaganda tools, the Somalis were aware of the establishment of the United Nations in 1945 and of its programme calling for the independence of peoples under colonial rule. One of the foremost topics of discussion among the four major powers in the world (Britain, France, United States of America and the Soviet Union) was the future status of the former Italian colonies, one of them being Somalia. This new circumstance stimulated the Somali Youth Club members as they realized that the nation could not move forward without guided political agenda. Debates among members convinced that the time was ripe for the Club to become a political association. Among the items debated was the name of the new party.

The delegate from Belet Uen, Aden Abdulla, who was knowledgeable about development in Pakistan and its dominant political party (the Islamic League) suggested the name Somali Youth League and the Congress duly accepted the proposal.[39] The SYC was thus transformed from a simple social Club to a party of mass appeal. The official newspaper of the time, the *Somalia Courier*, reported the momentous event in its article heralding the changes. "On the 1st April 1947 a new era started for the Somali Youth League. In fact it may be said that childhood was over and manhood was reached. On that date the name was changed from Somali Youth Club to Somali Youth League, the latter being more suitable for the widening interests and development. The foundation date of this League is still considered to be the 15th May 1943 but the 1st April is the date that marks the renaming of the Club, the passing of a new constitution and framing of a wider programme. This will be an important date in the history of Somalia".[40] His articles from Belet Uen, penned under the pseudonym of Adab were known for their strong influence on the growing nationalism, and regularly appeared in the Italian language daily newspaper *Il Popolo*.[41]

## UN Trusteeship assigned to Italy
## Mixed reactions over the UN decision

At the end of the World War II, the disposition of the Italian colonies posed a problem for the Allied victors. At Yalta, the Allied victors discussed the Italian colonies but they could reach no agreement about their future status. In September 1945, at the first session of the Council of Foreign Ministries in London, the United States proposed a collective trusteeship for the former Italian colonies under Article 81 of the United Nations Charter. The following session of April, held in Paris, the British Foreign Minister proposed, on condition of Ethiopia's consent, the union of the Ogaden, British Somaliland, and Italian Somalia to form a "Greater Somalia" under British administration.

But the other Allies—namely, France, Soviet Union and United Stated—declared their opposition to the plan for varying reasons. Emperor Haile Selassie of Ethiopia, from his side, declared that his country would never give up its claim to the Ogaden.[42] The General Assembly created a Trusteeship Council to oversee the administration of the colonized or "non-self-governing peoples", whose wellbeing and self-government the UN Charter had pledged to promote. The Four Powers, as part of consideration of the disposition of the Italian former colonies, sent a Four Power commission of Investigation to Mogadiscio on January 6, 1948, to ascertain the desire and aspirations of the local populations. Failing to reach agreement, the question of disposal of former Italian colonies was referred to the UN General Assembly pursuant to Article 23, paragraph XI of the Peace Treaty with Italy.[43] This formal delivery of the problem to the United Nations publicly proclaimed the failure of the Big Four to reach an agreement, after negotiations which have been in progress for more than three years. The Four Powers were bound to by the Treaty to accept the recommendations of the General Assembly and to put it into effect.

In the Peace Treaty signed in 1947, Italy renounced the ownership of its colonies but that did not mean that it had abandoned the idea of regaining them by any other means. When the campaign for maintaining its pre-war African colonies ended badly, Italy tried to conquer at least one place in the decolonization process and managed to become the guardian and custodian of Somalia in the phase that would have preceded independence. In the end, and after nearly one year of intensive debate, on November 21, 1949, the General Assembly adopted a resolution recommending that Italian Somaliland be placed under an international trusteeship system for 10 years, with Italy as the administering authority, followed by full independence.[44] To avoid words like "protectorate" and "mandate", the term "Trusteeship Administration" was coined: and, to prevent the temporary nature of the trusteeship administration from becoming permanent, it was decided that the Italian mission would last ten years, from 1950 to 1960. One of the most painful and prolonged state of uncertainty over the future of Somalia had finally came to an end, ushering the country in a new era full of hope for the Somalis who for many years had been longing for a regular government and for normal condition of life.

Under the Trusteeship Agreement, the Italian Trusteeship Administration (A.F.I.S.) was required to "foster the development of free political institutions and to promote the development of the inhabitants of the territory towards independence". The agreement also contained as an annex a "Declaration of Constitutional Principles" guaranteeing the rights of the inhabitants and full implementation of the administration's obligations, sponsored by India[45]

In comparison to other trusteeship administrations, the regime placed on Somalia presented a unique feature, for it was the only case in which trusteeship responsibility was assigned to a defeated former colonial power which was not even a member of the United Nations. This particular situation led to the approbation of stringent trusteeship arrangements for Somalia compared to those elsewhere. These strict conditions included a specified duration of ten years set for the mandate given to Italy, followed by independence after this period,[46] the first example in the history of the UN of a target date being imposed on a Trusteeship Power.[47] Other trustee countries (Australia, Belgium, Britain, France, New Zealand and the USA) were given indefinite duration and the Trusteeship Agreement made reference to 'self-government' and not to full independence as an alternative solution.

Another unique feature of the Trusteeship Agreement for Somalia was the provision for an Advisory Council to assist the Administering Authority in the control of affairs in the Trust Territory. "No other Trust Territory has been watched over so jealously by its guardians as has Somalia, which has long been viewed as the special ward of the United Nations," commented Alphonso Castagno.[48] The effect of this UN presence in Somalia was also further strengthened by the provision of regular visiting missions which, like the Advisory Council, reported to the Trusteeship Council of the United Nations.[49] Throughout the period of the mandate, three missions visited Somalia between 1951 and 1957.

However, these political and civil guarantees did not make for smooth

Italian-Somali relations from the beginning. The Lega, or more precisely, its radical wing, distrusted the new Administration, suspecting it of having a hidden colonial agenda despite the fact that a process of decolonization of non-independent territories had been put in place by the United Nations Organization and the Atlantic Charter. The radical wing of the party was utterly against any form of co-operation with the incoming administration and contemplated approaching the Ethiopian government with a view to make sure of their help should a form of resistance to the Italian authorities be adopted. Earlier contacts of Abdulkadir Sheikh Sakawaddin, the first President of the party, with the Emperor of Ethiopia in August 1946, indicate that the Emperor was in full sympathy with the principles of the Somali party and expressed his readiness to accord them any assistance in his power. It is reported that the Emperor seized the opportunity to state that "the flag of Ethiopia was the banner of all Africans".[50]

British intelligence reports indicate increasing evidence of contacts established between the SYL leadership and Ethiopia at several centres. According to the same sources, the Somali Youth League considered, among other issues, the possibility of exodus to Ethiopia in the event of Italy returning to Somalia. The radical faction went further, requesting Ethiopian administration as an alternative to the Italian option. "It is now the wish of the Somali people that I should make on their behalf the following petition to the Assembly, namely, that the administration of Somalia should at once be transferred to and vested in Ethiopia, or alternatively, Great Britain and Ethiopia jointly," wrote Ali Nour Elmi, one of the representatives of the SYL and Hamar Youth Club on December 1949 to the Secretary General of the United Nations.[51] However, within the SYL, there was a considerable body of opinion favourable to the idea of cooperation with the Trusteeship Administration.

The official and final position to be adopted vis-à-vis the UN decision was discussed in a meeting in Mogadiscio in November 1949 to which all branch secretaries of the party were invited. Three options were on the table: (a) to remain in Somalia and fight it out with the Italians; (b) to transfer the HQs to Ogaden and link up with the Ethiopians and, (3) to co-operate with the Italians and capture the best positions under the Trusteeship to be leaders of the country when independence would be granted.[52] Each option required hard and informed decision. At the end of a prolonged and charged meeting, the opinion of the moderates, led by Aden Abdulla, the SYL delegate from

Belet Uen, prevailed.

He reminded his party fellows that the Somali public was ill-prepared to engage in armed resistance against Italy, and to challenge the world body's decision on behalf of which Italy was coming to administer Somalia as a trustee. The best course of action, he suggested, was to wait and see how the new Administration would respect its international obligations under the Trusteeship Agreement.[53] Essentially, what Aden Abdulla was proposing to his fellow party members was a "conditional co-operation", very much contingent on the proper fulfilment of the Administering Authority of its international obligations. He understood the political implications of his recommendations on the future of the country. He thoughtfully assessed his choice and managed to convince others that his proposal, in the circumstances, was the decision that best served the interest of his country. From that time, his reputation mounted among his party fellows, and a feeling of mutual respect developed between him and many of the rising young members of the party.

In compliance with this policy decision the President of the SYL, Haji Mohamed Hussein, in his tour of the Upper and Lower Juba Provinces, called on SYL members to maintain order during the period of handover and to "collaborate with the incoming Italian Administration if they respected the obligations under the Trusteeship Agreement."[54] However, not all Somalis opposed the Italian trusteeship. Italy counted many friends in Somalia among the Conferenza somala party, who laid no smaller claim than the SYL to represent the people of the territory. Pro-Italian political parties, under the umbrella of the Somali Conference, whose active members included prominent tribal chiefs (traditionally well-disposed towards Italy) as well as former servicemen, hailed the return of Italy with enthusiasm and a sense of pride for their "victory" over their rival parties at the United Nations. In 1950, the Conferenza was an alliance between the following political parties: Comitato Progresso Somalo (CPS), Unione Patriottica Beneficenza (UPB), Gioventù Abgal (GA), Hizbia Dighil Mirifle (HDM), Unione Africani Somali (UAS), Scidle e Mobilen (SM), Giamiya Bimalia (GB) and Lega Progressista Migiurtina (LPM).

Although Italy did not acquire influence and/or prestige enough to pave the way for a return to Africa, it left an imprint on the Horn's institutional, social and economic structure. Traces of the Italian presence were still visible, particularly in terms of urban solutions, food, and even, to a certain extent, linguistic and cultural expressions. The formal proclamation of the termination of British Administration was made on March 30, 1950.[55] On 1 April 1950, as provided by the General Assembly Resolution, the transfer of administration from the British to the Italians was formalized with a solemn ceremony. An exchange of military courtesies and a guard of honour marked the handover to the Italian authority. The status of Italian Somalia changed thus to that of a Trust Territory under Italian administration.[56]

The handover process took place without incident all over the Territory. In Mogadiscio, the ceremony of the lowering and hoisting flags took place in the courtyard of the Palazzo Governo, the Government's Palace. The last Italian flag in the wider Horn of Africa region was memorably lowered at Gondar, in north-western Ethiopia, on November 27, 1941 but with the return of the Italians, that flag was again hoisted in East Africa within a decade, on April 1, 1950. In its editorial comment, the official daily newspaper *Corriere della Somalia* wrote triumphantly: "Nine years of British administration over the territory of Somalia ended this morning in accordance with the decision of the General Assembly of the United Nations at Lake Success on 21 November 1949. Above the administrative buildings in the capital, Mogadiscio, there now flies the tricolored flag of the Republic of Italy. The Union Jack is lowered. With dignity and simplicity, in harmony and friendship, Britain transferred, at the wish of the United Nations, the administration of Somalia to the Republic of Italy. All was completed without incident and in harmony".[57]

A large crowd of Somalis, including religious and tribal chiefs, attended the historic ceremony. Top officials from Britain and Italy were present to witness the occasion. The outgoing authority, the British, were represented by Gen. Dowler, Commander-in-Chief of the East African Troops, and Gen. Geoffrey Gamble, Chief Administrator of Somalia and Italy by Acting Administrator, Pompeo Gorini, and the Commander of the 'Corpo di Sicurezza' [Security Corps], Gen. Arturo Ferrara, in addition to the Italian Liaison Officer in Somalia, Ambassador Raimondo Manzini. With the same modality, the transfer of power took place in all parts of the Territory, and the day passed without incident, except for a brawl which broke out between elements of the Conferenza and the Lega dei Giovani Somali at Bardera (Upper Juba). The brawl, which later degenerated into shooting, claimed the lives of three persons; a few more were slightly injured.[58]

Immediately after the establishment of the Administration, and in accordance with the Trusteeship Agreement, a consultative body known as the Territorial Council was established.[59] The first Territorial Council was composed of 36 members appointed by the Trust Administrator, of whom 28 were Somalis. Twenty-one seats were held by tribal representatives, 7 by political parties, four by the Italian community, two by the Arab community, and one from both the Indian and Pakistani communities. This step represented an expression, for the first time in Somalia, of direct involvement of the local population of the administration of the country.

Opening the first session of the Territorial Council on 29 January 1951, the Trust Administrator, Ambassador Giovanni Fornari, said: "In a few hours' time, the news of our meeting will cross over the frontier of the territory to convey to all neighbouring and distant countries alike that Somalis of each group and party have started meeting together in an assembly, jointly with exponents of the minority communities. This is still a small assembly, but you should bear in mind that all modern States derive their democratic origin from assemblies like yours".[60]

## Showdown: Brusasca-Aden Abdulla

In the eyes of the SYL party, the new Italian administration in Somalia was identical, in its structure, to the old Fascist era. Most disturbing, among other things, was the large number of civil servants who had once been in Somalia during the Fascist period, now returning to Somalia into the Italian Trusteeship Administration (AFIS), putting doubt in their minds—as the saying went—that the leopard could ever change its spots. Echoing widespread Somali concern, Aden Abdulla made an appeal to the then Italian Premier, Alcide De Gasperi during a visit in Rome on March 28, 1954: 'Your Excellency, if Italy really wants to show good faith towards the Somalis, call home those who are putting obstacles in the way of collaboration between us and the Administration, those who have "baksheesh", paternalism and a kick in the pants as a system of government. The rest will go of its own accord'.[61]

With the exception of the Chief of the Administration and few others, the bulk of the personnel recruited for Somalia, particularly the top ranking officials were staff of the "Ministero dell'Africa Italiana".[62] In a letter to the Administrator, Sig. Giovanni Fornari, the SYL complained the behaviour of some AFIS personnel: "Despite your Excellency's efforts and good intention, we do believe that your staff are of the old Fascist system, whose character will not allow them to adapt to new conditions, Your task will not be made easy and you will never be able to know the real situation".[63]

On the eve of Brusasca's visit to Somalia in May 1950, the SYL Central Committee itself drafted a letter for circulation to all SYL branches north of Belet Uen in which members were instructed to avoid any disturbance of the peace or anti-Italian acts, but also to "not go out of their way to be friendly." Members were also encouraged to accept employment if offered on sufficiently good terms. "The majority of the League Committee and members have taken up a sane viewpoint which reflects to their credit," observed a British diplomatic source in Mogadiscio.[64]

Against this backdrop of growing political tension, the SYL urged Aden Abdulla, who was then the head of the SYL branch in Belet Uen, to come to Mogadiscio and lead a committee of the party for talks with Giuseppe Brusasca, Undersecretary of State for the Ministry of Foreign Affairs of Italy, who came on visit, less than a month after the establishment of the Trusteeship Administration. The talks were expected to be tough for the Italian delegate since the positions of the two sides differed starkly. Ultimately, what stood at the heart of the matter was the fact that Somalis were eagerly anticipating independence and the day Italians would leave Somalia, therefore being unable to think about working with the Italian administration. In those early days of the Italian administration, the SYL was generally doubtful about the sincerity of the Administering Power in fulfilling its international obligations under the Trusteeship Agreement with the United Nations. The few days before his trip to Mogadiscio, Aden Abdulla spent in silence and meditation. He was thinking about how to approach the negotiations with Brusasca at this crucial stage and secure a successful outcome. His feelings towards the Italians were cool but courteous.

At the beginning, the dialogue between Aden Abdulla and Brusasca was not easy, as the SYL delegation assumed an attitude of scepticism, if not outright criticism. A straight-talking man, Aden Abdulla harshly reminded Brusasca of all the wrongs Italy had committed, ranging from the genocide to forced labour, from encouraging tribalism to keeping Somalis in utter ignorance,[65] things he himself had seen for himself as a young man in different parts of the country in previous decades. The conversation between the two men was terse and uncompromising. In a brusque, matter of-fact manner, and reflecting the League's reservations about the Italian return, Aden Abdulla started the conversation by asking, "We wish to know on what basis are you returning to Somalia?" [*Vogliamo sapere che cosa è venuta a fare l'Italia in*

*Somalia*]. Brusasca's response was calm and concise: "We are here on behalf of the United Nations with the task to organize your State".

But unconvinced, Aden Abdulla probed further: "You are not going to use this mandate as a pretext for maintaining your colonialist pretensions, are you?" [*Non farete di questo mandato un pretesto per poi rimanere come colonizzatori?*]. Brusasca, struggling to find an adequate rebuttal in the face of this barrage of accusations pointed out the public infrastructure realized by Italy during the colonial era (particularly the Fascist years). "All that is here has been done by Italy: roads, hospitals, public services, waterworks and sanitation, quite honestly, everything".

Aden Abdulla's reply was curt and to the point. "This is true, but those who came after you granted us something immensely much more important than that. They gave us freedom of expression, freedom to establish political parties, freedom to work for the future of our country" [*E' vero, ma quelli che sono venuti dopo di voi ci hanno dato di immensamente piu' importante , ci hanno dato la liberta' di esprimerci, di costituirci in partito, di lavorare per il future del nostro paese*]. After the initial difficult round, the meeting ended more amicably, with a commitment from the *delegazione leghista* [the SYL or Lega delegation] for frank cooperation with the Administration. This received the blessing of the Central Committee of the party on 9 June, who all, as an indication of the warming of relations, went to the airport to see off Brusasca.[66]

## From confrontation to collaboration

The initial days of the Trusteeship administration were characterized by uneasy relationship between the Administering power and the SYL party, and there were many moments of tension, as a result of which, the stand-off between the two parties had brought relations close to breaking point, causing valuable time to be lost in the first crucial years of the new administration. Aden Abdulla was elected to the first Territorial Council, as part of the SYL party list, which was assembled in 1951 and towards the end of 1953 he was elected Vice President of the Territorial Council.

Sometime in 1953 and before the first municipal elections in 1954, the party asked him to conduct a mediation process to break the impasse. There are good reasons to believe that the Egyptian member of the UN Advisory Council in Somalia (UNACS) was actively involved in pushing the idea of opening a constructive dialogue with the administering authority. It seemed that there was a strong support among the party members for an official revaluation of their policy towards the administering authority. Aden Abdulla was convinced from the beginning that his party had nothing to lose if it co-operated with the Administering Power. He had largely succeeded in convincing his recalcitrant fellow party members to open a channel of dialogue with the administering authority. Gradually, the SYL came to realize the advantages of moderation and constructive dialogue with the Administering Authority, and started opening up from its initial rigid positions.

The Italian Trust Administration of Somalia [Amministrazione Fiduciaria Italiana della Somalia (AFIS)] mirrored, at least in principle, Italy's new democratic profile. Italian authorities put aside the hate and the intolerance of the past and took effective steps in order to seek reconciliation with the most dedicated and militant Somali movement, the SYL. The election for the leadership of the SYL party, held in the territory in 1954, resulted in a sweeping victory for Aden Abdulla, who gained sixty per cent of the seven thousand five hundred votes cast. To many observers, Aden Abdulla's overwhelming victory was a very good sign that the party had come to recognize the advantages of a policy of moderation, and could appreciate "a man of real ability who is capable of holding independent views".[67]

Abdirazak Haji Hussein, a former Prime Minister of Somalia, described Aden Abdulla as "a moderate and practical man, one of the most sensible and sensitive figures to appear in the political scene. Better educated than almost any Somali at the time, he brought a new sense of dedication and nationalistic fervor to the office of President of the party. He was a man ahead of his time, and he influenced me greatly, as he did everyone who associated with him". [68]

In the same year, the inaugural municipal elections were held in Somalia, the first step in the difficult democratization process and an early opportunity to test the degree of maturity achieved by the local population, fewer than four years from the establishment of the Trusteeship Administration. The election results gave the SYL a comfortable majority, 141 out of 281 elective municipal seats. The municipal elections proved to be a key factor in the blossoming of the relationship between the SYL and the Italian Administration, having strengthened the party by making them the most well-represented and hence the principal political party in the territory.

According to British diplomatic sources, Aden Abdulla's policy of moderation and cooperation with the Administration over the previous years had been a success for the party as a whole.[69] The SYL's election victory precipitated a *rapprochement* between the party and the Administration. Apart from being the principal, most well organised political association in the territory, securing the majority of votes in the electoral exercise validated their party's claim as being the voice of the Somali people, an assertion the Administration now seemed to accept. For their part, opting for the path of collaboration with the SYL demonstrated the Administration's genuine desire to find partners with whom it could work in the development of the country in the latter half of its ten-year tenure. A direct consequence of this warming of relations was that conversely the so-called pro-Italian parties lost the political and financial support they had traditionally received from Italy, leading to their disintegration and decline.

From 1950 to 1956, Aden Abdulla divided his time between Belet Uen, where he was local party leader, and Mogadiscio, as one of the SYL representatives in the Territorial Council, the representative organ for the entire territory which was consulted by the Trusteeship Administration on all issues apart from the reserved areas of defence and foreign affairs policy. In the critical pre-independence decade, he emerged as one of the most enlightened members of the Council with ability to analyze issues of political, social and economic nature presented in the Council for debate. For his active participation in the Council's works and grasp of the issues debated at the United Nations, he was chosen, on different occasions, to represent Somalia at the annual discussions taking place before the Trusteeship Council of the United Nations in New York and other international Conferences like the Islamic Conference in Pakistan. His selection as a representative of Somalia in international fora came as a result of endorsement he received from the entire spectrum of political parties present in the Territorial Council, including his long-time political rivals, the Conferenza Somala.

## The 1956 general elections
## Serving as Speaker of the Parliament

Events began to move fast towards self-government. The municipal elections of 1954 were followed two years later by the first parliamentary election in the country held in March 1956.[70] This was a daunting task, not only because it was a new experience for the Somalis, but most importantly because it was scheduled to take place without a clear picture of the size of the population eligible to participate in the election process. In the face of the difficulties involved in organizing a credible census of the nomadic population, AFIS had introduced a mixed election system under the terms of which residents living in the cities and in possession of an electoral card could directly cast their vote, while nomadic populations living in the rural areas expressed their vote through their tribal leaders. This arrangement resulted almost in two categories of electors, which differed from each other in a stark way: while the town dwellers were registered in the municipal electoral roll, were more politically mature and with experience acquired in the 1954 municipal elections, the latter were not registered, largely illiterate and less familiar with the modern political systems.

The Administration advanced a number of detailed arguments in favour of the indirect "second degree" elections among the rural population including the lack of a credible population census. The absence of electoral certificates—and the consequent difficulty of identifying electors—made it difficult to control how the rural population would cast their vote. Using the *shir* system was seen as the only appropriate system, through which each tribal unit would nominate one electoral representative who would subsequently present himself at an electoral college on a date set for the voting. Despite these arguments, Aden Abdulla and his close colleagues in the Territorial Council, such as Haji Mussa Bogor and Haji Farah Ali Omar of the SYL, in agreement with other political parties, persisted in their strong opposition during the discussion in the Territorial Council over the electoral law suggesting the postponement of the political elections until it would be possible to conduct the elections through a direct vote system.[71]

However, to allay these concerns, AFIS proposed, and the SYL accepted, a compromise formula on the basis of which new municipalities were created and the jurisdictions of some already existing were enlarged in order to allow as many voters as possible to take part in the 1956 indirect elections. To this effect, eight new municipalities were established and four existing ones were expanded, bringing the number of new electors casting a direct vote to 35,000.[72]

The election was a success to the SYL, which won 43 of the 60 elected seats in the Parliament. When the party, convened a congress, after the elections, to discuss, among other issues, the formation of the future government, Aden Abdulla, proposed a multi-party cabinet so that other parties could gain experience in executive responsibility, but the party congress voted down the proposal. He always exhorted his fellow party members to acknowledge the presence of lawmakers in the legislature representing the opposition because he believed that the Lega, the majority party, had nothing to worry about. He favoured the institutionalization of a competitive multiparty democratic process with electoral and constitutional accountability.

The congress endorsed his candidacy as President of the Legislative Assembly, a position he could utilize in shaping a future independent Somalia. In fact, as President of Parliament and majority leader, he launched an ambitious campaign to generate ways to reform the structure of his party and improve its cohesion. In his inaugural speech in the Legislative Assembly, he said: "The date of 30 April 1956 will remain engraved in golden characters in the first pages of the history of this country, but will also remain engraved in the hearts and minds of all Somalis grateful and appreciative of Italy and the United Nations who have made such a big step possible".[73]

In the wider sequence of events in 1956, the most significant was the establishment of the first Somali government, led by a Somali Prime Minister, a government enjoying very wide powers regarding internal administration of the territory.[74] A second critical event was the transformation of the Territorial Council into a fully-fledged elective legislative body, with full statutory powers over legislation dealing with domestic affairs.

After the election of the first Somali Parliament and government in 1956, Aden Abdulla reminded the new Somali government that political independence was not enough as many had understood it as the replacement of white masters by black masters with all accompanying privileges. The President urged the new government to do away with the malpractice of offering foreign currency to persons with no regular import and export trading licenses and that the use of official government cars be limited to official purposes in order to reduce the cost to the taxpayer. In the economic field he encouraged the government to fight against profligate spending and take measures to ensuring that the revenue and expenditure shown in the national budget be kept in balance.

## Census of the population residing outside the municipal areas. Failure of the process

One of the most difficult tasks, which required urgent attention before independence, was the issue of the population census of the Trust Territory, particularly regarding rural dwellers. There had never been a proper census although the Italian Trust Administration tried to count the population of the urban dwellers in anticipation of the 1954 municipal elections. The issue had been a subject of intense debate since the early years of the Trusteeship Administration and before the 1956 general elections. However, while all the concerned parties, including the United Nations, the Administering Authority and the Somali political parties, were in full agreement as to the necessity of carrying out an official population census, they seemed to be lacking a clear idea of how such a complicated process could best be executed.

Acting under growing pressure, the new government introduced a draft law in 1956 on population census limited to the rural population. The Somali Legislative Assembly approved the law with minor amendments on September 6, 1956 by 33 votes for, 25 against and one abstention.[75] In practice, the survey required by law was a mere registration of population rather than a real census of the population residing outside the municipal areas, and the process, as predicted, ended in total failure.[76] Apart from establishing records of the rural population, the exercise was also considered as a means of identifying those nomads entitled to vote in the political elections scheduled for 1959 and to whom an electoral certificate would be issued in order to overcome the unsatisfactory indirect system of voting through electoral representatives.

Both AFIS and the Somali government made costly efforts to secure a registration of the nomads and to complete the process within the time limit assigned to it. It was clearly an ambitious and complicated operation and many, including the United Nations, expressed reservations about its success from the outset. One obvious shortcoming was the absence of qualified personnel to carry out such a sophisticated operation. The census law provided for a registry office for the extra-municipal population to be set up in each district and for the census-taking operation to be completed in 12 months.

Started on January 10, 1957, it was to have been completed on December 31 of the same year. The exercise was to be conducted in three phases: direct survey carried out by salaried tribal chiefs acting as census-taking chiefs; registration and control carried out by the district officers and finally, revision and inspection entrusted to regional officers. The resulting documents would be firstly, the census list, compiled by the census takers, which would include various data (sex, name, patronymic name, paternal grandfather) and secondly, the population registers, filed on a card index system, which would be kept in the district offices.[77]

As predicted, and despite the efforts made by the Ministry of the Interior, the census count was not successful in all six regions. At the very outset, it was realized that the operation would be fraught with many serious difficulties, particularly if the chiefs did not give their full co-operation. In the capital, for instance, many of the inhabitants gave false names because they feared the collected data may be used for taxation purposes or military recruitment. In three regions (Benadir, Hiran and Upper Juba), there was a considerable degree of success; in the other regions (Migiurtinia, Mudugh and Lower Juba), there was a failure to obtain accurate results.[78] The census, intended to produce electoral rolls for a poll on the basis of individual participation under terms of secret ballot to all those eligible, had been a farce.

The United Nations Advisory Council for Somalia (UNCAS) confirmed the failure of the census operation, reporting: "It is significant to note that the most sparsely settled region, Migiurtinia, by November 1957 had recorded no fewer than 889,000 persons".[79] Another UN document reported that the most sparsely settled regions together (Migiurtinia and Mudugh) had listed more persons (1,295,000) than the rest of Somalia, where population was estimated to stand at 1,070,000.[80] In 1941, the British Military Administration estimate was approximately 971,000 in 1947, though with regards to the nomadic population, the estimate was considered by the Administration as susceptible to a margin of error of up to 20 per cent. The Italian Trust Administration considered 1,250,000 to be a more reliable figure.[81]

The only known census conducted in 1931 showed that the lowest population density was registered in Migiurtinia and Mudugh because of the aridity of the terrain (0.8 persons per $km^2$), while the highest level of density was registered in the inter-riverine areas (3.5 persons per $km^2$).[82] According to analysts, the failure of this exercise was caused by "reasons of prestige and [...] failure to understand the significance of census taking. Tribal Chiefs in the nomadic areas were eager to report impressive numbers of tribesmen. Many of them filed lists containing the names of non-existing tribesmen".[83]

## The first fissures

## Italy threatens to relinquish the trusteeship mandate

In-fighting within the Somali Youth League party began immediately after the formation of the first Somali government in 1956. The infighting turned bitter and the party began to fracture. Halfway before the expiry of the Trusteeship mandate, the foundation of the future Somali state was laid down, and the Trust Territory was rapidly moving towards its full independence set for December 1960. However, the summer of 1957 and autumn of 1958, a complex political and institutional crisis brought the SYL under the control of the pro-Nasserite party faction led by Haji Mohamed Hussein. With sound backing from the Egyptian government, Hajj Mohamed Hussein was elected leader of the party on July 28, 1957 while he was residing in Cairo thanks to a scholarship from the University of Al-Azhar. Aden Abdulla was elected Vice President of the party.

By the time Haji had returned from Egypt, the country had changed a great deal. There was a functioning government, led by his own party, in charge of the domestic affairs of the territory; his party held the majority of seats in the Legislative Assembly; the administration underwent a process of Somalization to replace Italian personnel with Somali counterparts, faster than many had predicted, and the political atmosphere between AFIS and the ruling party was one of co-operation, with a focus on the target date of independence and a smooth transfer of power even ahead of the date originally sanctioned by the United Nations.

However, the newly elected president of the ruling party soon found himself out of step with the thinking of the mainstream of party members and the government. He started delivering inflammatory statements against the Trusteeship Administration and the Somali government alike, accusing the latter of "betrayal" of the party principles. Since his return from Egypt, he had been a thorn in the Administration's side and an embarrassment to those party fellows who did not share his radical views. Hajji's populist calls to expropriate Italian-owned farm land, without compensation, had become a source of frustrations for Italy, at a time when she was even ready to put the independence date forward, should the Somalis make such a request. "His venomous attacks created a strong feeling of resentment within the party. The fact that he had been elected while he was out of the country gave him an overinflated sense of his popularity, and he had no fear of counterattack".[84]

In October 1957, Administrator Anzilotti declared before the Legislative Assembly the need for collaboration between the ruling party and AFIS, referring also to the possibility of Somalia attaining its independence before December 2, 1960. In his statement, he said: "Should such collaboration between the Administering Authority, the Somali people and the political parties disappear, it would only remain for Italy to inform the United Nations of the impossibility of honouring the international obligations, the Italian government stated, not long ago, it would completely fulfill until the expiration of the mandate." He added: "The same would be all the truer should the Somali people manifest expressly through legitimate channels their will to obtain full independence before 2 December 1960".[85]

On February 7, 1958, the Somali Prime Minister received a chilling letter from the Administrator stating that clear action by the Somali government was essential to clarify its official policy towards Italy and restore confidence in foreign investors. The letter concluded: "As it is evident, the President of the SYL, after his return to Somalia, continued doing what he used to do through Cairo Radio, making public speeches in open contrast not only with the commitments and the assurances given by the party in its electoral platform, but also with the Legislative Assembly and the Government, with regard to the protection of the life and property of aliens resident in Somalia, and to the guarantees offered to foreign capital investment in Somalia; furthermore these statements constitute a threat to public order". Anzilotti made it clear that, if the prevailing uncertain situation was to continue, the Italian government would be obliged to report to the United Nations on the situation that was developing in Somalia, and urged the Prime Minister to obtain from the Legislative Assembly "an unequivocal statement regarding the value of the assurance which the same Assembly formally reaffirmed on various occasions concerning the protection of the life and property of foreigners residing in Somalia and the guarantees afforded to investments of foreign capital in the Territory.[86]

The firm Italian position raised the real prospect of the Territory being abandoned without direction. The government, reacting to Anzilotti's request, addressed a letter to the Central Committee requesting clarification of the party's position vis-à-vis the statements of the newly elected President. Faced with the prospect that Italy might surrender the mandate before the target date for independence, the Central Committee of the ruling party hastened to take measures to avert the worst.

The British government which was closely following the internal political situation in Somalia suggested that, should the state of affairs develop in a way such as to render Italian position in any way untenable, could the United Nations be persuaded to appoint a Somali, say Aden Abdulla, Administrator for Somalia for the remaining period until December 1960".[87] At this juncture, Aden Abdulla was both displeased with Haji Mohamed's stance for his Egyptian stance and for his well-known pro-Communist policy and frustrated with certain members of the executive committee of the party "for their factionalism, incongruent with the party's policy".[88]

The crisis within the ranks of the ruling party had assumed new dramatic dimension when Aden Abdulla resigned from his position as the party's Vice President after publicly denouncing the bickering, radicalization and dangerous polarization within the Central Committee between Darod and Hawiye clans, the latter ethnic group forming most members ready to support the government for good or bad. He went as far as invoking Allah's wrath upon those party members who encouraged tribalism. Indeed what was most worrying to Aden Abdulla was the pro-communist Egyptian policy of the party's President and his overtly anti-western hostility at a crucial time when wisdom would have dictated the maintenance of a more balanced policy towards the major friendly foreign powers.

However, the Central Committee had rejected outright the resignation. A three-member delegation composed of Sheikh Issa Mohamed, Mohamed Ossoble Adde and Haji Jimcale Barre, was tasked to convince him to rescind his decision.[89] The resignation was later withdrawn on condition that the President of the party changed his policy and returned to the fold.

## The SYL party dismisses Haji Mohamed

An extraordinary party congress was convened in Mogadiscio from 28 March to 26 June, 1958, with the party crisis at the top of the agenda. Some 116 delegates took part, including 19 Central Committee members, 43 MPs and 47 branch secretaries. There were also a delegate from British Somaliland and several delegates from the Ogaden tribes, none of whom had a right to vote. During the debate Aden Abdulla, in his capacity as deputy leader of the party, delivered an acerbic, point-by-point takedown of Haji Mohamed's worldview and brand of nationalism.

'It is true that from the beginning until the last elections of Haji Mohamed to the presidency, this happy organization [the Lega] has always been managed in a comradely way and there has never been any necessity for us to defend ourselves against the ambitious deviations and "personality cult" that seem to be the chief aim and tactics of Haji Mohamed.

'The current President left Somalia for Egypt in 1952 of his own free will, abandoning the post of president that he had held for several years. It is the opinion of many that he ran away from difficulties. He did not ask himself whether he should remain to help in the fight. He followed his personal interest.

'In 1957 once again the question of the presidency of the party was raised. Nobody opposed his nomination although he was abroad. He was elected and the first thing he did, by means of Egyptian radio, was to make believe that all the leaders in Somalia were traitors paid by the colonialists whom they served, and that our people were living under the worst kind of colonialism.

'According to Mohamed Hussein, to work in politics means to scheme against one's own friends in their own party, as he did over the Egyptian radio and has done since his return.

'Till now I have refrained from contradicting him publicly as I hoped the members of the party should condemn him, but nobody can have patience with this man.

'I have twice made speeches without first consulting the Central Committee and I am ready to suffer the consequences. I did it to provoke the reactions of the President, but Haji Mohamed Hussein has not reacted, and his bad faith is manifest.

'The President continued to do this because evidently, as he declared in Aden and Hargeisa, he was not afraid of the government or the Central Committee in which he had no confidence, but counted on the people who he pretended had given him their confidence, and had no confidence in the others.

"It is not by inciting the people against foreigners that we can gain the confidence of those foreigners. It is not by awakening the jealousy and envy of the masses that the interests of Somalia will be advanced.

In response to the President's call for the forcible nationalisation of Italian-owned farmland, Aden Abdulle said: "If, as is meant to be, and justly so, we wish the majority of Somali firms to be owned by Somalis, this can be realized by means of a law that we can pass, but no other way can succeed. Haji Mohamed has used a battering ram on open doors. For example, he has said that any contributions from individual foreign states towards aid to Somalia must be given through the United Nations: Haji Farah Ali, Minister of Economic Affairs, had already said this to the United Nations on instructions from the Somali government. He has said that the independence of Somalia must be declared after the election and the mandate ended: this is a matter that was already decided and it is quite clear that the Administrator made his memorable declaration only after consulting the Lega dei Giovani Somali.

"The Administratoi had naturally made such declarations with the full consent of his government, and which we are counting on, the anticipated independence of Somalia is already endorsed and can materialize without any difficulty.

"But if Italy, as she threatened to do, renounces the mandate for the Somalis' fault, have you thought of the risk we are running?

"In every country of the world, for imperative monetary reasons, the State tries to compel the country from which it buys to give an amount equal to what it has spent. Italy, therefore, is within its rights if in exchange for our exports it asks that we respond with equal imports from Italy.

'On the border question, Haji Mohamed said, if I am not mistaken, that England told us that without her the Abyssinians would not spare us. Are we inferring this or have we any proof of such a thing? We have had several talks with English personalities and also with personalities from several other countries, and nobody has yet told us to seek the protection of their country against the Ethiopians or anyone else nor have any of them shown any preoccupation at the danger of Ethiopian aggression against Somalia. And I remember very well several of them advised us to do our utmost so that we and Ethiopia could diminish our mutual mistrust by at least half.

'To speak like that is, in my view, dangerous for Somalia and amounts to nothing less than trying to discredit the policy of independent powers that have their own good reasons for following a certain policy.

"If, in reality, Haji Mohamed wishes to follow a neutral policy, why speak evil of certain powers and well of others. Is this neutrality?

"One last word: I have already pointed out to Haji Mohamed one of the results that could emerge from his conduct, a result none of us would like to see. We are grateful to Egypt for all she is doing and do not wish the Somalis to be divided into pro- and anti-Egyptian [camps]. But as Haji Mohamed began his campaign in Egypt and has now come from that country, rightly or wrongly, it will be inevitable that someone will blame Egypt for what he says and then create enemies for Egypt herself. You must judge".[90]

While the party Congress was still in session, Aden Abdulla arranged a meeting with Haji Mohamed; this informal encounter, in the mind of Aden, was meant to clarify some of the misunderstandings arising out of the political crisis. The tone and the substance of the conversation between the two men was recorded in Aden Abdulla's journal thusly: "Dear Haji, since your return from Egypt you have been behaving badly and I had noticed that you perceive me as your worst enemy and I do not really know what I did against you. I want to start by saying that you should be grateful to me as I, on more than one occasion, extended financial support to you and paid a visit to you as a token of sympathy when you had been wronged by the SYL government which supported the opposition leader, Mohamed Sheikh Osman "Edmondo" by publishing his criticism against you and refusing to accept likewise the publication of a letter from Sheikh Mohamed Issak and company in your defence.

'You cannot boast of a single favour you did to me. The ill feeling you harbour towards me cannot be interpreted if not in relation to your ambition to become, in the future, President of the Republic, and you think that I might be among those, if not the only one, who may overshadow you. If this is the case, I swear on what I most value in the life that it had never crossed my mind to compete with you and that I have no obsession or anxious to become President, even if I would not mind having such an honour. The policy that you are engaged in will cause split among the SYL ranks; some will follow you and the rest will be with the party leadership whom you refer to, in your speeches, as traitors notwithstanding that they took Somalia and the party, during your 5 years of absence, to the current level of self-government and position of strength in the political struggle.

'Somalia today can be compared to someone locked up and whose release is in the hands of 60 persons who must agree to free the country from the prison. We cannot afford the luxury of criticizing some UN members nor is it convenient for us to scare away the Italians in Somalia". Haji Mohamed's reaction to this frank statement was concise and challenging. He said "When the water stagnates, it becomes breeding ground for larvae and therefore we have to keep going ahead"; Aden Abdulla interpreted these words as refusal to his advice.[91]

Haji Mohamed was expelled from the SYL party on grounds that he "impaired the unity of the party, showed dictatorial tendencies, and had acted contrary to the party statute".[92] The resolution issued by the party Congress read: "Taking into consideration the fact that the current President does not intend to observe the democratic practice which is the essence of the life of the party; taking account also of the attitude assumed by Mr. Haji Mohamed Hussein, not only in the capital city, but also up-country, where he delivered speeches and made declarations, with no consideration for general interests not only of the Party, but also of the country of which the Party is a vigilant protector; in consideration of the demonstration organized by Mr. Haji Mohamed Hussein, designed to influence the decision of the Congress currently in session, and of the speech he delivered to the demonstrators in which, with no consideration for the consequences that could come upon the country, already on the verge of independence, he incited the public to "spill blood" for freedom.[93]

Without running for leadership and, notwithstanding the clear arguments he put forward for not seeking office, Aden Abdulla's name was included in the list of candidates. On June 9, the party congress elected him to succeed Haji Mohamed as party leader by a bare majority of 44 to 42 votes.[94] His closest contender, Sheikh Mohamoud Ahmed Mohamed Adddan, "Kutubaxoor", a deputy representing Adale district, received 42 votes. However, immediately after his election, Aden Abdulla declared before the Congress that he would not accept the responsibility bestowed on him. The Congress unanimously and repeatedly asked him, insisting even threatening him with expulsion from the party, to accept the responsibility to lead the party for the good of the party and the country. Aden Abdulla reiterated his decision not to accept the responsibility to lead the party.

It was only following increased pressure brought to bear on him from many quarters and groups, that he reluctantly accepted the post, with the proviso that: (a) the election process be repeated so that he might get a full endorsement from the Congress, (b) the Central Committee of the Party to support his reform policy, and (c) the government to assure collaboration with the Party, and with him in particular. When the election process was repeated for the second time on the night of June 11, by open ballot, Aden Abdulla received a quasi-unanimous vote: 66 votes out of some seventy voting members of the Congress.[95] Italian diplomatic sources based in Mogadiscio, described him as the only man with the highest degree of personal qualities needed to bring back the party, out of its current crisis "to concord, unity and cohesion".[96]

This was the second time Aden Abdulla was being elected party leader after 1953. His election was a surprise because of the unusual circumstances that precipitated it. To start with, he did not run for the position. At the time, he was holding the office of president of the Legislative Assembly and was tormented by two main preoccupations: firstly, that the accumulation of the two functions as President of the Party (if he were elected) and President of the Legislative Assembly might undermine the efficiency of one or both bodies and secondly, as one of the strongest critics of Haji Mohamed's policy, he did not want to be seen as coveting party leadership.

## The 1959 political elections

## Aden Abdulla reconfirmed President of the National Assembly

The 1959 political elections, the second held under the trusteeship regime, started on 4 March and were spread out over the following four days because of the largely nomadic or semi-nomadic character of the population who cast their votes without electoral certificates. The elections, which ended peacefully, were for the first time held on a universal adult franchise, meaning that the right to vote was extended to women.[97] Out of the 30 constituencies nationwide, 19 were presented with party lists only by the SYL in a practice described as *Lista Unica* [sole list of candidates], a fraudulent system which obviously favoured the SYL.

In areas where only one list was registered, the Minister of the Interior was empowered to enact provisions in order to prevent electors from one area going to vote in other areas. On the face of it, that sounded reassuring, but these provisions were defined in such a loose way as to render them almost meaningless. As there was no system for the registration of voters, repetitive voting was controlled by the application of pigmentation on the back of the voter's hand; but various ruses were adopted by voters to overcome this prohibition. Both the opposition parties and the United Nations Advisory Council, based in Mogadiscio, expressed concerns over whether elections would be free and fair.

In the general elections of 1959 the SYL won the majority of seats in the parliament. However, political commentators, including the United Nations, accused the party of winning through the use of intimidation tactics and electoral malpractices. In fact, the voting pattern in many areas showed that 100 per cent of the vote was cast for the ruling party. Ultimately, when the ballots were counted, distribution of seats in the legislature among the political parties was 83 to the SYL, 5 to the HDMS and 2 to the Liberal party. Systematic electoral fraud including double voting in many constituencies, stuffed ballot boxes, and electoral officials changing electoral results had a decisive impact on the outcome of the 1959 elections. Aden Abdulla, who was closely following the election process, made this comment in his diary: 'I rejoice at the victory of my party, but at the same time, I would have been equally glad had there been strong opposition and had the "unopposed" list not been a product of fraud'.[98]

Deprived of the victory it was confidently expecting, the Hisbia Destur Mustaqil Somali (HDMS), cried foul, asking the courts to annul the results of a number of districts including Lugh Ferrandi (Upper Juba). As a result of this legal challenge, the electoral results of this district were invalidated by the judicial authorities on grounds of irregularities.[99]

Soon after the elections, a serious, unexpected crisis surfaced again within the ruling party leadership, resulting in petty feuds. In the Central Committee, the members remained split on two key proposals put forward by the President of the Party: (a) to convene a Congress and involve the party members up-country in the selection process for the future Prime Minister and the President of the Legislative Assembly after the general election, and (b) to form a coalition government with the participation of all the parties represented in the National Assembly. When the first proposal was put on vote, it was rejected by 10 votes, 7 in favour and 2 abstentions. Similarly, within the government there were divergent views over the convening of the Congress. Aden Abdulla felt uneasy at the way the party leadership failed to engage with the membership in a meaningful way: "It is with regret that I note that we resort to them when we need their support, but exclude them from taking part in important political decisions".[100]

In reaction to this result, he submitted his resignation from party leadership, later withdrawn when the reasons which caused it were eliminated and a consensus was reached to convene an extraordinary party congress.[101] A communiqué printed by the government's official newspaper, the *Corriere della Somalia*, announcing the end of the crisis caused by Aden Abdulla's resignation, read: "The Central Committee of the Lega announces that it has resolved the internal crisis affecting the Party leadership since March 26, 1959. The leader of the party has in fact withdrawn his resignation. [...] The Committee re-examined the reasons that prompted the crisis and adopted measures including the convening of a congress limited only to a single representative from each of the outpost districts".[102]

The highly anticipated Congress of the party, was finally convened on May 22, its immediate task being, among other things, to designate the president of the Legislative Assembly and the future Prime Minister, two positions which had become vacant following the general elections in March. At the end of a marathon session lasting from 9.30 a.m. to the following morning at 12:35 a.m., the results of the vote for the premiership were: for Abdullahi Issa, 68; and 52 for Aden Abdulla, In the same session, the Congress designated Aden Abdulla as President of the Legislative Assembly.the results of the voting were: 66 votes for Aden Abdulla, and 38 for Abdullahi Issa, The proposal for forming a coalition government was defeated and the Congress instead passed a motion in favour of an SYL government.[103]

When the new Parliament held its first meeting on May 26, Aden Abdulla was, for the second time, elected President of that body, obtaining 76 votes out of 87.[104] On the same day, two Vice Presidents were elected in the persons of Abdulkadir Mohamed Aden "Zoppo" (HDMS) and Haji Bashir Ismail Yusuf (SYL).[105] The division of functions within the presidency of the Legislative Assembly clearly reflected a tribal balance as the President belonged to the Hawiye and his two deputies to the Rahanweyn and Darod respectively. In June 1959, the leadership of the SYL passed to Sheikh Issa Mohamed Abukar, who had been on the board since the establishment of the party in 1947.

However, Aden Abdulla's difficulties with his party did not end there as a bizarre situation emerged on the heels of the invalidation of Lugh Ferrandi's election results. Prior to the judicial revision, the two seats of Lugh were allocated to the SYL party represented by two MPs hailing from the Darod clan family. Soon after the Court ruling was made public, an angry Darod clan group, all associated with the ruling party, met Aden Abdulla in his office at the National Assembly on April 11, 1959 to claim the "right" of their clan to secure the two seats invalidated by the Court.

Aden Abdulla, still Leader of the party, gave the following account in his journal of the atmosphere which prevailed in his meeting with the group: "This morning at 10:00 a.m., I received in my office at the National Assembly:

Messrs Haji Dirie Hersi, Haji Mohamud Abdille Dirir, Haji Mohamud Abdi Dheere, and Sugulle Habsey, accompanied by Haji Mussa Boqor. It was Haji Mussa who at 9.00 a.m. informed me in advance about the desire of the group to see me together with Abdullahi Issa, the Prime Minister. Abdullahi was nowhere to be seen". Of the group only Haji Mussa Bogor was a member of the Parliament, the others were long-standing members of the SYL party.[106]

Aden Abdulla added that, "On behalf of the Darod, they spoke angrily about the invalidation of Lugh election decreed by the Court of Upper Juba asking the Court decision to be reversed whether rightfully or wrongly. They intend to get their way, by hook or by crook. If I understood them well, as [a] Darod [group], they would denounce the entire election process. I tried to explain to them that it was inappropriate to present the case in that way; that what happened was not nobody's fault because the Hisbia had the right to seek redress from the Judge and [it was] for him to decide [the case] after ascertaining the facts. Anyway I told them to bring the matter to the attention of the Prime Minister, but not in the way they had presented to me i.e., in the name of the Darod! I was unable to conceal my anger and went as far as to say that I could not intervene in the matter unless they recognized the two seats were claimed on behalf of the SYL party and not of the Darod. Having made my position clear, they changed their attitude, displaying a more reasonable tone",[107] and it seems they did not pursue the matter further, as Aden Abdulla did not produce any entries on later developments.

## Leadership challenge
## Splits within the SYL along clan lines

As the country became increasingly jittery on the eve of independence, a behind-the-scenes struggle started for leadership of the post-trusteeship regime. A major political development after the elections was the formation of the second Somali government. Premier Abdullahi Issa formed his second government, a fifteen-strong Cabinet reflecting tribal balance on June 16, 1959. The broad-based government gave proportional share to all three major contending clan families represented in the Parliament. However, the government soon came under fire from a faction of mainly Majerten Darod MPs of the party, led by Abdirashid Ali Sharmarke and Abdirazak Haji Hussein. Their criticism to the Prime Minister focused on three key points:

(a) the way the government had handled the parliamentary elections of March 1959, which they held had been rigged in many areas of the country; (b) the enlarged Cabinet which, in their view, was a burden on the small national budget; and (c) the moral standard and professional qualifications of the ministers, considered to be below the required stand for them to discharge their ministerial duties effectively. In truth, however, there was an underlying tribal feeling and much personal bitterness moved by different interests and different aims.

Aden Abdulla urged the dissident group to cast aside revenge, resentment and retributions and appealed for co-operation between the party members.[108] He spared no efforts to bring the parties and factions together in reconciliation but all his efforts failed. He was disheartened and felt he was facing one failure after another expressing his disappointment. "We created the Somali Youth League and for this party we have made all form of sacrifice to see Somalia united and free from foreign shackles. But, now that we are on the eve of being fully independent, we are risking everything we have done through our own egoistic and factionalist actions" [*Abbiamo creato la Lega dei Giovani Somali; per essa abbiamo fatto ogni sacrificio onde vedere i Somali uniti ed indipendenti dal giogo straniero, ed ora che siamo alla vigilia di essere completamente liberi, con le nostre stesse azioni, di egoismo fazioso, stiamo rischiando di rovinare tutto*].[109] He accused his colleagues of playing political games, susceptible of tarnishing the country's image abroad ahead of the approaching Independence Day.[110]

When all attempts to solve the crisis failed, the party's bickering eventually landed at the United Nations. In fact, a defiant Abdirazak Haji Hussein, together with his colleague Mohamoud Ahmed Mohamed Addan "Kutubaxoor", travelled to New York in July to challenge the legitimacy of the Somali government before the United Nations Trusteeship Council.[111] Protesting before the United Nations against the Somali government were also representatives from the traditional opposition parties: Hisbia Destur Mustaqil Somali (HDMS), the Somali National Union (SANU), and the Greater Somali League (GSL). In reality, although the President of the Parliament shared some of the grievances aired by the dissidents, he firmly believed that the matter could have been better addressed through political processes rather than taking it to the United Nations.

In a move designed to pre-empt the dissidents' plan, the government, in addition to the strong delegation already present in New York, urgently dispatched two more MPs, assisted by a Police Officer, Lt. Col. Daud Abdulla

Hersi to the United Nations.[112] The irony was that the two MPs sent to New York (Ali Mohamed Hirabe, known as "Ali Hagarey", and Abdullahi Haji Mohamud Jama, known as "Insaaniya") were in the past well-known prominent members of an anti-SYL front.[113] The two were carrying with them written statements, bearing many signatures of ordinary persons to prove the popular support the new government was allegedly enjoying. Many feared that the concerted protests before the United Nations might call into doubt whether the country was ready for independence, and this was the last thing any Somali in his right mind would have wanted to happen. Luckily, however, there was no disposition among the members of the UN Trusteeship Council to interfere with the internal affairs of Somali politics, and no delegation made any attempt to seriously embarrass the SYL government. Even the USSR was very mild in their criticism, which was directed carefully at the administering authority and not at the Somali government. "The demands of the petitioners were not, therefore, taken up, and they made little impression", commented the UK delegate to the United Nations.[114]

Realizing that his arguments were unlikely to cut much ice with the members of the Trusteeship Council, Abdirazak Haji Hussein refused to be drawn into any general indictment of the Somali government. Instead he made a face-saving statement on July 25 on behalf of all Somali petitioners present at the UN in which he said, "All Somalis were one in pursuit of certain general aims for the future of Somalia which would be achieved with the harmonious cooperation of all segments of the people".[115] Most Somali breathed a collective, heavy sigh of relief that wide-scale violence and chaos were mercifully avoided. Yet the country remained badly split, largely along clan family lines.

## The Legislative Assembly becomes a constituent Organ The drafting of the Constitution

The Trusteeship Agreement provided no clear indications as to whether the Administering Authority was expected to prepare a constitutional charter for the Trust Territory or whether this was an issue to be tackled by the Somali government after independence.[116] However, the Administration started drafting a Constitution, with the aim of having it ready before independence. Much time was devoted to this work in the last three years of the Trusteeship period and for this purpose, two committees were appointed: a Political

Committee and a Technical Committee.

The Legislative Assembly was therefore to carry out two functions: that of approving the Constitution as a constituent body but also continuing its law-making duties as the nation's legislature. In his capacity as President of the Assembly, Aden Abdulla became Chairman of the Political Committee and Professor Giuseppe Aurelio Costanzo (Dean of the Somali Institute of Law, Economics and Social Science) Chairman of the Technical Committee.[117] A second step towards self-government came in January 1960 when the Legislative Assembly, elected in the 1959 elections, was formally transformed into a Constituent Assembly for the purpose of framing and approving the constitution of the future state.[118]

The draft provisions became the source of a controversy over the form of government that the new nation would adopt. The Hisbia Destur Mustaqil Somali party (HDMS) advocated a federal government, a principle enshrined in the statute of the party.[119] This preference derived from a deep-seated fear of dominance, by the northen pastoralist clans generally supporting the SYL. By contrast, the SYL advocated a unitary form of government, arguing that federalism would encourage clannishness. The federal system was seen as a dangerous principle that clan and regional groups could resort to, with potentially destructive effects on the integrity of the country.

In the end, political and numerical strength enabled the SYL to prevail and the unitary system was adopted. The 1960 Constitution also adopted the unicameral instead of the bicameral legislature which exists in many countries, including Italy. The rationale behind the choice rested on its relative advantages because the process in such a legislative system was quicker; bicameral legislatures, for instance, were susceptible to deadlocks, the inability to pass legislation because neither house was willing to compromise on its version of a bill. Similarly, having two Houses would constitute a greater strain on the country's budget.

In view of the fact that the Somali Legislative Assembly was almost entirely composed of Lega members, the UN Trusteeship Council recommended in 1959 that the composition of the Political Committee and Constituent Assembly be broadened to include representatives of all existing political parties and other important social and cultural organizations of the Territory.[120] Aden Abdulla came to prominence again when, during the debate on the draft Constitution, he strongly supported the UN recommendation calling for broadening the Political Committee and the Constituent Assembly to include representatives of political parties, having no representation in the Parliament.

The Somali government was highly suspicious of the proposal which it saw as a clear sign of the Trusteeship Council's long-held reservations on the fairness of the 1959 general elections.[121] Aden Abdulla led the MPs in favour of the UN proposal arguing that the National Assembly, elected in 1959, was expected to deal only with ordinary legislation and as such it had no mandate to draft a constitution, hence the need to include in the representatives of all existing political parties. Pressured by different parties, the government eventually accepted the UN recommendation to include two members of each existing political party in the Constituent Assembly.[122]

Between October 1957 and May 1959, the Technical Committee prepared a preliminary draft constitution of 141 articles, accompanied by a 316-page commentary. In parallel, the Minister of the Constitutional Affairs produced a shorter draft constitution, with 64 articles. Both drafts were examined by a Drafting Political Committee of fifty Somali members between 4 April and May 1960. The Committee approved a new draft of 100 articles and submitted it to the Constituent Assembly, for it to be considered by the 90 deputies of the Legislative Assembly who were joined by twenty additional Somali members.

Deliberations began on 23 May. With only a few changes, the Assembly approved the draft of the Political Committee which was then later adopted by acclamation by the Constituent Assembly on 21 June 1959.[123] After being issued by the provisional President of the Republic, it came into force on July 1, 1960. Eighty-seven deputies were present during the approval of the final text of the Constitution. It had taken one year and several sessions to complete the work. In fairness, some of the delays were the product of attempts to find a compromise with the members of the Assembly, who were conservative (both religiously and culturally). The scholarly work of the Techinical Committee facilitated the rapid conclusion of a highly successful debate that produced the constitution of 1961. "The Constitution thus prepared was essentially a democratic instrument based on Western, and especially on the model of the Constitution of Italy. It represented the culmination of the efforts to evolve a modern political structure for a traditionally democratic society".[124]

# SECTION 1

# PART 3

# SECTION ONE, PART THREE

# INDEPENDENCE COMES AT MIDNIGHT

## Aden Abdulla elected provisional Head of State

In Law no. 643 of June 28, 1960, the Italian government decreed the termination of its Trusteeship Agreement of Italian Somaliland. The UN Trusteeship Administration (AFIS) thus formally ended its trusteeship administration in Somalia at 1630hrs on June 1960,[125] six months before the time stipulated in the Trusteeship Agreement, and the last administrator, Ambassador Mario Di Stefano, left Mogadiscio on board a plane bound for Nairobi, Kenya. At 6 o'clock in the evening, in all centres of Somalia, the Italian and UN flags were lowered for the last time. The date for the independence of the Trust Territory of Somalia was originally scheduled for December 2, 1960 but was brought forward by a Resolution of United Nations General Assembly,[126] given that the main objectives of the administration had been reached.

Despite the SYL's initial misgivings, the 1950s were something of a golden age for Somalia. With UN development funds pouring in and experienced Italian administrators who had come to see Somalia as their home, infrastructural and educational projects flourished. This decade passed relatively without incident and was marked by positive growth in virtually all parts of Somali life. Meanwhile, the politicians of Italian Somaliland were already in discussions with leaders from British Somaliland about the prospect of the unity of the two entities, a plan which was agreed in April 1960. With Italian Somaliland's independence scheduled for 1 July, the British relinquished claim to the British protectorate in the north and both joined to form the new-born republic. The legislative assemblies from both met in the red-brick building in Mogadishu, hitherto the home of the Legislative Assembly, for the first time on that day. In that meeting, Aden Abdulla, 52, was elected with 107 votes out of 115 deputies present and voting, as provisional Head of State for a period of one year, until the time when the Constitution would be approved by referendum. He promulgated the Constitution, and from that date, the Constitution provisionally came into force throughout the Republic.

Describing the qualifications which might explain his election, Angelo Del Boca, the Italian historian who was present during the independence celebrations, described the new Head of State, in the following words: "If there is a man who can claim the status of determined and coherent nationalist, in addition to being a moderate, this man is Aden Abdulla" [*Se c'è un uomo che può vantare la qualifica di nazionalista risoluto e coerente, ma anche quella di politico moderato e conciliante, quest'uomo è Aden Abdulla Osman*].[127]

The boy whose first memories included watching his village of origin destroyed by the invading alien forces and who went on internal exile with his father, grew up to become one of the most prominent political figures in modern Somalia. In his rise to the presidency, Aden Abdulla held a various key positions over the years. He served as local Secretary of the SYL in Belet Uen, two times Leader of the SYL ruling party and Member of the Territorial Council (Consiglio Territoriale) for ten years as well as President of the Legislative Assembly. Strikingly, he had never run for or sought any of the positions he had served in during his long political career. His sense of the State and his political integrity were the base for his election to all the positions he served in.

At midnight on the 30th of June 1960, the Somali flag was hoisted atop the National Assembly building. The Provisional Head of State, Aden Abdulla, appeared on the terrace of the building's tower where he was greeted by a very large crowd of happy and cheering Somalis below. When the people gathered in the main square facing the Parliament, the African Solidarity Square, and saw the hoisting of the flag above the National Assembly building, cannon salvoes numbering 114, equal to the number of chapters in the Koran, marked the occasion.[128] That night was gentle by the standards of the summer monsoon, the Crux—or the Southern Cross, which gave its name to a hotel in the centre of town built in the colonial era in the Modernist style—beaming in the dark sky. When calm returned, Aden Abdulla started his speech. "Fellow Somalis, in this moment in which I am announcing to you, with the heart brimming with joy, the birth of the Somali republic, allow me to congratulate you for the struggle we have jointly conducted to witness all united this historic moment. The history of our young Nation abounds with sacrifice, expectations and hope; these facts and situations are engraved in our hearts as one."

As he spoke, the one hundred thousand standing below were banging from his every word, as he deliberately chanted the proclamation announcing the birth of a free and independent Somalia: "Today, we are Somalis, independent and sovereign. Finally, we have our own state, our own flag and with God's leave, we must preserve it".[129] He added: "We call the world represented here today, to bear witness of our firm desire to have friendly relations with all. Our first words to the world delivered, like the intensive, initial call of a new-born, is for peace and prosperity to all".

"Fellow Somalis: Wherever you may be rejoice with me and give all your energies, to the defence of the sacred values of democracy, respect, peace, and justice. Our course of action in foreign policy is to reflect our domestic policy. Let us honour and respect our democratic institutions and model them on our relations with the rest of the world. We sincerely say to the world who is now listening us that we are proud of our achievements and jealous of our newly acquired independence".

Despite the auspiciousness of the occasion, Aden Abdulla invited then the crowd to turn their thought to "the millions of our African brethren still languishing under the yoke of foreign rule and injustice and left in a state of utter disorientation" and as he said the words, it was felt as though the sky was ripped in half by the shrill, passionate response of the crowd. "We renew our appeal of peace and justice to the world which is listening to us for these brothers of ours since it is good and just that the entire world knows that we Somalis, being part of Africa, feel mortified to the point of death by their plight and the inequity that prevails in the world more generally".

"Fellow Somalis: On your behalf I thank the very kind guests who from far away countries came to rejoice and celebrate with us this happy occasion which marks this special year for Africa, of 1960, a starting point leading to a new era of peace and prosperity in Somalia, in Africa and the world. May God protect the Republic".[130]

It was the speech in which Aden Abdulla set out his vision for the nascent Somalia, a nation he hoped would be prosperous, tolerant and where corruption would find no home. His brief speech, interrupted again and again by shouts of "Somalia Hanoolaato" [Long live Somalia], marked a turning point. In that breezy night of July, in front of the African Solidarity Square, an emotional bond was forged between Aden Abdulla and the cheering public that ushered the country towards unification. His speech shows that he was mindful of the political evolution in other African countries and kept repeating that his country would only be truly free and independent if all of Africa were too. His pan-African views and actions granted him extra-national prominence as his message was the basis for the Organization of African Unity that later became the African Union.

Aden Abdulla asserted that the Republic would maintain good relations with all nations and defend "the sacred values of democracy".[131] The President's speech was followed by that of the head of the Italian delegation. When the time came to hand over Somalia to the Somalis, a Minister of the Republic of Italy was sent to Mogadiscio. It was Senator Giuseppe Medici, Minister of Education, an old-fashioned Modenese notable with a chin adorned with a pointed goatee. During the ceremony, the Italian flag was lowered, scrupulously folded and handed over to the minister who would take it back to Italy.

Senator Medici read a brief but significant message from the Italian Head of State to the President of the Somali Republic. He said: "Being aware of the significance and importance of today's celebrations, I have the privilege to notify you with sincere congratulations that Italy, in compliance with the Resolution adopted by the United Nations General Assembly, has ended at zero hundred hours of today, 1 July 1960, the Trusteeship Administration assigned to her by the United Nations on November 21, 1949. I have therefore the honour of declaring that Italy extends, as from this moment, its recognition to Somalia as sovereign and independent. Italy is convinced that she is transferring sovereign powers to a State based on the democratic and modern institutions, albeit embryonic, of an adequate administration. I do moreover confirm that in the future also Somalia can count on the support and friendship of the government and the people of Italy".[132] Constantin Stravropoulos, a representative of the United Nations, said, "Independence could never have been achieved without an enthusiastic spirit of the Somali people and Italy's enlightened leadership".[133]

All United Nations members, except for South Africa, Byelorussia and Ukraine, were invited to attend the independence celebrations. Representatives from the British Commonwealth and Colonial Territories included Kenya, Aden, Sierra Leone, Tanganyika, Uganda and Nigeria. Over 400 guests were invited to the celebrations. Everyone was eager to observe this unique country which had defied all predictions and attained its independence. As the official celebrations came to an end, and the independence of Somalia was declared, ambassadors were to present their credentials to the Provisional Head of State from 17:00 on July 1, 1960 at Villa Somalia, the former residence of the Italian Administrators which became the residence of the Provisional Head of State. The Italian Ambassador, H.E. Silvio Daneo, was the first, followed by Britain, France, and West Germany. The American Chargé d'Affaires presented his credentials as the first Ambassador to Somalia on July 11, 1960.

The year 1960 is referred to as the Year of Africa because of a series of events that took place during the year, namely the independence of seventeen African nations that highlighted the growing pan-African sentiment in the continent. The independence of these countries was in part the result of a long process that began fifteen years earlier in the tumult of World War II. In the chronological list of independence, Somalia took place in the 5$^{th}$ position after Cameroun, Togo, Madagascar, and Congo Kinshasa (now the Democratic Republic of Congo).

Most of the African countries were free from their British or French colonial masters by the second half of 1960, often following prolonged struggle for independence. There was not one process of decolonization. In some areas, it was peaceful and orderly. In many others, independence was achieved only after a protracted revolution and military confrontation. These nations joined the United Nations General Assembly adding weight to voice to the Third World countries. At the end of the Second World War, there were only two independent countries in Africa: Liberia, which had been founded by freed slaves and declared its independence in 1847 and Ethiopia, which was an ancient territory and had never been colonized by a European power, despite attempts of the Italians in 1880s and 1930s. However, newly-received freedom to control their resources did not always bring direct benefits as the infant nations frequently lacked the stable institutions they needed to manage their economies and public services. Not least of the challenges left in the wake of decolonization was that of arbitrary national borders, left behind by the departing powers, creating time bombs for future conflicts.

President Aden Abdulla was the contemporary of African leaders like Kwame Nkrumah of Ghana, Sékou Touré of Guinea, Jomo Kenyatta of Kenya, Kenneth Kaunda of Zambia, among many others who emerged in the 1960s as leaders of their respective countries. While for most of the post-independence period, all these African leaders shared an unmistakable similarity of approach: the absence of even the most essentials of democracy. Somalia, however, stood faithfully by the model of parliamentary democracy which it had adopted. The new Republic adopted a constitution which legalized opposition parties; imposed term limits on presidential tenure; granted independent courts and constitutional review and, guaranteed civil and political liberties. This explains why the Republic had no political prisoners. The separation of powers among the three branches of the government, namely the legislative, the executive and the judiciary was embedded in the Constitution. The President was the Head of State while the Prime Minister had full executive powers and was a Head of Government and assisted by the Council of Ministers.[134]

While the independence celebrations continued for four days with a round of parties and dinners, a behind-the-scenes struggle, for the post of Prime Minister, was underway. As widely predicted, President Aden Abdulla, in his capacity as provisional head of state, had on July 6, 1960 designated Abdirashid Ali Sharmarke, a long-time member of the governing SYL party and one of a handful of Somalis with a university degree, to form a new cabinet.[135] It appears that, although endorsed by the Central Committee of the party, the President did not select Abdullahi Issa on the grounds firstly that, he had been Prime Minister for the last four years of the Trusteeship period and secondly, because Issa and Aden Abdulla both hailed from the same Hawiye clan family.

The President held, as a matter of principle, that it was time to give a chance to others. In certain circles, the expectation was that the premiership should have been assigned to Mohamed Haji Ibrahim Egal, the leader of British Somaliland when it joined with Italian Somaliland. This, however, could not be the case because, in a parliamentary system of government, the premiership belongs to the party holding the majority of the seats in the National Assembly, which was the SYL. Egal was a leading politician but he was not affiliated to the majority party. He was a member of the Somali National League (SNL), one of the two northern political parties alongside the United Somali Party (USP), who were the junior partners in the SYL-led coalition government formed after independence.

## Full term in presidential office

One of the first actions taken by the new government was the organization of the referendum on the Constitution which had so far been adopted as a provisional charter. On 20 June 1961, the Constitution, as contemplated by Section III of the Transitional and Final Provisions, was submitted to a popular referendum and passed almost unanimously, with 90.6% of the electorate in favour.[136] With the approval of the Constitution, and the expiry of the one-year provisional period, the National Assembly was required to elect a new president.

Unlike the rest of Africa, Somalia had adopted the parliamentary system of government, meaning that the President of the Republic is elected by the Parliament, not by the people, for the duration of six years.[137] By virtue of this system, the executive power was vested not in the President of the Republic but in the government led by the Prime Minister.[138] The President had the role of representing national unity and guaranteeing that politics complied with the Constitution. On July 6, 1961, the day set for the presidential election, three deputies were selected by the drawing of lots as vote counters: Abdinour Mohamed Hussein, Salad Elmi Mohamoud and Mohamed Ahmed Hajj Salah.

The candidacy of the incumbent President, Aden Abdulla was supported by the Central Committee of the ruling party, but he refused to campaign, believing it improper. "He believed that campaigning for himself would convey a feeling that anyone who held office would not want to leave it. It was up to the members of Parliament to decide whether, in view of the interests of the country, he was the most qualified candidate", as Abdirizak Haji Hussein recalled.[139] The Prime Minister and the Cabinet members however campaigned for his election. He rejected the idea of making promises to MPs in return for their votes, a position he would maintain throughout his long political career. On the contrary, the presidential hopeful, Sheikh Ali Jimale, extensively and intensively campaigned for his election with the assistance of his group, which used every means, both personal and clan, to further their cause".[140] To his friend, Hussein Abdi Abdulla "Farmacia", a member of the SYL party who would later serve as SNC deputy for Bulo Burti in the third legislature (1964-1969), who offered his support in soliciting votes from the parliamentarary group of their native Hiran for his re-election, Aden Abdulla said: "In my life, I have never solicited votes for getting elected, and I see no reason why should I do now for it is undignified thing for a self-respecting person" (Diary June 10, 1961). Days before the presidential election, Aden Abdulla took the initiative to meet Sheikh Ali Jimale, his long-time friend and now contender, to reach an understanding that they would work together irrespective of who won the race. The conversation between the two which took place during the independence celebrations in Villa Somalia, the official residence of the President, was recoded verbatim in Aden Abdulla's diary of July 4, 1961.

"I told him that life often plays tricks of the kind we are currently experiencing, putting friends and brothers against each other in competition for position of responsibility and that the present confusion will be over in few days' time when one of us will win the election. I said that if he is elected President, I am ready to extend to him my full collaboration, and I expect him to do the same in the event I win the election. Sheikh Ali felt instead that two individuals, divided by serious contrast, could not collaborate. I explained to him that, as far as I am aware, nothing serious had happened between us that could not be forgotten. The conversation ended there as other guests joined us".[141]

Thus, on 6 July 1961, the National Assembly started the process: the election was a two-horse race between Sheikh Ali Jimale and Aden Abdulla. According to the Constitution, a two-thirds majority (82) is required in the first and second ballots and an absolute majority (62 votes) in the subsequent ballots. Since the Parliament could not possibly accommodate each and every Somali who wanted to watch this significant event, Radio Mogadiscio provided an extraordinary live transmission in which every word said in the Parliament could reach the animated citizenry.

The correspondent covering the presidential election for the *Somali News* newspaper reported that the counting of the first ballot papers revealed that there were two political giants locked in a close race. Both candidates got equal votes (60 each) which held the balance, with one vote in dispute. The contest, too close to call, in a way indicated how the political culture which had developed over the last ten years had not produced clear favourites. The party leadership, for instance, had been held on a rotating basis through the

1950s by different members, which did not provide any single leader a platform through which to dominate or at the very least become synonymous with the institution. Indeed, although they possessed markedly different political styles, both candidates shared a number of similarities.

They were born, for instance, of the Hawiye clan family within a few years of each other in the environs of Belet Uen—Sheikh Ali Jimale in 1905 and Aden Abdulla in 1908-9—where decades later, they joined the Somali Youth Club (Aden in 1944 and Sheikh Ali two years later), both serving on the Central Committee of the local branch before and after it became the Somali Youth League in 1947. That they were the only two contenders running for the presidency in 1961 was a consequence of the age of candidacy for the role, which the Constitution set at 45 years of age.

This provision had been the cause of much debate during the drafting of the Constitution. Although there was no concrete, irrefutable ground for its inclusion, the rationale offered in discussions was Islamic custom and the precedent found in the life of the Prophet Muhammad, who received the call to start his mission at the age of 40. Unsatisfied at setting the age requirement there, it was ultimately agreed to raise it to 45, a decision some believed was to be politically motivated and an underhand tactic for disqualifying many eligible aspirants; indeed, there were many examples in early Islamic history, where younger people were entrusted with leadership, even by the Prophet himself.

Nevertheless, the fact that Aden Abdulla and Sheikh Ali Jimale, both from the same [electoral] district, were running in the contest appeared to attest to the ascendancy which the Hiiraan region enjoyed since the birth of modern Somali politics. The region's distinction also rested on the fact that the Prime Minister of the first Somali-led government, formed in 1956, was Abdullahi Issa Mohamud, who also represented Belet Uen.

Although the prominence which Belet Uen and its politicians enjoyed may appear like pure accident, there were also practical reasons for why it commanded the attention of colonial and post-independence governments. Firstly, lying between Somali- and Ethiopian-controlled areas in the Horn of Africa, it had been sought after—as discussed earlier—by the forces of Sayyid Mohamed Abdulle Hassan and the Italian forces in the early twentieth century. Later, once under Italian control, it became a tactical site from which both to defend the colony against Ethiopian incursions but also ultimately launch assaults as part of the Abyssinian War.

On the eve of the tenure of AFIS starting in 1950, the armed infantry, known as Terza Battaglione [the Third Battalion], established itself there in March of that year. The unit settled in the military camp, built a few decades earlier. Completed in 1931 and named then after "Generale Pantano", the Italian general who was involved in the Battle of Adwa, the dedication-inscription could still be made out on the gate to the Lama Gala (or Lama Galaay) military camp.[142] At independence in 1960, the commander of the unit was Major (later General) Abdulla Barre Sabrie and his successors in subsequent decades there included Colonnel (later General) Mohamed Ali Mire; Colonnel Elmi Nur Tarambi "Tarey" and Colonnel (later General) Mohamed Nur Galaal.

By virtue of its position in central Somalia, the town was considered a gateway, sitting on the road network connecting not only north and south of the country but also Somalia and Ethiopia. The *Camionable,* macadam road suitable for the use of trucks, began in Mogadiscio and came to Belet Uen, 330Km away, via Jowhar, following the course of the Shabelle River for most of the distance—including the one hundred and fifteen kilometre stretch between Bulo Burti and Belet Uen, vividly known as the Centoquindieci. Realised in stages in the 1920s and known as Strada Imperiale, on one side the road entered the areas of Ogadenia, reaching Gabredarre in the northwest after 205 miles (via Fer Fer) on a rougher, all-weather road, which followed the slopes of the hills, before branching out later on: one route leading to Harar and Dire Dawa, where it connected with the highway running down to the port of Djibouti while the other turned to Hargeisa and the port of Berbera.[143]

Along the Somalia north-south corridor, the road from Belet Uen ran in another direction for 360 kilometres to Galkayo, an important centre. Important to the region's trade networks, the thirty feet wide road was also used to convey the produce from Hiiraan's fields. In order to manage the seasonal inundation and drying up of the Shabelle River, a stream was introduced in the 1950s, known locally as "canale", to divert waters to a reservoir and away from the city when the river was in spate. Three other similar canals followed in the 1970-80s.

In the election, neither of the two contenders managed to gain the two-third majority of the 123 deputies required for an outright victory in the first two secret ballots. The deputies had to go to another round of voting when Sheikh Ali Jimale superseded his opponent and got 61 votes against 59 votes for Aden Abdulla with yet one vote in dispute. Tension mounted in the overcrowded House as ballot papers were distributed to the deputies for the third time. This time, the President of the National Assembly, announced that a simple majority of 62 members out of the 121 votes would decide who would be President.

The monumentality and importance of the occasion weighed heavily on almost every Deputy and silence reigned and everything came to a standstill as the ballot papers were finally handed to the three Deputies chosen to count the voting and the three witnesses who supervised the counting. At exactly 11:25 hours, the result of the last voting was announced by the President of the National Assembly, Jama Abdullahi Ghalib which drove Aden Abdulla to power in, what the *Somali News* described as, the most fantastic and probably the closest fight for a presidency in history.[144] The President of the National Assembly declared Aden Abdulla Osman as the new President of the Somali Republic, with 62 votes against 59 in favour of Sheikh Ali Jimale. "Enthusiastic rejoicing ran high as news of Aden's victory reached the public who were gathering outside the National Assembly".[145]

Ten minutes later, the fifty-three-year-old Aden Abdulla who had not been in House earlier, was ushered in by the President of the Assembly, Jama Abdullahi Ghalib. The President of the Republic took his seat at the Assembly President's desk, to his right. After the swearing-in ceremony, the first citizen of the Republic pronounced a brief, moving speech. The President's victory speech was characteristic of his style: "I thank you all Deputies with saddling me with responsibilities and honouring me, for the second time, in electing me for such a high position. I, on my part, solemnly swear and declare that I will endeavour to promote the good interest of our country and beloved nation and that I will try to be worthy of this high and most coveted honour.

"I see that the future will be difficult and [there will be] challenging years for us all and supreme national effort will be needed in the years ahead to move our country on the road of the economic emancipation and eventual prosperity for our beloved people. I ask [for] your help and the support of our people whom you represent here, in this effort and I can assure you that every degree of mind and spirit that I possess will be devoted to the long-range interests of the Somali Republic. I will also make it my duty to promote mutual understanding coupled with goodwill and friendly co-operation among you since we can only hope to discharge our national obligations by sincere collaboration". The speech was followed by rapturous applause.[146]

The live radio broadcast of the election, followed with passion throughout the country, was a powerful instance of civic education. "Sheikh Ali Jimale was one of the first to come to congratulate me. I hope his move was dictated by the heart", commented the chosen President.[147] Others soon followed in offering their congratulations: the President of the National Assembly with all the Vice Presidents; Prime Minister Abdirashid with members of his Cabinet; many deputies and thousands of members of the public as well as delegations from political parties, dignitaries and local notables.

While there seemed to have been none of the vote rigging that had troubled the general elections, it was widely rumoured that vote buying tactics had been used to influence the outcome of the election. It is widely believed also that Jimale received his support mainly from the Hawiye deputies, who blamed Osman for "abandoning" his own ethnic group (the Hawiye) and from a group of Issak deputies, who felt that Somaliland's (or rather the Isaak's) interests were being subordinated to those of southern Somalia. Although Aden Abdulla himself may have received the favour of different groups in the Parliament, he was nevertheless a man capable of holding independent views, who in the decade of Trusteeship, had emerged as the most respected statesman in Somalia and an astute arbitrator who could reach beyond partisan politics to reconcile conflicting factions.[148]

After his election, the President started a cycle of complex informal consultations with party leaders and key political figures in Parliament and outside. This was technically an exploratory phase during which public opinion was consulted regarding the person who might be best placed to form a government and obtain a confidence vote in Parliament. At the end of the consultation Abdirashid Ali Sharmarke, a graduate of Rome University, who had been Premier from 1960, was again asked to form a government. In announcing the re-appointment of Abdirashid as Prime Minister to the press representatives, the Head of State said: "I have the pleasure to communicate that, after having carried out consultations, I have decided to invite Honourable Abdirashid Ali Sharmarke to form a government with the hope that he will accept the task and do whatever is possible to form a government which will obtain the approval of the people. I am sure, as I was in July last year, that Hon. Abdirashid is the most qualified for this task".[149]

A coalition government was formed by the SYL party and the two leading northern political parties, the Somali National League (SNL) and the United Somali Party (USP) as junior partners. The President was deeply convinced that the MPs should not be seen as divided between those who elected him and those who did not. He felt that the criteria for the membership of the government should not be based on the way individual lawmakers had voted in the presidential election, but instead on their honesty and competencies required to exercise their ministerial responsibilities. As a result of his indirect influence, Sheikh Ali iumale, Abdullahi Issa and Mohamed Ibrahim Egal and others, who did not support Aden Abdulla's candidacy for the presidency, became members of the new cabinet.

Immediately after the cabinet was formed and sworn in, the President addressed the new government calling their attention to the need to work as one team, preserve the confidentiality of the decisions taken at the Council of Ministers meetings until a decision was taken to announce them and make them public knowledge. He expressed his readiness to offer them advice and guidance every time the need arose.[150]

It soon emerged that Sharmarke's government did not, by any stretch of the imagination, come close to the President's expectations regarding competence of cabinet ministers. Commenting on the formation of the government, Aden Abdulla wrote in his diary, "With the number of cabinet ministers and the inclusion in the government of certain individuals, Abdirashid made me swallow a bitter pill; for fear of who knows what, he left some good men out. I am sorry, but this is a disappointment and a disservice to his honour". The President also recalled the hostile campaign of Abdirashid and some of his colleagues against Abdullahi Issa in 1959, on the grounds that the number of ministers in his government was excessive and the members generally had poor qualifications for the job.[151]

## A coup in the early days of Independence and the Union

The long sought-after but unplanned and hastily executed union of the two former colonial territories, North and South, in 1960, raised almost insurmountable problems of political, legal, linguistic, administrative and economic integration to give practical effect to the union. Amid this feeling of general uneasiness of the people, twelve young army lieutenants, trained in Britain, were aggrieved that the British officers, who had left the Northern battalion, were replaced by Somalis of field rank from the South, who had received paramilitary training in Italy. There was a feeling of widespread resentment among northerners that the major advantages of union lay with the south. The young officers thus planned and carried out a bloodless coup d'état in December 1961, to overthrow the government in the north but they failed to win the support of the soldiers and the coup collapsed within a day.

The Defence Minister, Sheikh Ali Ismail Yaqub, a deputy who represented a constituency in the north (Burao), delivered an address at Hargeisa football ground on 11 December. He was accompanied by the Interior Minister and the two generals commanding the army and the police. "I deplore and deeply regret this plot attempted by certain youth", he said, "without regard to [the] future and without taking into consideration the need of this nation for progress and the urgent call for the unification of those of its sons who are outside the republic with their brothers".

'In addition to this regret, I would like to express sympathy and condolence to the Somali nation. The Somali nation does not need misfortunes or the division of the two united regions at a time when some of its sons are still under the imperialist yoke...I have always been convinced that the Somali people would oppose anyone who attempted to use them and misled them by such statements as "Nobody has done or is doing anything for us; therefore let us secede from them". What benefit would the division of the two regions bring? Each one of them would be half-naked.'[152]

Later, the officers were charged, before ordinary Court, with waging war against the state, punishable by death under Section 121 of the Indian Penal Code. In strict adherence to the spirit of the Constitution and respect for the rule of law, Aden Abdulla rejected calls for a military tribunal to be established for the trial of the rebellious officers "to ensure long and deterrent punishment rather than bringing it before an ordinary court", as suggested by the Commander of the National Army.[153] The Court comprised of an English Judge and two Somali Assessors. The trial was removed from Hargeisa Tribunal to Mogadiscio Court on basis of "legitimate suspicion".

Although the Hargeisa Court was physically located in Mogadiscio, the trial was governed by the Northern law which, at the time, was the Indian Penal Code and the Indian Code of Criminal Procedure. (The integrated Somali Penal Code and Criminal Procedure had not yet been enacted when the trial took place.) To the consternation of the Prosecutor, the Court threw the case out, claiming that the accused had not committed a crime against the State and discharging them on a technical point of law.

The crisis in the North was further complicated by the government policy aimed at bringing northern import duties in line with those in force in the South. The legislation on import duty, introduced in 1963, had thus caused further turmoil in the north and deepened the social crisis among northerners, already unhappy about the hasty union with former Italian Somaliland. Predictably, this unpopular law had triggered widespread disorder and strikes in Hargeisa and other major centres in the north. The police interfered in the matter and, in dispersing the group of rioters, killed four people and injured 17; all the casualties were civilians. This continuing rift between north and south is partly the consequence of the two separate colonial legacies and of the lack of adequate preparation prior to unification. But it was certainly this antagonism which was the main factor in the serious discontent in the north which led the Government to dispatch three northern Ministers to try to remedy the situation.

The team of Ministers was empowered to take measures to rectify the position, but a dispute later developed about their precise terms of reference. The mission ended in failure as its members could not agree on certain aspects of the recommendations to be presented to the government. The Minister of Agriculture, Ali Garad Jama, of the Dulbahante clan, disagreed with the other two members of the mission, both of the Issak clan, on the disciplinary transfer of four senior staff in Hargeisa. The Minister of Agriculture made direct contact with Mogadiscio from Hargeisa, expressing his displeasure with the disciplinary action proposed against the District Commissioner of Hargeisa, a fellow Dulbahante. The position of the two Issak Ministers was further undermined by the hasty decision taken by the government to appoint and promote as Governor of Mudugh the very officer against whom disciplinary action had been recommended. This prompted the resignation of the two Ministers, Mohamed Haji Ibrahim Egal and Sheikh Ali Ismail Yaqub.

In the morning of October 25, the SNL parliamentary group staged a walk-out—*"questa mattina il Gruppo SNL ha abbandonato l'Auola"*, as Aden Abdulla observed[154]—when their request for a debate was not taken up. They presented a motion asking for Parliament's ongoing discussion on recruitment to the army to be interrupted and for the legislature to have a debate on the composition of the government. They had made a similar request days earlier and quit Parliament then as well, on 23 October, after the Vice President of the Assembly rejected their call. On 30 October, the President of the Assembly told the deputies who had asked for that debate—on whether the government was constitutionally composed and in which the different political parties were represented equally—that parliamentary business should not be stopped for such a request and that the deputies should instead reach agreement on the matter through private talks with the other groups.

The SNL deputies and other parties, however, insisted that "unless our motion is discussed and we are satisfied with the discussion we stand by our demand, and we are ready to stay away from the session of Parliament if Parliament continues with its business". When the President of the Assembly replied that he would continue with ordinary business, the deputies, joined by others from various parties, walked out of the sitting.[155] However, the USP parliamentary group did not follow the SNL, thus splitting the northern parties along tribal lines. Instead, a group of southerner MPs closed ranks with the SNL in a show of solidarity, a move evidently aimed at giving the crises a national dimension. The general situation in former British Somaliland became volatile, in the wake of the aborted military *coup* representing a source of real concern for Mogadiscio which was undermining the very foundation of the union between the two regions of Somalia, further exacerbated by the resignation of the two ministers, one of whom had been the leader of British Somaliland before the union.

The President of the Republic was thrown into the fray and embarked on a long tour of all major urban centres of the North which ran from 10 to 24 September 1962,[156] the general success of which must be partly attributed to his high personal reputation.[157] In an address to the people, the President pleaded with them not to resort to violence. 'My purpose for coming here was to see the leaders and to have a frank and forthright exchange of views with them. We talked of ways to improve conditions in the Northern region, particularly in education and health. These problems and difficulties are not confined to us alone but are common to all new African states.

"Our principal objective was to find ways of bringing together the two countries previously divided by the imperialists... Our country can proudly claim that it has kept internal peace and stability since it achieved independence, unlike some other African states which did not but are now envious. There is no more tribal fighting as there used to be under colonial rule. The people now cooperate with each other, as can be seen by the Taleh and Mijjertein agreements to stop tribal fights. They are now dedicated to peace. The government wants peace in the country because the foreign investors must be assured that the country is stable and that there is peace and understanding.[158]

"I have one more thing to add: for the gradual progress of the country towards economic, social and political development along democratic lines, we must have discipline. Without discipline, nothing can be achieved; lack of discipline and chaos will block the whole process and merely bring about what some would call a strong regime, but I would simply call dictatorship". His speech was hailed as a milestone in national reconciliation. One of the most pressing challenges the new Republic faced at independence was its clan dynamics. Because of the way in which the SYL party dominated the political scene, conflicts over outstanding political issues gradually began to surface within the party rather than between the ruling party and opposition parties. Internal divisions festered as factions within the SYL strove to win a greater say in the party for their interests or those of their clans. The President had largely succeeded in continuing to negotiate on this issue, saving Somalia (at least for a time) from the trauma of outright discord. Referring to the unsettling ethnic tension between politicians which reached a scale never seen before in recent memory, Aden Abdulla wrote in his diary, "I have to talk seriously to Abdirashid over the mistrust between the Somalis, particularly between Darod and Hawiya clan families, which continues to gain ground like climbing a devilish shrub. At times they cast aspersion even on me on the basis of suspicion. We have to take action and study in depth how to uproot this dangerous leech" [*Bisogna che parli seriamente ad Abdirascid. La sfiducia fra i Somali, specialmemte fra Hawie e Darot sta continuamente guadagnando terreno come un arbusto arrampicante, malvagio. A momenti, avvelenano anche me coi sospetti. Bisogna darsi da fare e studiare a fondo come sradicare questa piovra della malora*].[159]

## 1963 – The arms deal with the Soviet Union and the severance of diplomatic ties with Britain

Soon after independence, Somalia wasted no time in proactively pursuing irredentist aims by embarking on a programme of military build-up. At the outset, Somalia had approached the Western powers for military aid. In October 1963, during a state visit to Italy, the Italians briefed the Somali President on the ongoing consultations between Italy, the United States and the Federal Republic of Germany on the issue of military aid to Somalia. The Somali delegation met Ambassador Giovanni Fornari, Head of Political Affairs of the Italian Ministry of Foreign Affairs, who had served as the first Administrator during AFIS's tenure between 1950 and 1953, ahead of his mission to Bonn.

Ambassador Fornari wondered whether his planned visit to Bonn to meet the three Western powers to discuss the military aid to Somalia would serve any purpose, in the light of intelligence reports from Italian Embassy in Mogadiscio indicating that Somalia had already ratified a military agreement with the Soviet Union. The meeting between the President and the Ambassador was less than cordial as Aden Abdulla made a blunt statement of facts: "Mr. Ambassador, firstly, I am not the one sending you to Bonn, and secondly, I believe that if the West were ready to draw up an urgent plan of military aid within a clear timescale, the Somali government might be in a position to thank the Soviet Union for their favourable disposition and decline their offer".[160]

Fornari aired potential adverse political and economic repercussions Somalia might suffer in the event it accepted Soviet military assistance. Aden Abdulla perceived that Fornari's statement was designed to scare him into total acceptance of the Western military offer to Somalia and took exception to the Italian diplomat's concerns as he felt that the responsibility for any steps taken by the Somali government would fall squarely on the Western powers who, for over three years, either in bad faith, or in their own interest, failed to meet Somalia's urgent military needs.

In the meantime, news started trickling into Italy of the departure of 60 Somali army officers to the Soviet Union for training purposes, some of whom had initially been expected to go to Italy for the same purposes. Taken by surprise while still in Rome, Aden Abdulla made the following long entry in his diary: "Abdirashid has forgotten that I had warned him not to get into commitment with the Soviet Union before my return from the state visit to Italy, during which time I would be gauging what the Italians and their Western allies were thinking of providing in terms of military assistance to Somalia. Abdirashid did not think that, after all, I am the one who should sign the agreement, even though the idea of refusing to sign it never even crossed my mind".[161] The President was annoyed by the fact that the arms deal had been negotiated and formalised with the Russians when he, with the knowledge and prior agreement of the Prime Minister, should have still been in the process of negotiating with Western powers about their offer.

On 19 October, one day before leaving Rome for Mogadiscio, Aden Abdulla was again contacted by the Italian authorities for an unscheduled meeting with President Antonio Segni at the Palazzo del Quirinale, the official residence of the Italian Head of State. It was in that meeting that the level of Western military aid to Somalia was finally disclosed. The three Western powers offered Somalia arms for a 6,000-strong national army – a package worth $18m, far below the level of assistance already offered by the Soviet Union. "If the Somali government was ready to accept this offer, the material would start arriving in Mogadiscio no later than the coming December", Aden Abdulla was told. Upon his return to Mogadiscio on October 21, the Head of State received detailed briefings from General Daud Abdulla Hersi, Commander of the National Army on the latter's recent mission to the Soviet Union where, acting under instructions given to him by the government, he initialed an agreement with the Soviet Union on military assistance for 10,000-strong Somali national army in addition to ShSo 200 million worth of materiel which included 23 military planes (20 of which would be jet fighters), 100 tanks, some cannons and other military equipment.

General Daud concluded his briefing by announcing that the same agreement had been signed by the Parliament Speaker, Jama Abdullahi Ghalib. On paper, this did not sound like much when compared to the Ethiopian army of 40,000, equipped with modern United Sates weaponry, and advised and trained by United States experts. By African standards, Ethiopia had a formidable air force, using American jets. The President briefed the Prime Minister on the outcome of his discussions with the Italian authorities. In an effort to avert possible deterioration of relations with three major Western powers, he recommended the government open further talks with them on the issue and accept their offer should it proved acceptable.

On the other hand, Jama Abdullahi Ghalib's exercise of the functions of the Head of State sparked off a constitutional clash over the President of the National Assembly's right to replace the President of the Republic during his absence. Under the 1960 Somali Constitution, the power to ratify international treaties was vested in the Head of State (Article 75 (e) of the Constitution of 1960); the President of the Parliament did not dispute this, but claimed that "he came under pressure from the Prime Minister to sign the document because he was made to believe that the matter was urgent". This however was denied by the Prime Minister, who declared he had even warned Jama Abdullahi that the latter would "take all the responsibilities arising out of signing the agreement".[162]

Acting on the recommendations of the President, the Prime Minister, the Minister of Defence and the Commander of the National Army met the military attachés of Italy, the United States and the Federal Republic of Germany. However, the three Western powers seemed unwilling to increase the level of military aid and warned the Somali government that their offer was not to be taken as complementary to the Russian offer, as the Somali government evidently wished. The three Western countries, in separate meetings with the President, did not conceal their worries over the impact that communist ideology might have on the young Somali officers being sent to Russia for military training and on the danger that they may, in the future, act to undermine Somali civilian governments. Aden Abdulla referred to all these statements as part of a familiar and cliché Western tune expressing concern about the possible negative impact that such sizeable Soviet military aid might have on relations with the neighbouring countries and on the Somali budget. "This is the result of years of hesitation by the West in addressing the Somali request for military assistance, and they are now overreacting in the face of the new developments".[163]

As there was no disagreement that the President of the National Assembly had acted *ultra vires*, the same agreement with the Soviet Union was signed afresh by the President of the Republic and the matter was finally put to rest. Unable to obtain support from the Western powers for development of a large army, the government turned eventually to the Soviet Union, which willingly provided military equipment, advice, and training. Moscow thus achieved an important strategic breakthrough within the moderate African camp in November 1963, when the Republic of Somalia announced that it would accept the military aid offer from the Soviet Union.

The Western power's tripartite plan came as friction increased between Mogadiscio and London over the final disposition of Kenya's Northern Frontier District (NFD). Before granting independence to Kenya at the end of 1963, Great Britain had to decide what to do about the NFD, an area comprising one-third of Kenya's territory, the majority of the inhabitants of which were ethnic Somalis. A British fact-finding Commission took testimony from the inhabitants of Kenya's North Eastern Province in December 1962, through a referendum, and found that 87 per cent of them were Somalis who wished to avoid association with an independent Kenya.

The UK did not act on the Commissioner's findings. In March 1963, London announced that the NFD would remain part of Kenya. British ineptness added to this mess, as London had long encouraged the Somalis to believe that the NFD would be given to Somalia before granting Kenya independence. Reacting to the British decision over the future of NFD, the Somali government submitted a motion to the National Assembly calling for the severing of diplomatic relations with Britain for failing to recognize the wishes expressed by the overwhelming majority of the people inhabiting NFD.

"Without rancour and with great courtesy, the Foreign Minister, Mr. Abdullahi Issa, handed to the Ambassador on March 18th the formal note breaking off diplomatic relations, and the rupture was complete", described, in the words of Briton, as "a most civilised rapture". Within a week, the British Consul-General in Hargeisa and his British staff left the Republic while the staff of the embassy in the capital followed a week later.[164] Mogadiscio's break with London cost Somalia £1.3 million in annual aid earmarked to cover part of the chronic national budget deficit and the Somalis were quick to ask the United States to fill this gap. However, the Americans made it clear that providing such kind of assistance under their programme was not a possibility, expressing instead their readiness to provide food supplies and military equipment. (*Government Republic, Activities from Independence until today, December 31, 1963, p, 88).* Alongside ongoing Italian support, China offered its support to help balance the remaining deficit.[165]

News of the arms deal with the Soviet Union came at a time when the Americans became deeply troubled by the pro-communist statements attributed to the Somali Prime Minister during his official visit to China. These concerns prompted an immediate meeting between Aden Abdulla and Mr Horace G. Torbert, the US Ambassador in Mogadiscio on 12 September 1963, before Aden Abdulla's planned state visit to Italy the following month. During the meeting, there were 'the standard recriminations on the part of the Ambassador on behalf of his country about the "Communist danger" – now understood as China – arising from the statements of the [Somali] Prime Minister and Minister of Information and from the Somali side of the lack of meaningful intervention from the USA around the aspiration of Somali unity and the reluctance of the West to provide proper equipment to the Somali army".

The Somali President raised Somalia's outstanding request for Western military assistance with the Ambassador, and his frustration and irritation with Western powers were palpable, insisting, that the US and its allies give Somalia the arms she needed for her puny army or leave her to get them from elsewhere *[All'Ambasciatore Americano ho detto che gli Stati Uniti ed i suoi Alleati devono armare l'Esercito Somalo cosí stremenzito (5,000 uomini) o di lasciare che la Somalia si trovi altrove le armi che le occorrono].*[166]

After the President returned from his visit to Italy, he received the American Chargé d'Affaires, Mr. Rogers, "upon his insistence (since I rejected him yesterday)". He said that the West was "embarrassed by the Soviet military aid to Somalia and hope[d] that Somalia would accept the military assistance from the West in the stead of the Soviet one" [*Questa mattina, dietro la sua insistenza (perché l'avevo respinto ieri), ho ricevuto l'incaricato d'Affari USA, Rogers. Quest'ultimo mi ha detto, per istruzione del suo governo, che gli Occidentali ono imbarazzati dagli aiuti militari Sovietici alla Somalia e spera che la Somalia accetti l'assistenza militare offerta dall'Occidente],* However things went, the diplomat reassured the President of continued support to Somalia in other areas, hoping that Italy and Germany – the other two countries contributing to the Western military aid offer – would do the same. Other arguments forwarded by the diplomat against the Soviet offer included the difficulties Somalia would face in efficiently running the huge Soviet military machine, which would burden the national finances to the detriment of economic development, not to mention the alarm it would cause to the neighbouring countries

The President, welcoming the prospect of continued American friendship come what may, highlighted that the recent development was the result of the "incomprehension of the West which, for four years, did not want to empathise with the needs of the small Somali army, which we still insist does not provoke fear in anyone" The President sincerely hoped that the Western offer would satisfy the Somali government and the army but – were things to go differently – the Ambasciator was assured that Somalia would not be linked inseparably to Russia and will know how to defend themselves from the Communist influence.

Addressing the point about the economic viability of the Soviet offer, the President used a Somali saying ("the hunchback knows best how he should lie down when he wants to sleep") to suggest that if the various difficulties which the diplomat predicted were to materialise, the very experience itself would be instructive since people adapt to their circumstances. He added that any problems or challenges faced along the way would allow the Somalis to get to know the Russians better, which in turn would put them in a position to avoid other similar mistakes in the future [*...da una parte ci servirà da insegnamento e dall'altra avremmo imparato meglio i Russi per non incorrere in altri errori*].[167]

Opposition to the military deal with the Soviet Union came also from influential Somali figures who voiced concern. One such figure was the chief of police, General Mohamed Abshir, who having closely followed the negotiations from his vantage point expressed strong opposition to Soviet military aid, recommending instead that the Western package be accepted. Abshir had a number of concerns, which revolved around the size of the forces proposed under the Soviet offer. Firstly, he felt the country's scant financial resources would make it difficult to maintain a force of such size. Similarly, he believed that, in the long run, "the army may represent a subversive threat to the democratic institutions of the Republic",[168] suspecting that officers in the oversized military, coming under communist influence, might prove difficult to control and manage.

The impact of the Soviet-Somali arms deal did not take long to be felt as fighting broke out between Ethiopia and Somalia a mere few months after Somalia concluded the arms deal with Moscow, over the dispute surrounding the Ogaden region. Soviet military equipment has been flown into the country since then, and Moscow has sent about 200 military experts to train Somali forces. About 400 Somalis went for military training to the Soviet Union (*Somali News January 13 1967 quoting an article which appeared on the Christian Science Monitor, an American and International weekly)*

While relations with Britain had deteriorated to the point of diplomatic rupture, Somalia's relations with Italy after independence remained stable and Italian influence continued in the modernized sectors of social and cultural affairs. Although their number had dropped to about 3,000 by 1965, the Italians residing in Somalia still dominated many of the country's economic activities. Italian economic assistance during the 1960s totalled more than a quarter of all the non-military foreign aid received by the country and Italy was an important market for Somali goods, particularly crops produced on the large, Italian-owned commercial farms in the river valleys. Italy's sponsorship enabled Somalia to become an associate of the European Economic Community (EEC), which formed another source of economic and technical aid and assured preferential status for Somali exports in West European markets.

## 1964 Parliamentary Elections
## Cry for free and fair elections

The 1964 elections were the first to be held since the merger of British Somaliland and Italian Somaliland in 1960. Eighteen political parties submitted their nomination lists of 973 candidates for 123 deputy seats in the National Assembly. After the union, the two territories' parliaments had merged, retaining the same number of seats as in the 1960 elections in British Somaliland and the 1959 election in Italian Trust Territory. The result was a victory for the Somali Youth League (SYL) which won 69 of the 123 seats. Of the eighteen parties participating in the competition in the south, only four had national significance: the governing Somali Youth League (SYL), the Somali National Congress (SNC), the Somali Democratic Union (SDU) and Hisbiya Destour Mustaqil Somali (HDMS).

Although, the role of the president in Somalia was often seen as largely ceremonial, the Somali Constitution granted him broad and discretional powers: he is not only an arbitrator and a guarantor, but also, as the case may be, one able to step in and influence political decisions. It was in the search for free and fair elections that Aden Abdulla made his most dramatic efforts when the holding of such elections still posed many problems in Somalia. Electoral fraud had become so brazen that few Somalis expected fair elections and there was widespread mistrust in the government's ability or willingness to ensure this. Aden Abdulla was aware of the major flaws in the electoral law which facilitated irregularities in the election process. But he was most worried about the government party using state resources and its control of the state's administrative machinery to gain undue advantage in the political elections of 1964. He spoke emphatically on several occasions of the need for free elections.

The President was firmly convinced, for example, of the fundamental importance of an strong Opposition in ensuring the successful functioning of a parliamentary democracy, particularly by keeping a constant check on government. One of the serious defects of the electoral law of 1964 was the excessive power given to polling station chairmen, who were often accused of rigging elections. To remedy this defect, the President of the Republic suggested the deployment of police with the task of keeping an eye on the ballot boxes from the time votes were being cast to when they were being counted. The Electoral Law, formally Law No. 4 of 22 January 1964 (Political Elections), however, as was common practice around the world, prohibited security forces from entering polling stations unless asked to do so by the chairman (Art. 34 (2), to ensure that electors could vote without interference from them.[169]

The law was approved without the amendments proposed by the President which were designed to improve the law. To express his frustration, the President summoned the Prime Minister and there was a bitter exchange between the two: "I received Abdirashid, the Prime Minister, together with the Minister of Grace and Justice, Ahmed Ghelle Hassan. In the presence of the latter, I urged [the Prime Minister] and his government to give solid assurances of propriety in the coming political elections or to step down, since I could not accept any repetition of the irregularities of the past political elections".[170] This was the first time the President had used such a strong language towards his Prime Minister.

This strong pronouncement led to a conflict with the Prime Minister, who expressed his readiness to resign from office. Indeed, for Abdirashid Ali Sharmarke, the President's move was tantamount to a breach of the constitutional division of functions between the president and the prime minister. Relations between the two were already strained, particularly since the debacle surrounding the Somali deal with the Soviet Union over military aid a year earlier when Prime Minister Abdirashid Ali Sharmarke had not consulted thoroughly with the President. Much of the friction between them rested on matters of policy on which the two leaders did not see always eye to eye.

The President gave the same strong message to an audience of provincial governors convened at the presidential mansion. Abdulla exhorted the governors to try to ensure fairer, 'one man, one vote' elections in the areas under their respective administrative control. The problem with the elections in Somalia was that the same party has been ruling since independence. Thus, there was some uncertainty as to whether elections were held in Somalia only because the ruling party was certain to win them and whether the ruling party would yield office if it ever lost. The repeated calls from the President for free and fair polls had also raised concerns among some Lega members, who feared that these calls for fairness may have adverse effects on the ruling party and, consequently, on their re-election as MPs.

The public, in general, and the opposition parties, in particular, had little faith in the government's ability or willingness to conduct fair and free elections. In fact, in the run-up to the March polls, the Somali Democratic Union (SDU) party executive, led by Haji Mohamed Hussein Hamud and Yusuf Osman Samatar "Bardacad" sought an audience with the President. The points the opposition leaders raised in the conversation included a proposal to appoint a government of only technocrats to replace the existing government [*"governo formato da tecnocrati, non membri del Parlamento"]*. To the President, the proposal seemed unworkable as the chances of the Parliament accepting such a government seemed highly unlikely.[171]

Continuing his efforts to improve the electoral law, the President of the

Republic addressed a letter to both the government and the Presidency of the National Assembly, stressing the need to reform the provisions of the electoral law barring civil servants from eligibility to the National Assembly (which in his view precluded the candidature of many qualified persons), the provisions governing electoral propaganda, and the casting and counting of votes. Sadly, not everyone in the government or in the ruling party seemed to value Aden Abdulla's cry for impartiality and justice in the election process, and some went as far as accusing him of harbouring anti-SYL sentiments and being biased in favour of the opposition. "This interpretation is obviously made in bad faith and does not remotely tally with my intentions," he noted in his journal.[172]

In another diary entry, Aden Abdulla referred to a heated discussion he had with two prominent members of the ruling party. 'I received in my office Sheikh Mohamoud Mohamed Farah "Malingur" and Sheikh Abdurahman Haji Moumin Mohame ], both of the Central Committee, who had the impudence of accusing me for allegedly "backing" Sheikh Ali Jimale's political party, and consequently "damaging" the Lega dei Giovani Somali'. The discussion with the two Deputies became, at times, very heated. "I invited the two gentlemen to read the provisions of Article 70 (3) of the Constitution dealing with the oath of loyalty of the Head of State,[173] and warned them that, if their intention was to deny the opposition parties their right for the convenience of the ruling party, they were wasting their time with me, as I would never accept such a thing to happen. There is nothing I desire more than the Lega winning and becoming strong, but not at the price they want".[174]

The two rebuked the President, accusing him of "exceeding" his legal authority as a President of a parliamentary regime. The President nevertheless received strong support in his efforts from his long-time friend and future Prime Minister, Abdirazak Haji Hussein, who proposed selecting "well-qualified and honest staff from the capital as polling station chairmen, particularly those destined to operate in outlying districts".[175] The first encouraging results came with the remarkable gains made by the opposition parties who, between them, secured a total of 54 seats in the 123 seats of the National Assembly, a level of representation never reached before. When the results were officially announced, 12 deputies from various parties crossed the line and joined the Somali Youth League Party, bringing the total number of SYL deputies an absolute majority of 81 deputies.

The first business of the National Assembly when it convened for the first time on May the 27th was to elect a speaker. Only 121 Members of Parliament formally gathered that day as two seats of the two-member constituency of Merca, in the Benadir region, remained vacant after the cancellation there of the 30 March results.[176] The Chairman of the Electoral Office in Merca had cancelled the results in the entire electoral district and a later Supreme Court ruling, delivered on 9 July, ruled that on the basis of a correction of valid votes, the two seats be allotted to the SDU and SNC lists. As a result, Haji Mohamed Hussein Hamud (the SDU candidate) and Haji Farah Ali Omar (SNC) became Members of the Parliament, bringing the membership up to full numbers with 123 deputies, due to take their seats within a few days of the ruling.[177] The Assembly unanimously elected Deputy Ahmed Sheikh Mohamed Absiyeh, a deputy from Berbera as president of the Somali National Assembly, who obtained the two-thirds majority at the first attempt, with 82 votes against 38 received by Ali Gerad Jama, the outgoing Minister of Agriculture.

The 49-year-old Absiyeh, like many of his fellow deputies, was a civil servant by background. Born in Sheikh (then British Somaliland), he joined the civil service in 1935, returning to the service in 1945 after six years of military service. In 1950, he proceeded to Khartoum University, where he obtained a diploma in Administration Science. He was later trained as an agriculturalist, receiving a similar qualification in that discipline in Cyprus. He ran in parliamentary elections for the first time in 1964, after resigning from the civil service, where he was the Head of the Agricultural Department of the Northern Regions.[178] He was the sole candidate to be elected on the SYL ticket in the north that year, his seat being in the Berbera district.[179]

The good showing of the opposition parties was undoubtedly made possibly thanks to the important mediation of the President on the election process. However, the President was well aware of the fact that the elections were conducted neither in strict conformity with the instructions he had issued nor in accordance with the law. Two weeks after, the President of the Republic Aden Abdulla Osman speaking about the recent general elections in the country said in a broadcast: "Logically, not everyone can be satisfied because there are clashes of many interests, and this may have been the cause of the nation not being completely satisfied and happy. There is one thing which requires to be considered, and that is that an aggrieved man will achieve nothing through force. If anyone feels that he is being denied his rights, there is a system in place: he should appeal to the Supreme Court and await its verdict. It is fruitless to arouse passions or incite trouble" (Radio Mogadiscio, April 19, 1964).

He could not but express his surprise that the electoral law had been allowed to remain for so long in its initial unsatisfactory state but he complained that the law had not gone far enough. In his diary entry of 30 April, 1964, he observed that, "Although my sincere and honest efforts intended to ensure clean elections, free of fraud, there had been persons who completely disregarded the law in spite of this, are unaccountable for their wrongdoing".[180] Despite the relative success enjoyed by the opposition parties, the SYL's authoritative command of the House was evident in the Assembly positions its members occupied. Along with Absiyeh, all of the Assembly's elected officers belonged to the majority party apart from one exception. Haji Bashir Ismail Yusuf (78 votes), Sheikh Mukhtar Mohamed Hussein (75 votes) and Ahmed Gumane Roble (68 votes) were elected Vice Presidents while Abdulaziz Nur Hersi (the only non-Lega figure, who represented the Somali Democratic Union (or the SDU)) and Sheikh Mohamed Yusuf were elected Secretaries. Haji Mohamed Nur Sheikh Hussein [Haji Mohamed Noor Sheikh Hussein] was elected Questor with Nur Mohamed Hussein Osman [Noor Mohamed Hussein Osman] and Haji Ali Ghedi Shador [Haji Ali Ghedi Shadoor] Vice Questores.[181]

## The search for a new Prime Minister
## Abdirizak designated Head of Government

Following the parliamentary elections of 1964, the President embarked on a cycle of complex informal consultations with party leaders and key political figures before announcing the designation of the new Prime Minister. The views and opinions he gathered in the course of the informal consultations carried no binding effect. Although the President of Somalia as the head of state has often been understood as a neutral power, being distinct from the actual seats of political power and above the fray when it came to political parties, the office holder was looked upon to play a role in managing conflicts that arose between them. This role, one of influence and mediation, often proved crucial during political crises. One of the most important of the President's functions, as described by the Constitution, was the appointment and dismissal of the Prime Minister. (Article 77 (3). The last word rested with the President to designate someone a Prime Minister who he thought could win the confidence of the Parliament. Although theoretically any citizen could be chosen for this role, on longstanding practice, Prime Ministers and Cabinet ministers were drawn from the parliamentary benches. As such, the President looked towards a Member of Parliament from the party which secured the most seats in the election and hence, held sway in the Hall. In other countries, for instance England, there is a convention that the majority party leader should be called to form the Cabinet but there was no such convention in Somalia.

The SYL Central Committee and Parliamentary group had passed a resolution endorsing the candidacy of Abdirashid Ali Sharmarke for the Premiership. But President Osman was convinced that the country was ripe for change. On Monday 8 June 1964, an announcement was made of the President's decision to designate Abdirazak Haji Hussein, the former Minister of Internal Affairs and Public Works, as Prime Minister.[182] Aden Abdulla believed that the responsibilities of head of government should be assigned to the most prominent party MPs on a rotation basis. This was not the first time the President had designated a Prime Minister of his choice not endorsed by the Central Committee of the ruling party. In 1960, immediately after independence, and again later in 1961, he designated Abdirashid Ali instead of Abdullahi Issa, who was proposed by the Central Committee and backed by more than half of the MPs.[183] Sharmarke, one of a handful Somali university degree holders from the South of the country, had served as Prime Minister from independence in 1960 to 1964.

But, while the 1960 designation and 1961 redesignation of Abdirashid Ali Sharmarke had raised only minor problems, that of Abdirazak Haji Hussein had stimulated a strong wave of opposition which ran through the ruling party and the Parliament. This challenge haunted Premier Abdirazak throughout his troubled tenure until he was voted out of office when President Aden Abdulla was defeated in the 1967 presidential election, for whose re-election he was campaigning. Abdirashid and Abdirazak shared, in common, origins in the Majerteen clan-family and a long militancy in the ranks of the ruling party. Yet in all other aspects they could not have been more different: while Abdirashid was one of the few Somali MPs with a university education and long experience in administration, Abdirazak was a self-made man with no or little formal education who had served as a radio and telegraph operator in the British Gendarmerie in the 1940s. One of Abdirashid's qualities was his ability to compromise, which had served him well in dealing with an often fractious Parliament.

By contrast, Abdirazak was widely seen as a confrontational man who treated his rivals in a rather abrasive manner besides lacking other necessary qualities: flexibility and the ability to reach out to hardline MPs. Abdirashid was also known for his close ties with influential religious sects based in the capital, which further enhanced his stature as a political campaigner. In addition to this, the two political giants disliked each other thoroughly as well as disagreeing on policy, and that made their battle in the National Assembly all the more spectacular. (By virtue of his association with the National Assembly, the author had witnessed heated exchanges between the two men in the debates in the Parliament)

The President was conscious of Abdirazak's Achilles heels. In his diary, he wrote: "I have always admired and liked Abdirazak Haji Hussein, even if I know he is resentful and vengeful towards those he thinks are his enemies, a serious failing, unbecoming of a Prime Minister. In spite of this, I have always held the conviction that he is a life-saving last hope for Somalia" [*Ho avuto sempre una certa ammirazione e simpatia per Abdirazak Agi Hussen, anche se gli conosco come difetto grave in un Capo del Governo (quello di essere astioso e vendicativo verso quelli che ritiene suoi nemici) e pensavo fosse un'àncora di salvezza per la Somalia*].[184] It was an open secret that the President had long been considering the designation of Abdirazak as an alternative to Abdirashid. In his diary for 12 November 1963, he reported: "This chap [Abdirazak] has the makings of a statesman; I need to nominate him Prime Minister at the next occasion. He is full of energy and he is honest. His weak point is the obstinacy and the tendency to demonize his political adversaries. But, to make up for that, he is honest and can be a good friend. [...] If Abdirazak made efforts to gain the confidence of his adversaries, instead of treating them harshly, I do believe that he would be a good Prime Minister".[185]

His friends believed he was firm but fair. His enemies believed that he was bitter and spiteful, some of whom felt that he in fact had the makings of a tyrant. Nevertheless, "Nobody dispute[d] his courage, nor the drive to work 18 hours a day, to the detriment of his health, even after a serious operation performed at Walter Reed Hospital in Washington, DC in 1962".[186] Although he had the constitutional power to sack the Prime Minister, the President was all the same convinced that dismissing a sitting Prime Minister, who enjoyed the confidence of the Parliament, was not in the best interest of the country. Despite that, he was waiting for the appropriate time for a change of premier and that time came with the general elections of March 1964.

A question worth asking is why Abdirizak had been chosen in the first place and why the political class of the day opposed him. He was chosen because of his personality and his approach to the administration of State affairs which distinguished him from his predecessors, who were often accused of condoning, or at the very least, not being tough enough on corruption and top-level, widespread maladministration. He was chosen because he represented corruption drive the centrepiece of his term of office. In fact, his first action was to request the members of his government to sign an undertaking not to engage in any professional, commercial, industrial or financial activities during their time of office. Most of the Somali political class were known to be corrupt and inefficient, inclined only to keep the status quo and resistant to any reforms and innovations which they feared might undermine their positions. In a country of unabashed kleptocrats, the designated Prime Minister shone like a beacon of probity. His opponents saw him as a threat to their dubious business interests and feared that he might undermine them.

In a major shift, the Central Committee and the Parliamentary Group of the Somali Youth League issued a statement on June 10, declaring that their support for the President of the Republic's decision and that deputy Abdirazak Haji Hussein should become the head of the new government. Admitting that although the decision of the President "had not been in accordance with the proposal expressed by the SYL that Abdirashid should become the next Prime Minister", the statement added that "after carefully examining the present political situation of the country, it has been decided to give the go-ahead to the formation of the new government headed by the Prime Minister designate, Abdirazak Haji Hussein Hassan".[187]

## Parliament rejects Abdirazak's government

The Premier designate presented the list of the 13 Cabinet Ministers to the Head of State 2 months after his designation.

The composition of Abdirazak's first government has provoked a feeling of genuine amazement. The Prime Minister had broken precedent in two ways: firstly, in the distribution of ministerial posts he departed from the usual practice of strict tribal and geographical balance. Secondly, he broke new ground by requiring Cabinet members to make a formal declaration of personal properties and business holdings,[188] turning the conventional acquiescence to ministerial pecuniary misconduct on its head.

Ability and education appeared instead to have been the main criteria in the selection process, leading to a relatively young ministerial cohort. Indeed, reinforcing the place of expertise in the selection process, the Prime Minister designate himself went as far as to refer to the new Cabinet on 15 June as a "working group", where quality rather than regional or ethnic balance had been the deciding factor. In their first Council of Ministers meeting held on 15 June, the day after they were sworn in, Abdirizak emphasised the importance of good conduct to the ministers, telling them, "We must set an example with our actions, both in the public and in the private life".[189]

The Cabinet included a number of deputies who defected from their original political parties to join the governing party. These were: Aden Issak Ahmed (Somali National Congress (SNC), Borama district), Sheikh Hassan Abdullahi Farah (SNC, Odweine district), Mohamud Issa Jama (Somali National Movement (SNM), Hargeisa district) and Yousuf Aden Mohamed "Bowkah" (United Somali Party (USP), Erigavo district). Like his predecessors, Abdirazak, too, faced a delicate task in assembling a cross-tribal team of Ministers that could win a confidence vote in Parliament. Finally, the members of the new government were sworn in on June 15, 1964, except for Abdullahi Issa, who seemed reluctant to take up his new post as Minister of Health, Veterinary and Labour, which he considered ill-suited to his political stature. He later accepted his new position and was sworn in a few days later, on June 18, 1964.

In an apparent move to alleviate the Issak "grievances", three Ministers from that clan family were appointed as against two in the ongoing Sharmarke cabinet, giving them important portfolios such as Foreign Affairs, Finance, Defence and Agriculture. Abdirazak's government, consisting of 13 Ministers, lost a vote of non-confidence on 13 July 1964, after which the Prime Minister resigned. Several powerful political figures, who felt they were not sharing in the spoils of political power, joined forces with loyal supporters of Abdirashid to form a strong opposition faction within the SYL ruling party. This was a vote which clearly cut across party lines. While 48 Deputies of the SYL party voted in favour of the government, 33 other members of the same party voted against it, among them the Secretary-General, Yassin Nour Hassan. Four SYL Deputies were absent, including the Ministers of Justice and Foreign Affairs, who were on official mission abroad, and the former Prime Minister Abdirashid Ali Sharmarke.

The major opposition party, the Somali National Congress (SNC) cast 18 votes against the government, but one SNC Deputy voted in favour and two were absent. Eight Deputies of the Somali Democratic Union (SDU) voted "No", and two voted "Yes". All the six Deputies of the Hisbia Destour Mustaqil Somali (HDMS) and the Partito Republicano Somalo (PRS) group supported the government. The criticisms mainly focused on faults which Deputies identified with aspects of the government programme, in particular with the provisions for the strengthening the national army which they considered inadequate and (sic!) for achieving Somali unity. Evidently, some were not satisfied with some of those chosen for ministerial positions. Whatever side they fell on the debate of the government programme, all those who made contributions to the discussion did so with strongly-worded statements.[190]

Criticism on the Assembly floor over the three days of debate also appeared to be fastidious in nature, focusing on the particular wording of the document. All Opposition speakers, for instance, chose to interpret the reference to "in Ethiopian territory, etc." as government acknowledgement of Ethiopian and Kenyan sovereignty over Somali-inhabited areas, inferring that the government had no intention to liberate those areas under foreign rule. The Prime Minister put this down to a misprint in the first published version of the programme and the reference was later corrected to read "the destiny of Somali territories under Ethiopian and Kenyan domination".

The fall of the government not only caused domestic political crisis, but it also generated repercussions on foreign policy. Without a proper government in place, the President of the Republic felt it was inappropriate to attend an international conference, and therefore, cancelled his attendance as head of the Somali delegation to the first OAU Conference scheduled to take place in Cairo. A more modest delegation was sent, headed by the new Minister of Foreign Affairs, 29-year-old Ahmed Yusuf Dualeh, who attended with observer status.[191]

A day after his defeat in the Parliament, Abdirazak, contending with many challenges, requested an audience with the President. During the unplanned meeting, he came up with a suggestion which bewildered the President: the suspension of the Constitution. The President took this as an indication that Abdirizak may have been pushed to his wit's end by the last few weeks: "I think that Abdirizak has been left shaken and disoriented by the general chaos of the last month, wanting me—with the help of the armed forces—to suspend the Constitution" *[Penso Abdirazak il marasma del mese scorso lo ha scosso e messo quasi disorientato. Vorrebbe addiritura che, appoggiandomi alle Forze Armate, sospendessi la Costituzione*].[192] This was a proposal which the President could not countenance, not only rejecting it outright but explaining in detail the legal consequences such a proposal might have entailed, had it been accepted.

"What Abdirazak has come up with yesterday i.e., suspension of the Constitution, constitutes one of the few specific cases for which the Head of State could constitutionally be put on trial for attempt against the constitutional order as provided by Article 76 (1-3 of the Constitution)", he observed, since a state of emergency—endowing the President with extraordinary powers—could be interpreted as despotic, adding: "Certainly the best thing is not to act illegally on impulse. For me, the essential thing is to get moving forward, stand firm against the blackmail emanating from the Deputies, let governments to fall till the Deputies will be convinced that they cannot win using corruption. It is through the firmness of purpose, in the framework of the Constitution and the law, that I will be able to square up to the situation. Only those who are not afraid of losing power can gain firmness of purpose" [É la fermezza, nell›ambito costituzionale e della legalitá›, che potrá dirizzare le cose; e la fermezza possono averla soltanto quelli che non hanno paura di perdere la posizione].[193] No one else appears to have been privy to Abdirizak's suggestion.

In a brief speech to the nation, after asking Premier Abdirazak to form a new government again, the President said: "I express my hope that the people and the Parliament will realize the fact that the country cannot continue in the current state of affairs which has practically left the nation without a government in the last ten months. I believe that the national interest should not and cannot be based on personalities. I would like us to get on with the formation of the government, a functioning government. Let then such government be seen functioning in the first instance and only when we see whether it is functioning in the interest of the country or to its detriment should appropriate action to be taken. I have deep confidence in Abdirazak's ability to solve some grave problems that have preoccupied me for a while and which by nature are domestic matters. Foremost among these problems is to dispel the belief – founded or not – held by the people who are accustomed to think that the personalities who hold public responsibilities, be they ministers or senior officials, only occupy their positions as representatives of a particular group or are working for the specific interest of that group. Hence, I say to the entire Somali nation and in particular to the men with parliamentary responsibilities (i.e. the deputies) to allow a government to establish itself and then to judge it based on its work when it starts to operate".[194]

In August, five months after the general elections, Prime Minister

Abdirazak presented a reconfigured Cabinet, with the intention of addressing the pressing issues raised during the July defeat of the first government in the National Assembly. The Cabinet was slightly larger than the original one. With more due paid to clan balance. The 12 ministers from the original Cabinet were reshuffled and handed new portfolios and were joined by three new ones, many of whom were elected for the first time in the parliamentary elections of 1964. This brought the size of the Cabinet to 16 rather than 13 ministers (inclusive of the Prime Minister in both cases). In the new government, Ismail Dualeh Warsame replaces his kinsman Mohamed Issa Jama as Ministrer of Agriculture and Animal Husbandery; Mohamoud Abdinour "Juju" and Abdirahman Sheikh Moumin are included in the new government, the firat as Minister without Portfolio in the Office of the Prime Minster, the second replaces Ali Omar Shego as Minister of Justice. Ali Omar Shego is moved to the Ministry of Planning. The SYL-dominated Parliament approved Abdirazak's second Cabinet by 91 votes to 23, without any abstentions late in the night of August 28. At the swearing-in ceremony of the new government, held at the presidential mansion, the President of the Republic said; "Today you have taken an oath to work honestly for the welfare of the country, to maintain its laws and to respect its constitutional precepts. Whereas the oath of office is both a symbol and constitutional usage, it is without any significance if it is not coupled, as I have said on many other occasions, with a genuine love for the country, a high measure of personal dignity, and a sense of fairness on your part. I am confident you have these qualities which are inalienable to the offices you have assumed".[195]

Although a government had been formed, an internal dissident faction, led by former Prime Minister Abdirashid Ali Sharmarke, missed no opportunity to challenge the government by introducing private bills aimed at embarrassing or weakening the Prime Minister and his administration. In Somalia, rebelliousness and squabbling became a common feature within the ruling party whose Members of Parliament, in the past, voted against the party's line, and against SYL governments led by Abdullahi Issa and Abdirashid Ali Sharmarke in 1959 and 1961 respectively.

## President clashes with the Parliament
## Demands for a 100% increase of parliamentary allowance

Across sub-Saharan Africa, in the two decades after many countries gained political independence (1960-1978), the Gross Domestic Product (GDP) per capita across the continent grew by less than one percent a year. At this rate, it would take more than seventy years to double average income,[196] almost double the life expectancy at birth for the region in 1960.[197] The Somali economy was no different and the new state lacked the administrative capacity to collect taxes from subsistence herders and farmers. The state could rely on the custom taxes from international trade, which were easier to collect, but tariffs failed to meet the needs of a government with ambitious development goals. Somalia therefore relied on Italian and British subsidies, which funded the new nation's budget in the first three years of independence.

The negative economic performance recorded in the first two years following independence was indicated by a budget deficit of over Sh.So 60 million for the 1961 financial year and an estimated deficit of Sh.So38 million for the following year. Worried by this trend, Aden Abdulla observed: "The level of foreign contributions needed to cover the national budget deficit, without taking into account the economic development, is really high, and to tell the truth, we should take the blame. It is inconsistent with the self-respect and dignity of independent people to rely any longer than is necessary on the generosity of foreigners for covering ordinary budget deficit and for providing fund for development projects".[198]

Italy and Britain were expected to cover the budget deficit for 1962 in the proportion of ShSo 23M and ShSo 15M respectively.[199] The Italian contribution towards the budget for 1963 amounted to ShSo. 42,285,000.[200] Aden Abdulla often warned the two Heads of Government who served during his tenure against reckless government spending which he saw as imposing an unnecessary burden on future generations, indicating areas of waste where government expenditure was ill spent like the excessive number of government-owned cars assigned to politicians and top officials or the creation of unnecessary diplomatic missions abroad. He encouraged the government to take measures aimed at reducing the nation's debt and place its finances on a sound footing. He also proposed the idea of multiple accreditations; where one embassy and ambassador could be assigned responsibilities for perform diplomatic duties in more than one foreign country in order to reduce the excessive budget involved in running two diplomatic missions.

He expressed concern over the excessive number of trips abroad undertaken by ministers and MPs, enjoying such trips for their own sake even when they had little practical benefit for the nation. He cited, for instance, the case of the Foreign Minister who, together with his entourage, including parliamentarians and support staff, spent 70 consecutive days on mission abroad, which cost taxpayers ShSo 65,800.[201] The President referred also to another case involving the President of the National Assembly who went on an official visit to China, and onward to North Korea, for 25 days, accompanied by 20 lawmakers and a number of supporting staff, including interpreters and translators. The mission cost taxpayers an estimated Sh.So100, 000.[202]

Despite the parlous state of Somali finances, in November 1961, the National Assembly had passed with an overwhelming majority, a draft law increasing the MPs' monthly allowance, from ShSo 1,000 to ShSo 2,000, an increase of 100%. The bill could not have come at the worst time, appearing at the very moment the country was struggling with unprecedented flash floods which had a devastating impact. The worst of the flooding was caused when the two main rivers, the Shabelle and the Juba, broke their banks and merged in a vast floodplain. The torrent of water submerged vast tracts of land, tore out communications, marooned towns and villages, destroyed homes and livestock, and ruined banana plantations. The extent of the disaster was far beyond the resources of the Somali government and people. Under the 1960 Constitution, the President had suspensive veto over laws passed by Parliament and thus the power not to promulgate a law but to send it back to the legislature for reconsideration.

When this happens the request for reconsideration must be accompanied by a message containing the reasons for the presidential action. Where the Parliament passes the returned law a second time, by the required two-thirds majority, the President must promulgate it within thirty days of the approval.[203] On the hand, the bill dies whether there is not enough votes to override the President. The President described the bill as "immoral", reporting in his diary entry of 30 November: "The Deputies have taken the decision to increase their allowance by 100% at a difficult time when the country is suffering catastrophic floods. However, as far as I am concerned, exercising my duty, I have returned the draft law, with a message stating the reasons why, to the Assembly for re-examination though convinced that they will not take heed my advice" *[I Deputati si sono aumentati l'indennita' parlamentare del 100%*

*ed al momento meno adatto colla caresdtia, etc., etc., ma io, per fare il mio dovere, non assendo convinto che mi daranno ascolto, ho rimandato la legge in Assemblea con messaggio motivato].*[204] This arose from the President's power, detailed in Article 61(3), that, "Within the period fixed for the promulgation, the President of the Republic may transmit to the Assembly a message stating the grounds thereof, requesting that the law be reconsidered". The message the President had sent to the Parliament emphasized that it was not reasonable to increase the MPs salary at a time of national crisis.

As feared, in December, the National Assembly voted overwhelmingly to override the President's veto of the legislation that would allow an increase of the parliamentary allowance. The vote in the National Assembly amounted to a sweeping rejection of plea from the President and with the government which was highlighting the strain the law would place on the national budget. In the face of this irresponsible decision of the Parliament, the President came close to start the procedure for dissolution of the National Assembly which technically meant dispersal of the legislature before the expiration of its constitutionally specified term followed by a call for fresh elections.

Before taking a final decision on the issue, the President summoned the Army Chief and the Police Commissioner to sound out their opinion on the idea of dissolving the current Parliament and eventually calling fresh elections. The two commanders, whose loyalty to the democratic institutions of the country over the years was beyond question, offered diverging solutions for the crisis. The Chief of the National Army, General Daud Abdulle Hersi, believed that for this first mistake, there was no need to dissolve the Parliament. According to him, it would be difficult to expect that any newly-elected legislature would provide deputies who were any better. He suggested working towards the cohesiveness of the SYL parliamentary group and also to dispel the feeling the Deputies held to shield themselves from the President and the government [*Daud é del parere che si cominci a costruire la coesione dell'SYL e si elimini anche l'impressione nei Deputati che dovono difendersi dal Presisdente della Repubblica e del Governo che non li riconoscerebbe*].[205]

The Police Commissioner, Mohamed Abshir Musse, instead was of the view that there was nothing positive to be expected from the legislators in exercise, therefore, it was a high time to dissolve the legislature as a deterrent force followed by fresh elections that may, generate a change of, at least, half of the current members with honest elements, a move that would create a precedent that will serve as a warning to the deputies in the future. (Diary

*December 10, 1961).* The Constitution of the Somali Republic provided that, "The National Assembly may be dissolved before the end of its term of office by the President of the Republic, having heard the opinion of the President of the Assembly, whenever it cannot discharge its functions or discharges them in a manner prejudicial to the normal exercise of legislative activity" (Article 53 (2). However, the President, after pondering the issue, reached the conclusion that dissolving the Parliament and calling for early elections was not in the best interest of the country and there was no public desire for this course of action.

## Controversial law on retail trade and the exodus of the Arabs

In 1965, the President clashed with the Parliament again when he refused to promulgate key draft legislation on domestic retail trade passed by the National Assembly by a strong majority arguing that the bill would contravene international agreements Somalia had signed. The draft law—nicknamed 'Legge Da'ar' after the MP, Mohamed Ali Nur "Dacar", who introduced it—originally approved by the Parliament at the end of 1964,[206] was designed to debar non-Somali citizens from engaging in retail trade within Somalia. The bill was approved by an absolute majority of 84 votes, more than two-thirds of the voting members of the Parliament. The bill would have affected the commercial business of thousands of Arabs resident in the country, 70 to 80% of whom—on an educated guess—were born in Somalia. The President of the Republic, defying a seemingly united Parliament and risking a public backlash, returned the bill to the Parliament for reconsideration with a message for why it was not promulgated.

Among the worries he expressed to the Parliament in writing was the potential for the proposed legislation to backfire, putting Somalis resident abroad, not least in the generally friendly Arab countries where they lived in large numbers, at risk of retaliatory and similarly punitive legislation and treatment as well as general apprehension at undermining the longstanding relationships with these countries. He was particularly referring to the communities of Somalis living and working in Aden, Yemen and the Hijaz. Votes from two-thirds of the members in the House would be needed to override a veto.

An article published in the independent, current affairs monthly magazine *Dalka (The Nation)* by the parliamentary correspondent noted that if promulgated by the President of the Republic, "The draft law would have in effect amounted to the expulsion of the thousands of little non-Somali shopowners – mainly of Southern Arabia origin – who have been here at least since the War. Such a whole-sale eviction would have had the most unfortunate consequences on our relation with many countries where a substantial Somali community lives". Agreeing that "[t]he President was, therefore, quite justified in returning it", the columnist highlighted that the presidential stance was vindicated by those observing the debate, adding that "Perhaps the most bizarre part about it is that the public at the gallery started clapping when it was finally defeated!"[207]

As feared, news of the bill triggered a mass exodus of Arabs from Somalia, and in the process, many of them hastily sold their properties below market price. Consequently, relations between Somalia and Aden deteriorated, as reflected in the virulent attacks levelled at Somalia in the Aden press at the time, reported in an adjacent article on foreign policy in *Dalka*.[208] When the bill was reconsidered by the Parliament, on May 27, 1965, the vote in favour of the bill fell short of the required majority of two-thirds to override the presidential veto, with 52 votes against and 48 in favour.

The bill, if approved, would have made it impossible for foreigners to obtain licenses for such commercial activities such as the selling of foodstuffs by retail, tobacco and matches, the cutting and selling firewood and charcoal, the public national services, (taxicabs, hired cars and buses), the selling of drinking water, export licenses, commercial agencies, commission services, butchery licenses and other similar activities.[209] Although the proposed legislation appeared to have been driven by nativism and isolationism, its supporters may have seen it as a response to some of the discontent felt by ordinary Somalis at the fact the lion's share of retail trade was still dominated by foreigners many years after independence.

Arabs and Indians, who had settled in the country many generations earlier, were relatively well-off and controlled most small-scale business. The more recent arrivals had built up capital through their employment in the colonial forces, having been recruited into the country for military service by the European colonisers, from around the early twentieth century, later settling in the country after demobilisation and establishing their own families, sometimes intermarrying with the local Somalis.

The trend of growing opposition to the Prime Minister waged by a dissident faction within his ruling Somali Youth League party reached a new height with the introduction of a bill providing for the Somalisation not only of the managerial posts but also wage earner and salaried posts of all private companies operating in Somalia, tabled by a group of MPs led by Mohamed Ali Nur "Dacar". The bill, which affected foreign-owned private companies, most of them Italian, was approved by the Parliament on 24 May 1966 by a large majority. The President of the Republic once again held back from promulgating the bill and returned it to the Parliament "on technical, juridical, economic and political grounds", requesting that Parliament submit the law to new discussion and deliberation. In his letter to the President of the National Assembly Sheikh Mukhtar Mohamed and dated 12 July 1966, the President of the Republic said that, among other things, the law was in contrast with international agreements concluded by Somalia with friendly countries.

Aden Abdulla cited, in particular, Article 5 of the bilateral agreement with Italy, approved by Law No. 28 of October 30, 1961 which said that "to citizens of each Country it will be guaranteed, in the territory of the other Country, protection and security for persons and their property and will be assured the same rights, privileges and treatment which the citizens of the Country enjoy within the law". The letter stressed that the law annulled the encouragement Somalia established by the Law No. 10 of February 18, 1960 on foreign investment, as the law itself created mistrust. The President also felt that the existing Foreign Investment and Immigration Law contains sufficient broad provision sufficient to control the employment of foreign nationals and to Somalise private sector jobs as and when required.[210]

The National Assembly began discussions on the draft law on 29 December 1966 and the bill was eventually rejected the following day, having failed to gain the required two-thirds majority (82 votes) to override the presidential veto, receiving only 67 votes in favour.[211] If approved, it would represent a source of embarrassment for the government, which may find itself in default on the international obligations it had accepted under bilateral agreements (Somali News January 6, 1967) All these bills were in substance designed to scare away potential and actual foreign private investors operating in Somalia, with the ultimate aim to cause the collapse of the government.[212]

In January 1967, just six months before the expiration of his tenure, the President refused to sign a bill adopted by the Parliament granting a lump sum payment of ShSo 24,000—or a year's worth of a deputy's salary—to each MP (or to his heirs, in the event he passed away during the legislature) or voted out by the electorate. The bill had been originally approved by deputies with 66 votes to 24 with three abstentions and was expected to come into effect from 1 January 1967.[213] Many expected that, in a crucial presidential election year, the President might be inclined to ingratiate himself with the MPs and sign it into law. But unwilling to compromise on his belief in fiscal prudence and aware that the country could ill afford such a measure, he sent the draft bill back to the Parliament for fresh deliberations.[214]

Towards the end of his presidential mandate, the National Assembly rejected a number of Legislative Decrees, delegating the government the power to issue four codes (Civil, Health, Navigation, Civil Procedure) and bringing up to date four other codes (Labour, Penal, Traffic and Criminal Procedure). The paradox was that these non-controversial Legislative decrees, after being approved article by article earlier in open voting, were rejected when secret votes were taken,[215] indicating that the Deputies' ultimate action was dictated not by the substance of the content but was instead a way of frustrating the government.

In June, the National Assembly also rejected a draft law concerning the appointment of temporary personnel (popularly known as "Giornalieri") for a period exceeding three months and the duration of each appointment to be determined by the Council of Ministers according to the nature of the particular work to be carried out. The government intended to amend existing legislation limiting the duration of the appointment of temporary personnel for a period exceeding three months.The draft law was first approved in opn vote but, when it was put in secret vote, it was rejected. (Soamli News June 24, 1966) The President had sharply criticized Parliament for failing to act reasonably. "[It] seems to me so stupid, irrational and unthinkable that the government bills could be disapproved by the National Assembly. I tend to believe the information brought to my attention according to which many MPs are determined to make the life difficult for the government during the next 12 months that separates us from the election of the new Head of State since I have no longer the power to dissolve the Parliament and call fresh elections", one of the President's powers expressed in Article 53 of the |Constitution.

He added, "I cannot still believe that the majority of the people's 123 representatives are harbouring bad faith. I cannot believe either that this majority are so stupid to believe that, acting in this way, they hurt the government and not the people, since they ought to know that the government would not fall by boycotting the legislation process, unless the government requested a vote of confidence on the approval of the law itself"[216]

In the National Assembly, the government was severely harassed at every possible opportunity by the dissident faction within the ruling party; this obstructionism was facilitated by the Assembly's practice of normally voting by secret ballot, thus making it extremely difficult for the Prime Minister to control his ill-disciplined SYL party fellows. Without a credible, organised opposition in Parliament represented by other parties, the practice of voting on draft legislation secretly eroded party discipline and made dissent difficult to identify, particularly since those voting against the legislation in the secret ballot often endorsed it in the division (or the earlier stage where the voting was declared openly). Once more, the situation reinforced the notion that the SYL Parliamentary Group was nothing but a collection of individual MPs asserting their individual, strongly held views and interest, unbounded by any clear political principles.

The Prime Minister's authority ebbed away as SYL MPs were pushing for different policies. Frustrated by the unorthodox behaviour of the legislators, the President went on to say, "The situation is grave of how things are going in parliament for the government. Two years ago I took the decision to give the country a courageous and honest Prime Minister, and today I do not regret how I acted. But now I am sick and tired of fighting with these irresponsible and corrupt so-called representatives of the people who systematically confuse their narrow minded interests and their dislike with the interest of the country and the people. They do not give a damn about the interest of the people!" [La situazione é grave. Come stanno andando le cose in Parlamento per il Governo Abdirazak. Due anni fa mi ero imposto a dare il Paese un Primo Ministro coraggioso ed onesto, e a tutt'oggi non mi sono pentito dal come avevo agito. Ma ora sono stanco e stufo di combattere con quei irrresponsabili e corrotti cosiddetti Rappresentanti del Popolo, i quali confondono sistematicamente i loro meschini interessi e la loro antipatia con l'interesse del Paese e del Popolo. dei quali ultimi interessi se ne fregano altamente].[217]

The President referred to those MPs who, in the secret ballot voted against the government despite voting with it in the open vote, as cowards and *franchi tiratori* [snipers or turncoats].[218] Fittingly, he borrowed the term from political commentary in Italy, a country whose political setup Somalia's mirrored and with which it therefore shared a number of similarities, which referred to a Member of Parliament who voted against his party in a secret ballot. The rejection of non-controversial legislation was a show of no confidence in the government, leading the embattled Prime Minister and his Cabinet to inform the SYL Parliamentary Group of their resignation on 26 June 1966, before formally presenting it to the President Aden Abdulla. In his letter of resignation to the President of the Republic, the Prime Minister stated: "Mr President, as a result of the unclear and unconceivable manner in which the bills have been rejected, I tend to be convinced that my government can hardly carry out its complex and delicate task in the face of the obscure and mysterious climate prevailing in the National Assembly" (*Somali News July 1, 1966*).

In comments to the press, Yusuf Aden Mohamed "Bowkah", the Information Minister tersely said, "We could not cope with the present attitude of our Parliament".[219] However, the President invited the Prime Minister to withdraw the resignation and seek instead a fresh confidence vote from Parliament. After receiving a letter from the President, the Prime Minister and the Cabinet agreed to remain in office in the meantime,[220] putting aside their reservations in time to present a united front at the sixth independent anniversary celebrations on 1 July.[221]

Quite apart from the challenges it faced on the floor of the Parliament, the government found itself fighting fires on different fronts. Firstly, earlier in the year, a number of Cabinet members—the Minister of Commerce and Industry and both the Minister for Agriculture and the Under-Secretary in the same department—had been dismissed on allegations of graft. The Finance Minister, under the spotlight for similar allegations, tendered his resignation without being asked. This all flew in the face of the Prime Minister's anti-corruption drive, a key policy of his administration, and his calls for an exemplary government with "clean" ministers. However, the reputational damage was slight and, *alla somala*, the ministerial seats they vacated were filled by deputies from the same clan.[222] As Prime Minister Abdirizak Haji Hussein wrote in subsequent years, after he had dismissed "three of my ministers for flagrant mismanagement and corruption", he also "requested Parliament to bring criminal charges against them". He added that, "There were also nine deputies who had been accused of stealing public money" but since "There existed a policy of parliamentary immunity, unless Parliament agreed to proceed against them, we had no recourse".[223]

Secondly, abroad, the government was caught in a clash with Kenya. Somalia's neighbour alleged that military aid, coming both from the Soviet Union and the Arab states, was being passed onto Somalis living in the Somali-inhabited regions under Kenyan control, who were continuing their struggle for their independence. Kenyan anxiety had been stimulated by the military gear on show at the anniversary celebrations, where they were the main feature and where they were on show for the first time: Soviet equipment which included tanks and MiG fighter aircraft, supplied to the Somali armed forces.[224]

The display was made all the more imposing by the fact independence parade took place, instead of along the *lungomare* [seafront], by a new, impressive square assembled for the purpose by the soldiers. The magnificent parade incorporated many parts of military drill—the rhythmic march and commands of the infantry, the roar of the engines let out by the artillery and armoured vehicles—which stimulated the crowd's cheers; the fly-past by the planes of the National Army continued for the entire duration of the event, whose daring manoeuvres aroused the admiration of all.[225] There was also the general sense that the military was up to full force; months earlier, in his congratulatory message on the sixth anniversary of the creation of the Somali Army, the Minister of Defence had said, "I wish to thank the Government and people of the USSR who helped our national force with [the] many things it needed for the defence of our country from its enemies".[226]

Upon the President of the Republic's advice, the Prime Minister went to the party in the first instance in an attempt to resolve the problem since most of the MPs belonged to the SYL.[227] A series of meetings were held between the Cabinet and the SYL Central Committee. The party executive decided to form a special six-member committee for these meetings, with Mohamed Sheikh Gabiyow as President, Deputy Ugas Yassin Abdurahman Vice President, Mohamed Ahmed Elmi "Ottavio" Secretary and Deputies Mukhtar Ibrahim Hussein, Ali Garad Giama and Omar Osman Yabeh as members.

A heated debate ensued. But, according to Abdirizak's recollection, "After a few days of ventilating their grievances, everyone more or less simmered down". When the general debate was over, it was decided to draft a final resolution taking into account the general tenor of the debate and the proposals and recommendations made throughout, which took two days to prepare. The resolution, which proposed that the government should be given a vote of confidence, was adopted in open ballot. However, to avoid a recurrence of what happened in Parliament—with an open ballot and a secret one which were at variance with each other—Abdirizak insisted that a secret vote should be taken, promising that he would resign if it did not get a two-thirds majority, which it nevertheless secured.[228]

In a meeting held on the evening of Thursday 7 July, the party therefore reaffirmed its confidence in Abdirizak's government. Of 85 members present—

from both the Central Committee and the Parliamentary Group—64 voted in favour, with 11 against and 11 abstentions. The meeting was the third held by the two party bodies in the past week. In comments to a SONNA journalist, the Chairman of the Special Committee raised the necessity of strengthening party discipline, a point raised by "speaker after speaker [and which] I [have also] emphasised".[229]

On 11 July, the government tabled a vote of confidence. In a speech to the National Assembly, Prime Minister Abdirizak Haji Hussein said that "Confidence [in the government] is of vital importance and essential for a government that relies on the support of the National Assembly, without which the government would not be able to perform its constitutional duties and its national and international commitments". He added: "I would like to point out to the National Assembly that the Government does not wish to see a shadow of doubt cast upon the Government by the National Assembly, which is the supreme legislative body on which the Government depends", concluding, "The Government does not intend to continue in its work without the continued support of the National Assembly". Reflecting the interest surrounding the vote, many deputies registered their names on the roll call to have their turn in the debate.[230]

After two days of the debate, the Assembly finally decided to renew its confidence in Abdirizak's government with an overwhelming majority on 12 July. On the day of the vote, the evening session opened at 6.30 p.m. and closed at 10.50 p.m., during the course of which the Prime Minister provided an update on the economic and financial situation of the country, speaking—remarkably—for more than two consecutive hours. When the time for the vote came, of the 108 deputies present in the Chamber, 74 voted in support of the government with 21 against and 13 abstained. The remaining 15 deputies were absent.[231]

# SECTION 1

## PART 4

# SECTION ONE, PART FOUR

# 1967 PRESIDENTIAL ELECTION

## The Six-Day War in the Middle East overshadows the election

The full six years term in office for Aden Abdulla was set to expire on July 6, 1967. According to the Constitution, new presidential election had to be organized. The election of president was not by popular vote, but rather an election by the Parliament, which consisted of 123 members. As in 1961, Aden Abdulla refused to campaign for re-election, thinking that it was improper to ask support from the Parliament or make any concessions or promises in exchange for votes. As Abdirazak Haji Hussein recalled in his personal account of the period, the President was lukewarm at best at the prospect of seeking a second term: 'In the beginning, President Aden Abdulle Osman had not even wanted to run for reelection. I remember one day when we were discussing local policies, the irresponsible behavior of many government officials, and the programs that were going badly. He said, "The best thing for us to do in the immediate future would be to watch through the windows rather than being conductors"'.[232]

In the run-up to the election, the President received a stream of visitors, including parliamentarians, businesspeople and old friends, all of them offering their moral and material support for his re-election. In their view, as the inaugural holder of the office, he had discharged his duties well, acting with sagacity through the different crises that faced the young republic and in the process, protecting the dignity and independence of the position of Head of State.

A group of MPs, all from the former British Somaliland, led by Hon. Sheikh Haji Yousuf Osman called on the President on March 6, 1967. The President jotted down the points discussed in the meeting. "From 9.00 to 10.15 a.m., I received in the office, the Honorable Sheikh Haji Yousuf Osman preannounced to me by Osman Ahmed Roble (*Deputy for Aden Yaval district*). I had half an hour but I could not disengage myself before an hour and a quarter. [He said] he and at least another 18 deputies from the North want me to remain as President of the Republic for another six years because they do not trust Abdirashid and they do not see anyone in the field who could adequately substitute me. There is, however, according to him [Haji Yousuf Osman] Mohamed Ibrahim Egal, to whom Abdirashid and his supporters had promised the office of Prime Minister if Abdirashid were elected president, and thus it had been decided to put Egal and Abdirazak in contact, etc., etc. As usual, I told them I do not seek re-election, explaining my motives. I told them that, besides me and Abdirashid, there were men that could be found worthy, but that, in any case, it is not in my character to bargain on such matters [*Non* è del mio carattere di fare baratto sulla questione], even if I were enthusiastic about getting re-elected, and we should not speak now about this, since I will seek re-election only if it imposed on me by those who believe that the country still needs me".[233]

Fewer than 30 days before the presidential election, Aden Abdulla received another group of legislators from the Issak clan. The group, preannounced to him by Cabinet Minister Mohamoud Abdi Nour "Juju" and led by Mohamoud Issa Jama and Mohamed Haji Dualeh, offered him the support of their group in exchange for the assurance that one of them would be appointed Prime Minister, namely Mohamed Ibrahim Egal, in the event he won the election. He told them that he was not accustomed to giving such undertakings although he was not ruling out *a priori* the possibility of what they wanted to achieve. He stuck to his guns, leaving them the freedom to act in the way they deemed was in the interest of the country.[234] The President threw the ball in the field of the legislators: if they wanted him as a president, he would be willing to serve. If they chose someone else, he would be equally happy.[235]

A number of wealthy businessmen, notably Haji Ahmed Abdullahi "Hashish" and Hagi Nasser Ali Hubeishi, offered to fund his re-election campaign. Haji Ahmed "Hashish", a businessman hailing from Hargeysa, pledged to make a donation of ShSo 100,000, a sum the President was free to spend the way he thought best, an offer he graciously declined. "I told him that I don't need money, for I believe it is not only shameful but unnecessary to do things using corruption".[236] Like "Hashish", a businessman of Yemeni descent, Haji Nasser Ali, in a separate meeting with the President, expressed his readiness to contribute to the funding of the re-election campaign. "I thanked telling him that I do not pay anybody in exchange for vote and, therefore, there is no need for money".[237]

In a rare heart-to-heart with his close confidant and friend, Mohamed Ali Dhorre "Agaweyne" (a Deputy representing Obbia), he explained the reasons why he would not seek re-election: "I do not consider myself indispensable, my advice and ideas are not appreciated [so] therefore I feel useless as Head of State. Consequently, I do not see why I should prolong my stay at the Palace".[238] To him, "Seven years [was] long enough to weigh up the pros and cons",[239] and to take stock of the failures and progress achieved in the immediate post-independence years.

Another reason why he did not engage in active campaigning was his deep dismay at the growing sectarianism within government and the nation. He despised the schism which afflicted the body politic, believing that clan differences should never become institutionalized and become such potent markers of political groupings. He strongly felt that political leaders should be free to debate important issues without being bound by clan loyalty.

"During the campaign, there was a distinct difference in methodology between the two opposing parts. Adan Abdulla and I were in complete agreement that we would pursue our goal with honesty, and fair play, avoiding any thing that even remotely would compromise the democratic system or set bad precedents". This included, for instance, avoiding fraud, coercion and public funds. While Aden Abdulla left the issue to the deputies if they wanted him as president, "Abdirashid personally decided to visit every deputy's house rather than make them come to him. He promised everyone a job, even using the oath of Allah [God] to sound more convincing, especially to those whose support was crucial".[240]

On 31 May, a meeting of a mini Congress of the ruling party was convened in order to designate the preferred candidate of the party for the upcoming presidential election. Two proposals were introduced; one suggesting that the party should endorse an official candidate while another advising that Deputies be given a free vote. When the two proposals were put to a vote, the option of designating an official party candidate received more votes, 59 votes to 16 and 2 abstentions.[241] This was then followed by a secret vote to decide the party's official candidate for the presidency, which saw 44 votes go to the incumbent Aden Abdulla and 30 for Abdirashid, his only contender, with 3 abstentions. Five SYL Parliamentarians did not attend the voting session,[242] namely Sceik Muktar Mohamed Hussein (Huddur), Osman Haji Hassan Jama "Jiis" (Galcaio), Ahmed Gumane Roble (Zeila, who was on a trip abroad), Muktar Ibrahim (Belet Uen) and Hared Farah (Belet Uen).[243]

Although the MPs were given a free vote in the Parliament, the SYL party leadership tried to ensure its deputies voted in accordance with this verdict. Addressing the party gathering after the verdict, the SYL Secretary General -

sitting Prime Minister Abdirizak Haji Hussein – spoke in strong terms: "With this [voting] decision, the Party chose Aden Abdulla Osman, who remains the only official candidate of the SYL. It is the unavoidable duty of all the Honourable Members of the party to work for his success and to vote for him and him alone [*Con tale decisione, il Partito ha fatto la sua scelta a favore di S.E. Aden Abdulla Osman, che rimane il solo candidato ufficiale della SYL.* È inderogabile dovere di tutti gli Onorevoli Parlamentari del Partito lavorare per il suo successo, e votare per lui e solo per lui].

"The Central Committee trusts that all the Honourable members who owe loyalty to the SYL will vote en bloc for the official candidate, giving up any personal or group preference in favour of the party interest... He must therefore be supported by all, completely, without any mental reservation".[244] The same edition of the newspaper ran an article under the title 'The necessity of party discipline'. Although it highlighted that "predictions on the possible outcome [of the presidential election] are the main subject of discussion, not only among the deputies whose difficult task is to choose the right person but also among the people whose interests will be served by the chosen man", the article appeared to advocate unity of purpose. Prefixed its remarks with the observation that "These notes have no particular reference to the upcoming elections expect as relates to all democratically organised elections", it recalled the words of Abdirizak Haji Hussein in the joint party meeting on 31 May, where he said, 'I don't think anyone thinks that "divided we will resist and united we will fall". It is unity which gives strength to a party, an organisation and a country" [*Ritengo che nessuno pensi che "divisi resisteremo ed uniti cadremo.* È l'unità, che dá forza *ad un partito ad una organizzazione e ad un paese*].[245]

Apart from the support of the ruling party, Aden Abdulla also received the endorsement of the main opposition party, the Socialist National Congress (or SNC, for short), known until it was renamed in 1965 as Somali National Congress but retaining the same initials by which it was widely known.[246] Speaking to Haji Osman Farah, the Director of the Radio Department, about forty days before the election, Hon. Sheikh Ali Jumale, the leader of the party, argued that "Each party should support one of the two candidates, H.E. President Aden Abdulla Osman or former Prime Minister Hon. Abdirashid Ali Shermarke". Asked what economic development and political stability he hoped the country would achieve in the next six years, he said that, "The most important thing that we can already be proud of [as a nation] is stability. What is going on in many countries has not happened in our country" for indeed, "In other countries, there are politicians who seek asylum in neighbouring States to propagandize their people; this has not happened in our country".

Indeed, "Here there is a real democracy and anybody – be he a party man or an individual in the street – can take the microphone and speak as he pleases. Here is the most important advantage, but perhaps not everybody is aware of its value: we have a Parliamentary democracy and yet since our Independence six year (sic) ago, there has not been a Parliamentary dissolution. This is the cause of much chaos in the world". Sheikh Ali Jimale added, "I feel that if Aden Abdulla Osman returns to power, the country will prosper both economically and politically, and in a stable manner".[247] A few weeks later, on 10 May, after an extraordinary meeting of its Central Committee, the Democratic African Somali Party (or H.D.A.S.) announced its support for Aden Abdulla's re-election,[248] following a similar announcement from the Somali Republican Party on 30 April.[249]

When the party officially announced the candidacy of Aden, the Central Committee called upon Abdirashid to withdraw his, even though his candidacy had not been made public. However, Abdirashid suggested he could not influence the decision and actions of his supporters. Some members of the Central Committee went as far as to suggest that Abdirashid be expelled from the party but the more dispassionate felt this would be a measure too far. Any such decision was also unlikely to influence the strength of his campaign.[250]

Unexpectedly, however, the presidential election process was nearly overshadowed by an event taking place beyond Somali borders, the war that had broken out between the Israelis and a coalition of Arab States in the Middle East. Known widely as the Six Day War, but known by the Arabs as 'the 1967 War' or *Annaksah* [The Setback]. The conflict began on June 6, 1967, just four days before the Somali presidential election. For the Israelis, who long thought of themselves as a democratic oasis surrounded by hostile neighbours in an unstable region, the war was a question of sheer survival while for the Arabs, it was a matter of credibility. Citing the military confrontation in the Middle East as a justification, the President of Somalia's National Assembly and the Prime Minister advanced the idea of putting off the presidential election at least to June 20, arguably to monitor the situation in the Middle East.

The President, however, saw things differently: "No, no, no, I see no link between what is happening in the Middle East and the presidential election here in Somalia", was his reaction to the proposal[251]. Nevertheless, just days before the presidential elections, on 7 June, the Parliament, in an emergency meeting convened at 9.00 a.m. at short notice to consider the Middle East War, unanimously approved the government proposal to support the Arab countries "against the Israeli aggression". The proposal of the government included sending troops to fight side-by side with Arabs, and opening registration centres for military volunteers, a move seen by many as an empty promise and a dangerous adventure. Addressing the Parliament, Prime Minister Abdirizak said that, "The situation is dangerous, but the breach of peace in the Middle East is solely the responsibility of Israel".[252] The Parliament had previously adjourned its sessions until 10 June,[253] the date set for the presidential election.

In his speech, the Prime Minister also asserted that "The Government and the Somali people have always maintained that, in the interest of justice, Palestine belongs only to the Arabs and, in support of this conviction, it has, in all sessions of the United Nations, condemned the deprivation of Palestinian Arabs by the Jews, of a land being but rightly recognised as other than the homeland of the Palestinian Arabs. There can only be a realistic solution to the Palestinian problem, namely the return of this land to its legitimate owners. Linking the suffering of the Palestinians to the Somali context, he added:

"Somalis are in the same condition as Palestinian Arabs because we too have been forcibly deprived of the possession of our lands by a state that is not only Israel's main ally in this part of Africa and the Middle East but also has an ethnic Jewish origin. Somalia and the Arab States are united in the fight against Zionism – your struggle and our struggle. We offer you all the assistance we can provide".

The following day, the Defence Minister, Hon. Abdurahman Haji Mumin Mohamed, together with the Foreign Minister Hon. Ahmed Yusuf Dualeh, had talks with the Egyptian Ambassador and his military attaché. Major-General Mohamed Siad Barre, Commandant of the Somali National Army, and two aides were also present at the meeting. Premier Abdirazak also told Parliament that a high-level military mission would leave shortly for the Arab world to discuss with the Arab High Military Command when and where Somali troops would fight in the war. He also disclosed that Somalia had requested Ethiopia to permit Somali military planes to fly over Ethiopia airspace on their way to Middle East.[254]

Somalia's armed forces had seen little action at home and even less abroad. While nobody provided an explanation of what irremissible national interest pushed Somalia to join a war, the risk involved was high, because Israel was, straightaway, legally entitled, to retaliate and attack Somalia as a belligerent party militarily. Indeed, this bravado became more evident when the government sent a long letter to Ethiopia requesting authorization to fly Somali military aircraft in its airspace,[255] in order to transport troops destined to fight on the Arabs' side. This request was ridiculed, coming as it did, at a time when Ethiopia was even refusing overflight rights to Somali commercial flights between Mogadiscio and Hargeisa. Ethiopia is known to have taken a neutral stand vis-à-vis the military conflict taking place in the Middle East. Seemingly driven by public sentiment, no one in the National Assembly was able to voice dissent to the proposals. As for the public at large, nobody seemed to take seriously the bravado displayed by a government which at the time was on the brink of being voted out of office.

Rather than committing to military action, in the circumstances, the Somali government could have given moral support to the Arabs as it had done in 1956, at the time of the Suez Crisis. Following Anglo-Franco-Israeli aggression against Egypt, the Somali government reacted in a manner which was much less risky. The government introduced a motion to the Legislative Assembly condemning the aggression and expressing solidarity with the government and the people of Egypt, which was adopted on 2 November 1956. The motion, which arose out of discussions in a Cabinet meeting a day earlier where it was accepted, read: "Faced with the serious development of the political and military situation in Egypt, the Legislative Assembly of Somalia, the Government and all the people send to the Government and people of Egypt expression of their solidarity and aligning itself with all the nations that have unanimously expressed abhorrence at the acts of aggression carried out by Israeli troops alongside Anglo-French operations".

It added: "They deplore that sudden attacks on small nations are still possible, ignoring their sacred rights of sovereignty". "They hope that these grave events which endanger security and peace and take away confidence in international collaboration will end as soon as possible, through the triumph of law and freedom, even for small countries", before concluding: "They are confident that the United Nations will be able to guarantee the free and peaceful coexistence of all peoples and of now express the gratitude of the Somali people who are yearning for their [own impending] freedom and independence".

First to have the floor was Deputy Vincenzo Calzia, a representative of the Italian community and an official in the Fascist era, who proposed to the Assembly that the motion be accepted by acclamation. All deputies duly stood up and applauded. Before the Government presented its own motion, Deputy Abdulcadir Mohamed Aden, head of the Parliamentary Group of the Hizbia Dighil Mirifle, presented one which said the aggression against Egypt constituted a violation of the United Nations Charter, noting the disappointment felt by the small countries who looked to the UN as an international guarantor of peace and the defence of their laws and sovereignty.

The motion also called on the Assembly to send a telegram to the UN Secretary General with a request to inform the General Assembly and another telegram to the Egyptian leader Nasser communicating the above. Deputy Nur Hasci Alas, head of the SYL Parliamentary Group, pointed out that the party had given its approval, noting that they expected the Government to present its motion and Deputy Calzia on behalf of the mixed Parliamentary Group. As President of the Legislative Assembly, Deputy Aden Abdulla Osman immediately sent a telegram with the text of the government motion to the Egyptian President and the Secretary General of the United Nations, pointing out that it had been approved by acclamation.[256]

The *Comitato della Somalia per soccorso ai martiri dell'Egitto* or the disaster fund for the Egyptian martyrs was set up later in the year, to which ordinary Somali people up and down the country contributed, with subscriptions listed in successive issues of *Corriere della Somalia* from December 1956 onwards.[257] The solidarity shown by the Somali public to the Egyptian people, seen as victims of aggression, was so strong that by the end of December 1956 an amount of ShSo 83,000 was collected for the Port Said victims.[258] The collected funds, amounting to $17,517, were transferred in May.[259]

Despite the reservations he expressed in personal discussions with the Prime Minister, President Aden Abdulla nevertheless spoke forcefully on the matter. In comments made on the night of 5 June, even before the Prime Minister had gone to the Parliament, he said, "We are ready to offer any assistance in our power for the defence of the Arab lands and the restoration of Palestine". In his message to all Arab heads of state and governments, he promised Somalia's full support for the Arab cause. Palestine, the President said in comments reported in the *Somali News,* had been usurped by Zionists with the connivance and assistance of foreign powers hostile to Arab unity who had created Israel for their own selfish interests.

Writing to the Shah of Iran, he said: "You are aware that Israel has waged armed aggression against Arab States this morning. Ever since the creation of the Jewish state in the midst of the Arab lands in 1948, Israel has always been the aggressor and you will remember that only a short time ago both Jordan and Syria were attacked without provocation"."We all know that millions of Palestinian Arabs have been made homeless and scattered in Arab countries, and that Israel has adamantly refused to honour United Nations' resolutions on the return of these Arabs to their homelands", he continued

The President said that the responsibility for the war rested with Israel and that the UAR had been justified in closing the entrance to the Gulf of Aqaba to Israeli shipping as it was not an international waterway but entirely within the territorial waters of Egypt, calling on all Muslims to stand by their Arab brothers both morally and materially in the just struggle. Aden Abdulla also asked the Shah to discontinue the supply of oil to Israel and in a similar telegram asked Archbishop Makarios of Cyprus not to allow British military bases in Cyprus to be used against the Arabs.[260] The President received responses to his telegram, including the Kuwaiti Emir His Majesty Sabah al-Salem as-Sabah, who wrote: "I received with appreciation and gratitude, your kind message supporting the Arab State against the brutal Zionist terrorism on Arab territory. I would like to express sincere thanks to our Excellency, the

Government and People of beloved Somalia for your courageous readiness to take up the restoration of the Palestinian cause, sacred to the Muslims".[261]

Besides the foreign policy dilemma, earlier, as everything was geared towards the election of the president, out of blue emerged a legal argument to impugn the eligibility of the incumbent to seek re-election, on grounds of constitutional provisions. The Constitution provided that "A person cannot be elected consecutively for more than one term" *(Art. 71 of 1960 Constitution)*, which some used to suggest that since Aden Abdulla had been elected in 1960 for one year as provisional President of the Republic, before being elected for a complete term of six years the following year, he was not in fact allowed to seek re-election. The matter was submitted to legal advice, which concluded that Article 71 of the Constitution should be interpreted "as applying to the case of a person elected for two full terms in office and not for shorter terms."[262]

## Election results
## A democratically elected African president steps down quietly

When the time for the election came, there were only two candidates running for the Presidency of the Republic: the incumbent and the former Prime Minister, Abdirashid Ali. At 10.10 a.m. precisely of June 10, the 123-man Assembly met to elect the President. Abdirashid Ali Shermarke took his seat as an MP and was entitled to vote, while Aden Abdulla (not a Member of Parliament) followed the election process from Villa Somalia via the live programme over Radio Mogadiscio.

At the start of the meeting, which ran for three hours, Assembly President Sheikh Mukhtar emphasised the significance of the election. Then, the Parliament selected a three-man jury as vote counters, who were Deputies Ali Alio Mohamed Barre (Bur Hakaba), Salad Abdi Mohamoud (Gardo) and Mohamoud Issa Jama (Chismaio). The Assembly also appointed five party representatives as election observers, one for each political parliamentary group: Mohamed Jama Badmah for the SYL, Ali Mohamed Ossoble "Wardigley" for the SNC, Ismail Hagi Uarsama (SDU), Aboukar Muddei (HDMS) and Abdullahi Ahmed Qablan (Independent).

The law provides for the President of the Republic to be elected by secret ballot, with a two-thirds majority on the first and second ballots, or an absolute majority in subsequent ballots. The incumbent and his former Prime Minister faced each other in a close competition which saw the former Premier winning, at the third secret ballot, with 73 to 50 votes. There were two previous ballots; in the first round, Abdirashid received 63 to Aden's 57 and in the second round, they received 67 and 55 respectively. Three papers were invalidated in the first ballot and one in the second. This was the second time in the history of the Republic that an important change has taken place in the highest officers of the realm. According to the Constitution, a two-thirds majority (82) was required in the first and second ballots and an absolute majority (62) in the subsequent ballots.

In a radio interview after the election was completed, President Aden Abdulla congratulated Abdirashid and confirmed his willingness to help the newly-elected Head of State. He said that he was satisfied with the democratic manner in which the Parliament had conducted the election. The smooth running of the process on the Parliament floor was ensured by the "efficient and straightforward Sheikh Mukhtar", who "directed the election proceedings strictly", helped by his juridical background, having served as a *qadi* before entering politics. He said that every MP should collect his paper from the jury – as names we called from a roll – and bring it back to the jury for counting as soon as the last MP had received his papers. "This", he reasoned, "was to make sure that each and every MP received his ballot paper". The President was signing ballot papers before the MPs and the audiences for the next ballot, as [they] receive the first", putting his signature to a total of 492 ballot papers, of which 369 were used in the three ballots (an additional 123 had been set aside for a possible fourth round).

The election result was notable for two reasons. Firstly, and of wider regional significance, conceding defeat and stepping aside, Aden Abdulla became the first leader in a modern republic on the African continent to hand over power to his successor, in his case his erstwhile political ally and former Prime Minister Abdirashid Ali Sharmarke. Secondly, on the domestic front, the election process demonstrated the continued widespread political awareness of the young nation. Large crowds gathered outside the Parliament and on the capital's streets, closely following every detail of the occasion, the proceedings relayed through loudspeakers or over the radio as it had been in the 1961 presidential election. The gallery inside the Hall was full, accommodating top State personnel, including high-ranking officers from the army and police as well as diplomats, political, religious and business leaders.

Members of the press were present in their numbers too. Radio Mogadishu, for instance, provided an extraordinary transmission which simultaneously broadcast every word. Outside broadcasting at the station had often been precluded by the lack of the appropriate facilities but had been successfully tried in 1964 and then again when station staff broadcast directly from Parliament Square and Independence Square during the 1966 Independence Anniversary Day celebrations. But such transmission was reserved for particular occasions and was possible "only after putting a number of public telephone lines out of use for the period".

Nevertheless, on the day, "all one had to do was to turn on his Radio and listen to the results as Hon. Ali Alio, a member of the jury, read each ballot paper into the microphone. There was only a fraction (sic) of a second between when those in Parliament heard Hon. Alio's readings and when those for example in Bosasso – [a] thousand of (sic) miles away! – heard it". As the newspaper reported, "In the tedious period while the ballot papers were being distributed on the roll-call the Radio entertained the public with light and patriotic songs". For its coverage, "the Radio deserved and indeed received public appreciation, which was shown by a shower of letters of gratitude".[263]

Moments after the results were out, it was clear, according to Abdirizak Haji Hussein, from how the numbers tallied up that some of Aden Abdulla's old friends had decamped to vote for the other candidate. He counted Mohamoud Abdi Nour "Juju" and Ibrahim Osman Abukar "Uunlaaye" among those parliamentarians who, despite encouraging Aden Abdulla to run for the presidency, voted for the rival candidate. It is likely that many factors could have affected deputies' (perceived) shift, rather than simply ascribing them to a lack of morals, conviction or being susceptible to having their vote bought by the highest bidder.

For instance, Abdirizak himself, recognised that "Uunlaye", a wealthy businessman from Kismayo, was "eventually neutralized by the opposition, which threatened to make him pay if they ended up winning the election and he had worked against them", implying that his business interests would have been targeted by the new administration. Similarly, the shift perceived in the allegiance of "Juju" may have been down to his long-standing rivalry with Abdulcadir Mohamed Aden "Zoppo", since both politicians—although from different clan families—were in competition for being the most prominent politician (and hence, eligible for a ministerial post) in the Upper Giuba where their constituencies were.

While Aden Abdulla was often perceived as a man above the parties, capable of taking unpopular decisions without compromising on matters of principle, his former Prime Minister and successor knew how to forge political alliances within and outside Parliament. These skills were tried and tested and had served him well in building a "big tent" Cabinet when he was reappointed Prime Minister after the 1961 presidential election, including in his ministerial team those from the rival camps in that contest.

Abdirashid's victory was made possible not only by his active campaigning, but also by his ability to capitalize on the government's unpopularity coupled with the lack of enthusiasm displayed by his contender. It believed that foreign countries had no any significant influence in the outcome of the presidential election. The tiny Arab States of the Persian Gulf were then very poor to be able to influence, with funds, the results of the election as the case has benn in recent years. After the election, there was much talk, including among the public, about who had voted for whom. The Abdirashid camp's success showed itself to be a curse in disguise; those who had dithered during the contest and whose conviction could not easily be read went to Abdirashid after the election to say that they had voted for him. "It was not easy for him to reject them because", as Abdirizak recalls, "some must have voted for him or he wouldn't have won", which led him to have some reservations, saying, "'If all these people had voted for me, I would have had more votes. Some of you must be lying"'. It was difficult to prove things either way and each deputy would demand (even expect) something in return.

The outgoing President reacted to the election results with serenity. "The government that has backed my candidature was double-crossed by people who made it believe [them] to be on my side, but as far as I am concerned, I consider the results as a blessing for me as that lets me return free". However, while the President expressed delight at having lost the election, he regretted that, with his defeat, Somalia lost as capable Prime Minister as Abdirazak Haji Hussein who, "with his unrivalled honesty and courage would have accomplished a great deal if he continued to guide the country for more years to come".

Aden Abdulla was deeply convinced that he occupied the Office of President long enough and felt no reason to ask for more time. Such a perspective was rare in the political climate of bombast and self-promotion in Africa at a time when African leaders appeared to be locked in a contest to see who could remain in power for the longest. Félix Houphouët-Boigny, after 29 years in power in Ivory Coast and already in his eighties, is reported to have said in 1988, "There is no number two, three of four (sic)", adding, "In Côte d'Ivoire there is only a number one: that's me and I don't share my decisions".[264] By the end of 1980s, not a single African head of state had yet allowed himself to be voted out of office. Of some 15 head of states that had trodden the African stage, only six had voluntarily relinquished power. They included Senegal's Leopold Senghor, albeit after twenty years in office; Cameroun's Ahmadu Ahijo, after twenty two years, and Tanzanian's Julius Nyerere, after twenty three years.

## Aden Abdulla resigns before time – Special tribute

After the results of the election were announced, the President of the National Assembly Sheikh Mukhtar Mohamed Hussein and the newly elected Head of State, called on the outgoing President. "I extended my congratulations to Abdirashid, promising him that he will have my collaboration if solicited. I felt that that was my duty towards him and to the nation to set Abdirashid's mind at rest". Late in the afternoon on the same day (10 June), Sheikh Ali Jiumale, a long-time friend, supporter and Member of Parliament, called on him. The discussion between the two friends was reflected in Aden Abdulla's journal thus: 'My friend seemed welcoming the idea of a "brief military take over with my involvement. Poor friend; he is out of his mind, for what happened. I told him this is something I would never wish on Somalia!' *[Sheck Ali considererebbe benvenuto un colpo di Stato da parte dei Militari, ed addiritura dovrei incoraggiare chi potrà. Povero amico, è fuori di se' per l'accaduto, e io gli ho detto che non è una cosa da augurare alla Somalia] (Diary 10 June, 1967).*

The following day, the ongoing Prime Minister and several other parliamentarians, including Cabinet Ministers paid him, in close succession, a visit in his office and his official residence. "All these friends came to see me here to comfort me, and instead it turned out that I had to comfort them because I got what I wanted deep down in my heart and that is to be free". Aden Abdulla, still popular, still optimistic bade farewell to the staff at the Presidential Palace. He urged them to co-operate with the incoming President.

On June 30, 1967, Aden Abdulla was escorted by police motorcade as President of the Republic for the last time, leaving Villa Somalia at 6.50 p.m. Displaying a marked degree of faith and foresight, as the first African head of state to hand over power graciously to his democratically elected successor, he not only conceded defeat but, even though his term of office was not due to expire until July 6, 1967, he wrote to the President of the National Assembly asking Parliament to accept an earlier transfer of power from June 30 at 6.00 p.m. He suggested this in order to allow the newly-elected President of the Republic to preside over the celebrations marking Independence Day on 1 July. The National Assembly approved the resignation of President Aden Abdulla, seven days before the official expiry of his term of office.

Arriving at the National Assembly, he was received by a guard of honour at the principal gate of the Parliament building. In accordance with the Constitution, a former Head of State becomes *ex officio* Member of Parliament for life (Article 51, Paragraph 4).At 7.20 p.m., Aden Abdulla took the oath as Member of Parliament, becoming the 124$^{th}$ Member of the Parliament, after which he made a brief speech, which drew a thunderous applause from the MPs present. He thanked the parliamentarians and the people for their collaboration over the years and the trust placed in him during his mandate. He also assured the new President of his full collaboration and allowed the Members of Parliament to enforce the Constitution in the interest of the country and the nation: "After seven years, I left all responsibility to my successor, democratically elected by our representatives in Parliament".

His successor was sworn in with impressive calmness and constitutional decorum. His decision to step down before the official expiry of his presidential mandate was hailed by all quarters as a good example of statesmanship. After taking the oath, the new President said, "We must forget the political campaign in the recent presidential election, and work together to develop our country" while for his part, Aden Abdulla said, "If there is sincerity of purpose, nothing can go wrong". Commenting on his seven-year tenure, he remarked, "Though a human being cannot be expected to be perfect, I feel that I did my best for my country and people during my term of office", adding, "I am satisfied that I have been replaced by legal and democratic means". He appealed to the nation to work with the new President and to preserve our democratic principles so hard to find in the continent of Africa. After the swearing-in ceremonies at the National Assembly, the two Presidents went to Villa Somalia where the outgoing President gave his successor a golden object as a gift. Later, at the presidential palace, the Somali government resigned, handing their notice to the Head of State, President Abdirashid, who in turn asked the Prime Minister to continue looking after the activities of the Government until new ministers were appointed.

The Council of Ministers recalled "the glorious record of public service of

Aden Abdulla, first as a prominent fighter for the freedom of the country and organizer of the premier national organization [the Somali Youth League], then as President of the National Assembly which enacted the Constitution; further as a Provisional President in which capacity he promulgated the Constitution; and last, and but not the least, as the first President of the Republic".

"His self-less dedication and excellent record of service to the country easily marked him out to be the First to occupy the highest offices the Nation could offer. His prudence, fortitude and sagacity and inspired leadership helped the country to overcome the birth bangs of a newly independent country and to launch it into a course of rapid transformation of a colonial order into a dynamic progressive society. His wisdom and mature judgment has been a constant guidance to the government and the country.

"By his exceptional personal qualities, Aden Abdulla enhanced the luster, prestige and dignity of the high offices that he had been holding from time to time. The government expressed its highest gratitude to the noble elder, wise leader and respected President, and wished him a long and healthy life. The Council of Ministers expressed its confidence that his wise counsels will continue for a long time to come to the benefits of the people".

# SECTION 1

# PART 5

# SECTION ONE, PART FIVE

# OUT OF PUBLIC OF OFFICE

Once voted out of office, the former President retreated from the limelight, scrupulously refraining from dabbling in politics to the great relief of his successor Abdirashid Ali Sharmarke. He did however attend sessions of the Parliament in his capacity as *ex officio* Member, continuing to give counsel, particularly to the younger generation. His comments tended to be focused on his passionate battle for the defence of the Constitution and in favour of an increasingly decisive advancement in the process of welfare of the people rather than sustained rebuttals and attacks on the new administration.

He quickly became acclimatised to his new role. When he attended sessions of the Assembly, he sat unassumingly among the deputies on the wooden-framed benches, something he had not done for over a decade not only because he did not have a seat in Parliament during his tenure as President of the Republic but also because he was routinely elected to an official position in the legislature, whether as President of the Legislative Assembly in in 1956-59 or as Vice President in its predecessor, the Territorial Council, in 1953-4. Still a member of the SYL, the party to which he had remained unfailingly loyal through his career, he advocated party unity, calling on fellow deputies to put aside their differences and support the newly-formed Egal government when its programme was brought before Parliament, after having been approved in a meeting of the SYL Central Committee and Parliamentary Group: "We must respect and follow the party rules which require every member of us to abide by the majority decision", he noted.

When it came to present his Government's programme to the deputies, in the preamble to his statement, addressing the National Assembly, Premier Egal spoke positively of Aden Abdulla's record: 'I take this opportunity to express my personal feelings, which I know are shared by you and by the whole nation, of respect and gratitude towards the ex-President of the Republic. Our new President has rightly described him as "the Father of the Nation". He noted in particular his faithfulness to the Constitution: 'His determination to stick to the letter and to the spirit of the Constitution, in order to consolidate that democratic stability of ours which is the envy of Africa, has been eminently successful. His dignity and humanity have been true symbols of all that is best in our people, and he has earned a secure place in the hearts of all his fellow countrymen'.

Styled Father of the Nation, Aden Abdulla received the title from the National Assembly with thanks, "as a token of appreciation of the esteem in which he is held by all his countrymen everywhere" (*Somali News June 28, 1967*) with a certificate of parchment bearing the signature of most of the Deputies (*Somali News January 3, 1969*). Although he was one of the most famous figures, he was humble, always humble to a fault. When he made mistake he apologized. In reading his daily diaries, one is struck by his honesty about his own personal and political shortcomings. Unlike many African head of States of his time, he has never become a focus of personality cult. Personality cult emerges, among other things, when an individual uses mass media, propaganda, or other methods to create idealism, heroic and, at times, worshipful image, often through unquestioning flattery and praise. The list of African dictators who are the subject of personality cult is long. President Mugabe of Zimbabwe already had been dubbed "the most authentic, consistent and revolutionary leader" in the ruling ZANU PF Party's newspaper advertisements. His Kenyan counterpart, Daniel Arap Moi, was known as "The Glorious" (*Mheshimiwa* in Swahili). The octogenarian Hastings Kamuzu Banda of Malawi was "The Lion of Malawi" or "Savior" (*Mkango waMalawi* or*Ngwazi* in the native Nyanja.) The Congolese President was known "Mobutu Sese Seko Koko Ngbendu Wa Za Banga ("The all-powerful warrior who, because of his endurance and inflexible will to win, will go from conquest to conquest, leaving fire in his wake"). Many of the attributes heaped on African leaders by their subjects compare their powers to those of God or of a dangerous animal. In contrast, Aden Abdulla was a very modest man, refusing to take any credit for his achievements.

## Moahamed Ibrahim Egal appointed Prime Minister

## SYL party infighting

After the ritual informal consultations, President Sharmarke designated Mohamed Haji Ibrahim Egal, a Lawmaker from Berbera, as his Prime Minister. The new Prime Minister was not a political novice in the Somali political scene, having led the short-lived State of Somaliland in 1960.

Upon being nominated Prime Minister, Egal had two key objectives before forming a government. Firstly, he wanted to secure the readmission into the ruling party of 13 deputies expelled in July 1966 and secondly, to allow willing SNC Deputes to join the party as well.

Since the election for the party leadership did not coincide with the one for the President of the Republic, Abdirizak Haji Hussein remained Secretary General of the party. This fact, however, displeased the Abdirashid-Egal team, who saw Abdirizak and the Central Committee as opposition. The new government wanted the party election, not scheduled for another six or eight months, to be brought forward as it wanted to gain control of the party leadership but the existing Central Committee was trying to establish its position as an arm of the government through the leadership of the party. For instance, the Central Committee had refused to accept the deputies from non-SYL parties, mainly members of the Somali Democratic Union (SDU) and Socialist National Congress (SNC), joining the SYL, who had been advised by Abdirashid and Egal to join the party before the formation of the new government with the view to them becoming members of it.

Abdirizak instructed the Central Committee to write letters opposing certain appointments on the basis that quality rather than political expediency should be the most important factor in selection for a ministerial post. Egal interpreted this as interference. This move, in blocking the applications for admission into the party of MPs whom Egal wanted to have in his Cabinet, essentially held up the formation of the new government. This changing of allegiance had been necessitated also by the fact the SYL rejected the idea of a coalition government with other parties, which Egal had originally proposed. Eventually, however, the new administration got its way, succeeding in getting the members admitted and in August, the government received an overwhelming vote of confidence from the Parliament with 119 votes in favour against one, with three abstentions. The tussle outlived the government's inauguration and, on 11 November, the headquarters of the SYL in Mogadiscio was temporarily closed upon the ordinance of the Regional Governor of Benadir, as a result of a speech delivered by Abdirizak Haji Hussein as Secretary General, "the consequence of which created a threat to public order and security".

The in-fighting led to the formation of a Conciliation Committee to narrow the differences within the party, namely between Abdirizak and Egal. This nineteen-man conciliation committee was formed and met for the first time on 19 November at the National Assembly building. An organising sub-committee [*Comitato dei Promotori*] was appointed from among the members, formed of Deputies Ugas Yassin Abdurahman and Garad Ali Garad Jiama, who were joined by Mohamed Scek Gabiou. The decisions of the Committee were decisive and to be accepted *a priori* by all those concerned.

## Foreign policy divides the party

The battle of personalities also came to be expressed in a struggle over policy, specifically the foreign policy pursued by the new government as it related to the fate of the missing Somali territories under foreign (French and especially Ethiopian and Kenyan) control. Contra the energetic activity of the previous Abdirizak administration in advocating for the cause of these territories, often against much stubborn regional and even international opposition, the Egal administration pursued a policy of détente, presented as a more pragmatic approach.

In responding to Egal's stance at the OAU summit held in Kinshasa in September 1967, Abdirizak Haji Hussein – still the SYL Secretary General – made a strongly worded statement at the party headquarters disassociating the party's policy from that of the government. Some believed that this new diplomatic approach was akin to renouncing the aspirations of the Somalis still living under foreign rule. At the meeting, Egal signed the Arusha Memorandum of Understanding between Kenya and Somalia, which promised to eliminate tension between the two countries by promoting understanding and good neighbourly relations, and asked President Kenneth Kaunda of Zambia to mediate between Somalia and Kenya, with a meeting set for late October 1967. A similar policy was pursued with Ethiopia.

The first set of talks took place in October in Arusha, with the Somali Premier meeting Kenyan President Jomo Kenyatta through the mediation of President Kaunda. The talks paved the way for resumed trade and diplomatic relations based on a Memorandum of Understanding in which both sides agreed to examine the possibility for ending hostilities referred to as minor issues. The MOU provided for the appointment of a working committee, with representatives from Kenya, Somalia and Zambia, "to examine ways and means of bringing about a satisfactory solution to major and minor differences between Kenya and Somalia".

On 18 November, Somalia's National Assembly started a debate on the Kenya-Somali conference at Arusha. Indicative of the polarisation of opinion on the floor, two motions were presented by deputies – one by Hon. Sheikh Abdulle Mohamoud, against the Arusha talks and signed by a group of eight deputies, and another which supported the Government's stand on the Kenya-Somalia talks by Hon. Said Farah Abdi, sponsored by 35 deputies. The key point of debate among deputies from both sides on the issue was whether the conference represented a move away from the ideals of pan-Somalism, with some seeing it as in line with Article 6 (4) of the Cons titution which required a settlement of the Somali cause by peaceful and constitutional means.

The debate was clearly marked by the tension and instability which, in particular, affected the NFD area for some time. For the past year, there had been frequent clashes between Kenyan security forces and the Somali NFD nationalists which led to numerous fatalities. Reports suggested that in one harrowing incident, the commander of the Kenyan forces in Marsabit "visited the scene of fighting, picked up the dead bodies of the Somali freedom fighters, stripped them of their clothes, and burned the bodies to ashes. [He] then sent the clothes by plane to Nairobi as proof of the men killed by his troops". The well-respected chief of the Rendille tribe was also murdered by Kenyan forces on instruction of their government "when he refused to lend a hand to men who were engaged in colonialist acts". Somalis were killed by the security forces and the livestock of otherwise uninvolved Somali nomads confiscated and sold "at the markets at dirt cheap prices" while Kenya decided to cut off trade relations with Somalia in 1966.

The SYL Conciliation Committee, involved more broadly in arbitration within the ruling party, also became drawn into the policy discussion. Opening the session of Parliament that morning, the President of the National Assembly acknowledged the role of the committee, noting that as a result of its work, a new modified motion had been drafted and presented to the Assembly.

Since the President of the Assembly, was Chairman of the Conciliation Committee, he gave the floor to Abdullahi Issa Mohamud so that, the new motion could be presented to the National Assembly. Speaking about the exploratory nature of continuing talks, Abdullahi Issa Mohamud – not a member of the Government but of the Conciliation Committee – said in the House: "Since a Tripartite Commission consisting of Zambia, Kenya and Somalia was provided for under the Arusha agreement to study and solve minor and major disputes between Somalia and Kenya, we do not wish to create obstacles to the initiatives of the Government, but to wait for a conclusion". He added that the Committee had decided to unify the two motions to permit the Government with its present efforts and finally to submit the results to the Assembly. Representatives of the opposition parties, Hon. Haji Mohamed Hussein Hamud of the SDU and Hon. Abdullahi Ossoble Siad of the SNC, fully supported the new modified motion.

When it was finally put to a vote on 23 November, the National Assembly approved a new motion "giving a full mandate to the government to continue its initiatives towards finding a peaceful solution to the problems of the Somali territories held by Kenya and Ethiopia", 89 votes to one, with four abstentions.

The blessing that Parliament gave to Egal was not, however, a blank cheque. The Premier was in fact required to seek ratification from the Assembly of any specific agreement reached with Kenya and Ethiopia. The motion's preamble reflected two key phrases in the government's policy statement of 8 August 1967, namely that the governments would "continue the policy of earlier governments" and "induce foreign countries to grant self-determination to the Somali territories still under alien rule".

Despite the best efforts of the Conciliation Committee, the disagreement between the *opposte tendenze* [different sides] remained, made more acute by conflicting views on the Arusha Understanding. A reflection of the general disorientation and lack of discipline within the party, and with the Party headquarters closed since earlier in the month, 12 members of the Central Committee, led by Abdirizak Haji Hussein, met at his residence and passed a resolution expelling Egal from the party. Three other members were also expelled from the Central Committee: Mohamed Abukar Ibrahim "Yero" (Wanle Weyn), Ahmed Hassan Ali "Giudicino" (Oddur) and Ali Ghedi Shador (El Dher). This was a big blow to Egal and on 25 November, the Central Committee met again and passed a resolution reinstating Egal and expelling Abdirizak.

After weeks of constant wrangling, in the afternoon meeting of the Conciliation Committee on 30 November, Abdirizak Haji Hussein announced his decision to resign from the position of Secretary General. At the same meeting, the Conciliation Committee adopted a number of decisions, announced in a statement issued on 2 December, bearing the names of Secretary Mohamed Scek Gabiou and President Scek Mukhtar Mohamed. This included the immediate reopening of the Party headquarters in compliance with the relevant laws. Although the body agreed to nullify the Central Committee's decision of 14 November to expel Egal from the party, it nevertheless accepted the removal of four members from the Central Committee and their replacement by four others, a decision also reached on 14 November. It was resolved that the SYL Central Committee would convene a congress of the party at a date to be fixed later.

Although Aden Abdulla did not take part in the Conciliation Committee's deliberations – being abroad at the time of its meeting – he was not happy that it had issued a resolution without first resolving the difference between the government and some of the SYL's governing body and before securing the reopening of the Party's headquarters, which had been closed in execution of an order coming from the government. The headquarters was eventually reopened on 7 December, with. Mohamed Jama Badmah provisionally becoming Secretary General while Aden Shire Jama (known as Aden "Low"), the Minister for Religious Affairs, was elected for the Central Committee post left vacant by Abdirizak's departure.[265] Despite losing leadership of the party, Abdirizak was allowed to remain a member but he decided to leave the party in favour of his own one: establishing the Democratic Action Party. The party's initials DAP or *Dabka* (the fire in Somali), proved apt, with the organisation channelling the passion of the many who found themselves disenchanted with the incumbent administration.

The party gave its name to the neighbourhood, in the heart of Mogadishu city, where it had its headquarters. There, hundreds or even thousands flocked in a kilometre radius to hear Abdirizak's fiery speeches characterised by bitter criticism of the government, which proved a cause of much concern to them. Perhaps, drawn as much by their sense of grievance as one of excitement, during election season, people gathered from different areas with the buildings and surroundings reverberating with ululations and the beating of drums. Some stood on the top of buildings to get a better view of proceedings.

In contrast, the former President Aden Abdulla remained characteristically mild-mannered. From the time he was voted out of office, he divided his time mainly between attending sessions of the National Assembly, meeting political figures and attending sessions of the ruling party (SYL) when he was formally invited to do so. Very often, he would make visit to the Head of the State, the Prime Minister and other Cabinet ministers in their offices, using these meetings to raise concerns about malpractices in the public administration, and offering them advice and guidance on how they might address these.

The entries in his diaries sometimes suggest the discussions were tough, pervaded by a sense of frustration. His participation in parliamentary debates was restricted, limiting his involvement almost to one of an observer, listening attentively to the discussion before casting his vote on the draft legislation. Nevertheless, he was appalled by the fact that very often bills presented by the government were approved by acclamation instead of being firstly debated, a practice at odds with parliamentary regulations. This may have been a convenient but undignified move to stay in the good books of the sitting administration given the political elections set for 1969 were soon approaching.

Sessions of the legislature, and hence its efficient running, were constantly interrupted when deputies abandoned the building for Mogadiscio airport, to see welcome or see off foreign dignitaries like the US Vice President Hubert Humphrey, the popular Italian Foreign Minister, Amintore Fanfani and the Zambian President Kenneth Kaunda, which meant that the Parliament lacked sufficient numbers to satisfy the quorum.

## The World Muslim Congress

**IMAGE 2:** 22-29 Sha'bān 1384, corresponding with 26 December 1964-2 January 1965 during the 6th Muslim World League Conference in Mogadishu. From left to right: Aadan Abdulla, the Syrian poet 'Umar Bahā' al-Dīn al-Amīrī, and Syrian Shaykh 'Abd al-Fattāḥ Abū Ghudda in Mogadishu. Both Syrian men arrived for the 6th Muslim World League Conference held on 22-29 Sha'bān 1384, corresponding with 26 December 1964-2 January 1965. Shaykh 'Abd al-Fattāḥ Abū Ghuddah, and others were the representatives of the Syrian government. The poet was a diplomat.

Over the two years,the former President had a number of trips abroad. In September 1967, the World Muslim Congress (WMC, *Congresso Mondiale Islamico, Motamar al-Alam al-Islami*) elected him as its Vice President.[266] Already due to travel abroad, Aden Abdulla agreed to pass through Beirut to meet Haji Mohamed Amin El-Husseini, the organisation's President and an enduring figure in its history stretching over many decades to the first meeting of Muslim leaders in Makkah in 1926, travelling there via Jeddah.

The article in the daily newspaper, *Corriere della Somalia,* had the subtitle "Un riconscimento per la Somalia". Somalia had previously hosted the organisation's biennial summit, the Sixth World Muslim Conference in Mogadiscio in 1964-5, the first time the *Mu'tamar* had been held in Africa.

The Somali government under Premier Abdirashid Ali Sharmarke had agreed to host the conference in principle but as a new government had to be formed after the recent elections in March, it fell to Abdirazak Haji Hussein's to honour this commitment and plan the conference. The conference was initially due to open on 1 December but was delayed due to domestic challenges, including a severe drought and widespread human and animal diseases, which demanded urgent and devoted attention.

There had been some reservations domestically about holding the conference in Somalia at all. The organisation's secretariat was Karachi and since Pakistan was known by more progressive countries to be in the American sphere because of the American military base there, the leadership of the organisation came to be seen as a kind of Western instrument. For this reason, Egypt decided to boycott the conference and tried to mobilise public opinion in the capital by labelling the conference an imperialist manoeuvre against the progressive Muslim countries. Besides, there were some anxiety about hosting an international conference in the country, prompted by the lack of dedicated conference facilities and experience in the country. Some of the Opposition members in the Parliament also opened a debate on whether it was politically opportune to hold the conference in Somalia at all.

A special budget, including funds to cover the expenses of the conference, was approved by Parliament on 26 November. Before the vote, in his speech, Prime Minister Abdirizak Haji Hussein mentioned the positive coverage that the World Muslim Congress had given to Somalia before and after independence. For instance, in 1952, the WMC meeting in Karachi passed a resolution supporting the cause of Somali independence. The 1962 session, held in Baghdad, passed a resolution which argued in favour of the reintegration of the different Somalilands (Greater Somalia). The Premier also recalled that the WMC weekly review, *The Muslmi World,* had published on 30 November 1963 a front-page article with the headline, "Somalia Turns East", in which it condemned the partition of the Somali nation under a new form of colonialism followed by another front-page article in September the following year supporting the Somali cause in NFD, analysing the results of the Anglo-Somali conference in Rome.

He added that a Somali delegation had always participated under Government auspices in the various WMC conferences, with previous representatives including Hon. Haji Ibrahim Osman Abukar "Uunlaie", Hon. Haji Mussa Bogor Osman, Hon. Haji Mohamed Hussein Hamud,

Mr Haji Abubaker Sheikh Omar and several others. As head of state of the host country, Aden Abdulla opened the Conference on 27 December 1964. The Somali delegation was headed by Hon. Sheikh Mohamud Mohamed Farah ("Maalinguur") and the other members were Sheikh Abdullahi Sheikh Mohamed Beghedi, Hon. Hassan Abdullahi Farah, Sheikh Abubaker Sheikh Omar, Mr Yusuf Ismail Samatar, Sheikh Abdurahman Farah Hassan, as well as Dr Mohamed Sharif Aidarus and Haji Mao Aweys too.

A committee to coordinate the activities of the conference was also appointed, consisting of Ahmed Shirreh Egal Lawaha as Chairman; Ahmed Sheikh Issa, Vice Chairman; Yusuf Dirir, Secretary and members Mohamed Musa Farah, Jama Ganni Ahmed, Dahir Haji Osman, Nicolino Mohamed, Hussein Nur Elmi, Ali Hussein Gurah, Ali Shido, Mohamed Ahmed Abdilleh and Amir Tarmoum.

Apart from discussing issues of concern to Muslim community around the world, two days at the Conference were set apart for African affairs. There were representatives from over 40 Muslim states and organisations as well as from the missing Somali territories. The delegation from Ogadenia was led by Sheikh Ali Sufi. Other members included Sheikh Mohamed Salah Said as Secretary as well as Sheikh Mohamed Aden Osman, Haji Issak Mohamed Daddeh, Garad Makhtal Dahir Ahmed, Abdullahi Hagi Abubaker and Sheikh Abdulghani Sheikh Mohamed.[267] The four-member delegation from the French-administered Coast was led by Mr Omar Ahmed Yusuf, with members Mohamed Absiye, Ibrahim Dahir Igueh, Mohamed Ali Dalhan, Mohamoud Caillard and Hagi Hassan Osman. The delegation from the NFD was by Mr Jatani Warko, with Abdulkadir Sheikh as Secretary and Abdulle Onshor, Mohamed Dualeh Hussen, Hajow Kassim, Swarre Hassaye and Aden Osman Issak as members.

Besides Aden Abdulla, the WMC in its 1967 meeting had also elected Dr Mohamed Natsir as its second Vice President. Natsir had been a former Prime Minister of Indonesia, where he led Masyumi, which, at its height, had been the largest Islamic party in the world with tens of millions of members. Fittingly and in a certain way, both Vice Presidents – personally – typified the shades of religious identity of their home countries. Natsir came from a long history of Islamic activism in different organisations, rising through the ranks of the young members of Masyumi in the 1940s eventually to take over the party leadership. On the other hand, Aden Abdulla, in the same period, had been an increasingly prominent member of the SYL, a nationalist organisation which, while lacking an overt religious aspect, sought to conform to the Islamic tradition, thus personifying the authentic yet gentle form of practice characteristic of his nation and indeed East Africa and the continent at large. Natsir would retain the Vice President position for most of the rest of his life. The other officer-holders were Abdul Latif Saduddin of Lebanon as Treasurer, Inamullah Khan (Pakistan) as Secretary General and Haider K. Al-Husseini (Iraq) as Assistant Secretary General.

To attend the conference, Aden Abdulla left Mogadiscio on 8 October for Jeddah travelling via Khartoum. At the airport in Khartoum, he was welcomed by two Somali diplomats, one of them being the Chargé d'Affaires at the embassy. The Sudanese President, Ismail al-Azhari, who paid a courtesy visit at the hotel where he was staying, seemed to make a good impression on Aden Abdulla. Entertaining him in cordial conversation, Aden Abdulla documented his impression in his diary: "What an honour, what a simple man!" When it came to check himself out, to his surprise, Abdulla learned that his hotel bill had been settled by the Sudanese head of state.

Leaving Khartoum for Jeddah on the following day, he was welcomed by two Saudi diplomats. At the time of his landing there, in the early morning, King Faisal was in Taif, busy in discussions with visiting delegations from Sudan, Iraq and Morocco about the withdrawal of Egyptian troops from Yemen. In the evening, Abdulla was escorted by the same two diplomats for a meeting with the monarch at 9.00 p.m., which was warm. On his visit, the former President observed the environment, reflecting on how similar it was to back home.

The weather in Taif was comparable to that of Mogadishu during the *Hagai*, the period of dry summer punctured by sporadic rains. Bonds of water along the road to Taif, he noted, were visible, sign that rain had not fallen for a while. There was no green grass or trees in the area except those planted by men. While in Jeddah, Aden Abdulla took the opportunity to perform the *Umrah,* the shorter version of pilgrimage which can be performed in Makkah at any time, as opposed to the obligatory *Hajj* whose rites are connected to a particular period in the year. He performed the *Umrah* in the company of Sheikh Hassan Abdullahi Farah, the former Minister of Justice in Somalia, who was in Makkah on his way to Mogadiscio from Amman, Jordan.

The former President's reflection on his experiences in Lebanon provides a striking example of how he was adjusting to life out of office. He felt a sense of discomfort travelling among strange passengers for the first time. "How boring is travelling alone, for the first time after seven years as head of state, always accompanied by an entourage of people whose presence I have often not appreciated or desired". This unfamiliarity also extended to logistical arrangements like finding the whereabouts of the Congress. Soon after arriving in Beirut, he started to search for the Mufti. After some unsuccessful attempts, he finally managed to learn about the preparations underway for a delegation from the Mu'tamar to undertake an extended mission to a number of countries (the US, the UK, Italy, France, Germany and Russia), the purpose of which was to canvass support for Jerusalem and the Palestinian cause.

Harbouring some reservations, Abdulla came up with some excuses including wanting to take some rest on a vacation, the desire to see his children and an expectation that the plan be shared in the first place with the Somali Government. "I hoped something to happen, something that would change the planned mission not only for the difficulty it would cause me but also because of my poor knowledge of foreign languages, although the people I was speaking to could speak English and French", On 14 October, he proceeded to Rome for a personal visit. At the time, a number of Cabinet members including Prime Minister Egal, Ali Omar Shego and Aden Issak Ahmed were in Italy and paid courtesy visits to him, as did other political figures who were in town including Abdulkadir Mohamed Aden "Zoppo" and Mussa Bogor. Aden Abdulla then returned to Mogadiscio on 20 November.

As former heads of government and state, in being elected to their respective positions, Aden Abdulla and Dr Natsir were also typical of the WMC's leadership, which besides religious scholars, intellectuals and serving political leaders of Muslim countries often included former ones in the last category as well. The first World Muslim Conference had been called in Makkah in 1926 by King Abdul Aziz ibn Saud, the first big effort to bring Muslims from far-flung places around one table. Some of those present were Umar Tgoromivoto, the founder of the Sarikata Islam of Indonesia; Mufti Kifayatullah and Moulana Sulaiman Nadvi and Maulana Shaukat Ali from India; Sheikh al-Azhar Zawahiri of Egypt; Adeeb Sarwat Bey of Turkey; Rashid Rida from Lebanon and Hassan Hakim, ex-Prime Minister of Syria.

The second Conference was called in Baitul Maqdis or Masjid al-Aqsa in Jerusalem by the Grand Mufti of Palestine, Sayyid Muhammad Emin al-Husseini in 1931 and a small secretariat was set up whose work continued until it was broken up by the war. The third Conference was called in 1949 this time in Karachi and it was there that the Assembly unanimously agreed to give the organisation the same name as the first World Muslim Conference, i.e. Motamar al-Alam a-Islami. With the formal revival of the organisation, a secretariat was set up, this time in Karachi, which called the fourth WMC in 1951, a much bigger affair than previous ones. It was at the fifth Conference, held in Baghdad in 1962, that proved to be a landmark, with the Mo'tamar accepting its new constitution, which replaced its earlier working rules and which required the Mo'tamar to meet in a world assembly once every two years. At its closing session on 2 January 1965, the Sixth Conference elected the World Muslim Congress's new Executive Council. Aden Abdulla was elected Honorary President of the Congress. Sayyid Mohamed Emin al-Husseini was re-elected President, with Ahmadou Bello, Prime Minister of Nigeria and Prince Badru of Uganda as Vice Presidents. Sheikh Abubaker Omar was elected a Member of the Council.

The Mo'tamar (or Congress) is not to be confused with the Organisation of Islamic Cooperation (OIC or *Munazzama al-Ta'aawun al-Islamiyy*), founded in 1969, which incidentally grew out of the suggestion of President Osman. In his opening speech at the Conference in Mogadiscio, he made a fervent appeal to all "our brethren to devise ways and means for all possible cooperation, and coordination, between all the international Muslim Organisations of the world so as to give strength to our voice and lend force to our demands, as also for the entire world of Islam to have the fullest benefit of all mutual Muslim co-operation at all levels, local, national, regional and international". This idea was then picked up by one of the Conference's resolutions on 'Cooperation between Muslim international organizations'. This call was echoed by King Faisal at the Muslim World League conference held months later in Makkah, in April, who endorsed the proposal of the Somali President.

Aden Abdulla made a few more personal trips over the next few years: in 1968, he returned to Italy, leaving Mogadishu on 23 June. At Rome airport, he was welcomed by his children; Ambassador Ali Hussein Gurra; former Prime Minister Abdirizak Haji Hussein; the Manager of FIAT (Rome branch); former minister, Abdurahman Haji Mumin Mohamud and some diplomats from the Italian Foreign Ministry (Department of Protocol). From Rome, Aden Abdulla then proceeded in the company of Abdirizak Haji Hussein, who was in town after completing the Hajj pilgrimage, on a version of *il giro dell'Europa*, the fabled Grand Tour.

He used the opportunity of being outside of the country to reflect on the situation at home. "I have been free from the grave responsibility of staying in

Villa Somalia for a year. I do not regret this and I do not want to return to that position but I am far from being happy with how things have been going since Abdirashid, Egal and Yassin Nur Hassan have come to power, the others not having much significance.

'The behaviour of those three big men [*quei tre "grassoni"*] is truly bizarre because they are destroying themselves [*si stanno demolendo da stessi*] with the injustice and nepotism they have established among the employees of the State, the constant travels of their acolytes and family members at the expense of the State and finally, their policy towards the problems of the Somali lands in the hands of Haile [Selassie] and [Jomo] Kenyatta".[268]

On 1 July, the two friends – Aden Abdulla and Abdirizak Haji Hussein – travelled by train to the northern industrial city of Turin. At Porta Nuova railway station, they were welcomed by Sig. Raimondo Priere, one of the FIAT managers. While in town, they were offered the opportunity to visit the car manufacturer plant. In Turin, the unexpected happened: Aden Abdalla had the pleasure to meet Dr Cotta Ramussano Ferruci, one of his teachers at De Martino hospital in Mogadiscio (ottobre 1928-febrario 1929). They had a happy discussion about the time they spent in the Somali capital and Aden was given a souvenir photograph with all the classmates and Dr Cotta himself.

On 3 July, the two friends now proceeded, by train, to Milan and, from there, they went to Belgium, Holland, Germany, Denmark and Sweden. At Brussels airport, they were received by two Somali diplomats, one of whom was the new Somali Ambassador Mohamud Mohamed Hassan Mussa in addition to a person from the Protocol Department of the Belgian Foreign Ministry. While they were in Milan, Ambassador Gurra passed on news of the attempt on the life of President Abdirashid to Abdirizak Haji Hussein. The President was returning from the airport to his official residence after seeing off President al-Azhari of the Sudan, who was one of a number of foreign dignitaries invited for the independence celebrations on 1 July. The assailant turned out to be of the Siwaaqroon clan. Two hand grenades were thrown at the President; the first failed to explode and the second exploded after the presidential motorcade has passed. The assailant who did not escape was arrested on the spot.

Days later, while still on his travels, Abdirizak received an anonymous, ominous letter: "They tell him in every way and threaten him with death that if something else happens, accusing him of having plotted the attempt of Abdirashid's life" [*Glielo dicono di tutti i colori e lo minaccono di morte se succedera' ancora qualche cosa, accusandolo di aver ordito l'attentato alla vita di Abdirascid*]. The following day, Aden also received a letter similar to Abdirizak's – it referred to the violence in Somalia fomented by me against the current regime. Signing off as "a group of Somalis who love their hand" (*un gruppo di Somali amanti della loro terra*), the authors promised that should anything happen, they will take out Aden, his family and friends [*se lo prenderanno con me, colla mia famiglia, e con i miei amici*]. But there were no further problems during the trip and Aden Abdulla returned to Mogadishu on 14 August.

The following year, in June, he spent a couple of weeks in neighbouring East African countries, Kenya and Tanzania, to escape as he put it "the monotony of life" at home. It is likely that his dim assessment of affairs at home was directly coloured by the tide of political events, which were affecting everyday life in the country and whose course would change in a decisive manner by the end of the year, with stark consequences not only for him and the nation but Somalia's place in the world at large.

# SECTION 1

## PART 6

# SECTION ONE, PART SIX

# THE PRESIDENT ASSASSINATED

The Italian historian Angelo Del Boca described the lack of direction and sense of general despair in Somalia in the late 1960s. 'By the summer of 1969, nine years after independence, in the country U Thant [Maha Thray Sithu U Thant, the Burmese UN Secretary General, 1961-1971] liked to define as "the darling child of the United Nations", nothing remains of the characteristics that made her an example. The democracy is a mere memory. The multi-party system is a mockery; the neutrality, a faded option and in the National Assembly, confusion reigns'.

Rumours of a military coup were rife but the government and the President showed no sign of alarm. The opposition remained largely divided without a common programme, fragmented, as had always been the case, along tribal lines. A foundering regime had weakened itself by discontenting everyone. Fraud in the March 1969 elections was not the only fuse that could lead to an explosion at any moment. Another was the rampant corruption in the public administration, which wasted vast amount of public money including aid from foreign governments and fuelled anger among the masses of Somalis, who resented economic deprivation and the opulence enjoyed by the political elite. Public unease mounted, faith in the regime waned and the optimistic mood quickly gave way to cynicism. By 1969, after nearly a decade of independence, Somalia was effectively bankrupt, shackled to foreign aid for survival and prone to sliding into a dictatorial regime.

On 15 October, Radio Mogadishu gave the shocking news that the President of the Republic had been shot dead at about 12.45 p.m. in Las Anod by a rogue policeman. The President was visiting the northern provinces of the country that had been hit by famine and drought. It is significant to recall that a year earlier the President had survived an assassination attempt when he narrowly avoided a grenade while being driven from the airport to Villa Somalia.

It is hard to believe but during the critical two weeks preceding his assassination, the President of the Republic – together with the Speaker of the Parliament – was on mission to the northern regions. At the same time, the Prime Minister was on a state visit to the USA. The military had obviously exploited these circumstances to stage the coup, which most probably would not have taken place had the three top State authorities not been absent from the capital city at the same time. Indeed, "[t]here could have been no better situation for the army and its Soviet advisors to hatch the coup d'état".

In the absence of reliable information, the tragic event had generated a jumble of contradictory accounts on the motives that might be behind the killing of the President. Among these, the one linking the criminal act to the way the general elections were conducted had gained the widest currency. According to this account, the killer appeared to have acted in reaction to the political violence which had caused the death of dozens of people, including some of his close relatives in the electoral district of Iskushuban (Migiurtinia). The accused denied this account before the court, citing instead different motivations for his brutal act.

A sense of lack of State authority was felt in the first hours following the death of the President, particularly when rumours started circulating that it had proved impossible even to send news of the tragic event to the Prime Minister, who was on a State visit in the USA. After the official visit, Egal appears to have taken some days off at Las Vegas, as a guest of the American film star William Holden. "The Somali Embassy in Washington took the trouble to seek the FBI's assistance in order to locate the whereabouts of our Prime Minister," wrote Mohamed Aden Sheikh.[269] When the missing

Premier was eventually located and informed of what had happened, he hastily returned from Washington to Mogadiscio.

In a statement issued days after the President's assassination, his predecessor Aden Abdulla released a heartfelt statement. "Although I am ten years older than the late President, we were among the first nationalists to devote most of their time and effort to the Somali cause from the start", he recalled, adding, "Abdirashid Ali Sharmarke was a true patriot". "The late President left no stone unturned for the country's development during his time as Prime Minister. When his term as Premier came to an end, after the general elections, someone else was appointed Prime Minister in 1964. But this does not mean that I, even for a second, doubted the nationalism of Dr Sharmarke but it was simply to test the ability of other Somalis, to assess them and to get to know them". He concluded that, "The memory of Dr Abdirashid will remain etched in bold letters in the golden book of Somali history".

Soon after his arrival, Egal and his party's leadership started the selection process for a new presidential candidate. The choice finally fell on Haji Mussa Bogor, a consummate politician and close associate of the slain President. The election was set to take place soon afterwards in compliance with Article 74 of the Constitution, in this case on the following day on 21 October. But no election took place and the National Assembly did not meet as planned. "When, at a late-night meeting at the party HQs on October 20, the party caucus reached agreement to present the nominee as their official candidate, thus virtually ensuring his election as President and Egal's reappointment as Premier, those army officers who were closely watching developments decided to act"

## The night the tanks rolled in

Thus, that which had been feared for some time had transpired. In the early hours of 21 October, the military sprang into account and put into motion their plot to bring down the civilian administration and usurp control of the state machinery, at first taking control of key posts including the Parliament building in the centre of town where deputies were due to meet in the morning to elect a new President; the Radio Mogadishu studio and other important buildings and posts in the capital. In different neighbourhoods, people were aroused from sleep by the throbbing caused by the army tanks rolling through the city.

Within twenty-four hours of the state funeral of the President, a self-styled revolutionary council seized power without bloodshed and would rule the country for almost 21 consecutive years, led by military officers who had donned civilian garb. This military takeover was quickly dubbed a "revolution". Explaining the difference between revolutionary movements and military takeover, Bernard Lewis wrote, "The word *revolution* has been much misused in the modern Middle East, being applied to, or claimed for, many events which would more appropriately be designated by the French coup d'état or the Italian *colpo di Stato*... Interestingly, the English language does not provide an equivalent term".

There had been murmurings about a possible military coup in Somalia since at least the mid-1960s. As the President of the Republic, in his briefings and encounters with General Daud Abdulle Hersi, Aden Abdulla would often try to gauge the sentiment of the military, posing the question directly to the General, who always insisted that his men were committed to serving their political masters loyally. In the morning of 21 October, the former President Aden Abdulla jotted down some notes at around 10.50 a.m. on the fateful events as they unfolded. "Somalia, since this morning, at 3.00 a.m., the country is under a military regime [*regime militare*]: a military coup has taken place. According the first radio broadcast, repeated several times from around 9.00 a.m., the army and the police are working together. The commanders of the army and the police both appear in the military council even if it is conceivable that the Police Commandant General Qorshel and his officers had nothing to do with the initiative and were forced to put on a good pretence and collaborate whether they wanted to or not [*che siano stati costretti a fare buon viso e collaborare volenti e nolenti*]".

## Old guard detained

It was only later that the politicians were interned. "It is rather incredible – yet true – but this afternoon (21 October), I was practically arrested and taken to Afgoye, to the presidential palace, which I built in 1965-67, together with my friend Abdirizak and a group of ministers from the dissolved Egal government". There, they found the other ministers – all twelve of them – as well as other politicians who were not part of the overthrown administration. Of the detainees, four were not members of the government: Aden Abdulla, Haji Mussa Bogor, Abdirizak and Omar Mohallim. The latter served as Somali Ambassador to the USA but, like his brother Hilowle Mohallim – the Defence Minister in Egal's government – had been elected as Member of Parliament in the March 1969 elections. Aden Abdulla and Abdirizak assumed that they were being taken for consultations but instead they were taken in a ramshackle coach and made to suffer the humiliation of being laughed at by the rabble on the way to the city even if the derision was directed at the other passengers from the hateful Egal government [*ci hanno fatto subire l'umiliazione di venire derisi dalla marmaglia durante il tragitto in citta' anche se sapevamo che la derision era diretta agli altri dell'odioso governo di Egal!*].

But on the same day, the two were taken back to their homes in Mogadishu in a Fiat 124 type car by Army Major Ahmed Saleebaan Abdalla (known as "Dafle") and Captain Abdirizak Mohamud Abukar in complete silence. Owing to this, Aden and Abdirizak thought that their first arrest was due to an error but soon afterwards, on the afternoon of 23 October, the army men came back to collect them again, before going onto the houses of Haji Mussa Bogor and Omar Mohallim, who had been released and sent home the previous day.[270] When Aden Abdulla was collected by the Police Land Rover this time, Abdirizak and the former President of the Supreme Court, Abdurahman Sheikh Ali – being collected for the first time – were already on board.[271] Now, they were all back at Afgoye and up to 24 in number, after having been joined by former Prime Minister Mohamed Ibrahim Egal.

The fact that some of the politicians had been detained soon after the coup released and then detained again suggested that the whole operation might have been haphazard. But according to Abdirizak, based on what he later discovered, when the leaders of the coup decided to intern the leading politicians without making a specific list, the man executing the order was Ahmed Saleebaan Abdalla "Dafle" was interested, primarily, in detaining Haji Mussa Bogor and Omar Mohallim. When Salad Gabeyre Kediye, the chief operations officer of the army, had learnt that his father-in-law Aden Abdulla had been detained, he ordered the men who had arrested him to release him, which is why he and Abdirizak were initially taken back to their homes. But soon afterwards, nephews of Haji Mussa Bogor must have complained to Mohamed Siad Barre, arguing that if the criterion for detainment was membership of Egal's government, then why had their Haji been taken in? Given Siad Barre's desire to keep both Haji Mussa and Omar Mohallim confined, it would be difficult to let Aden Abdulla and Abdirizak go which is why they were returned to Afgoye as well.

After the coup, the new order consisted of army and policemen as well as civilian figures. One of those in the latter camp was Abdulqadir Aden, the son of the former President Aden Abdulla, who accepted the role of Secretary of State for Public Works. During his internment, the father would usually receive a letter from his son once a week. As the eldest of the children, Abdulqadir was responsible for communicating family matters to his father. But when, once, two weeks passed without a letter from his son, the father started to worry and asked for news of his son from the guard. However, little was forthcoming until Aden and Abdirizak went on a hunger strike. After a few days, the officer explained to them what had happened. It was alleged that General Salad Gabeyre Kediye, with a few others, had been making preparations for a coup. Abdulqadir must have been incriminated by virtue of his association with Gabeyre, the General being married to his sister Faduma. When they received this news, Aden and Abdirizak ended their hunger strike. But ultimately, in 1972, General Gabeyre was executed, along with General Mohamed Ainaashe Guled and Lt. Col. Abdulkadir Dheel Abdulle, the last of whom had in fact left the army some years earlier and was running a pharmacy business.

## Regaining their freedom

The detainees would finally be released in 1973, helped by the decisive action and resolve of one of them. Sheikh (or Haji) Abdullahi Sheikh Ibrahim, known as Abu Sitta, was Minister of State for Religious Affairs in the last Egal government. This post had been newly created out of concern for public sentiment; the portfolio had been previously covered by the Minister of Grace and Justice. One day during their detention, Abu Sitta told the chief guard that if he was not given a reason for why he was being kept there, he would leave the building in defiance, even if it meant being shot. The Haji's plan got the support of some other detainees, who told the guards of their position. After a few days, he was taken to Mogadiscio and given a tour of the new improvements. When he returned, unshaken from his original position, he gave a date for his departure as a final ultimatum. Then, one night, according to Abdirizak Haji Hussein, two guards came to their floor and told the detainees to pack their things without saying anything else.

They heard the sound of cars entering the compound. Hours later, they were told to go to the dining area, where they met some officers, photographers, members of the media and security people. A makeshift court was set up in the dining area. Aden Abdulle, Abdirizak Haji Hussein and others were acquitted but six of the detainees were not: Mohamed Haji Ibrahim Egal, Yassin Nur Hassan, Aden Isaak Ahmed, Abdullahi Jireh Dualeh, Ali Aliyow Mohamed and Omar Mohallim Mohamed. Egal had been spoken about first; the prosecutor read out a long list of results from their investigation and recommended that Egal be remanded at the disposal of the public prosecutor for a trial before a court. These six men who were not being released were transferred that night to Laanta Bur, another prison in Afgoye, while the others boarded buses to go home. They returned home on 1 April 1973 although it is not clear whether the irony was intended or perceived and whether they thought they might be taken back into detention.

## Retreat to the Lower Shabelle

The former politicians, having regained their freedom, tried to keep a low profile and stay out of public life. Aden Abdulla, like Abdirizak Haji Hussein, settled into the life of a gentleman farmer, spending most of his days in his farm estate (Azienda Agricola) near Wagaadi and Mushaani villages, about 20 kilometres from Merca, the Lower Shabelle country he knew so well in his youth. The crops cultivated on the estate were grapefruit, coconut, mango and papaya as well as banana, the last of which was produced in a small quantity along with other farmers like the former minister Abdulkadir Mohamed Aden "Zoppo". Abdirizak, on the other hand, bought out the shares of some of his friends who owned a banana farm in the Lower Jiuba area.

Eventually, Abdirizak would accept an appointment as the Somali Ambassador to the United Nations in New York in 1974 until he submitted a letter of resignation five years later. Aden Abdulla, in contrast, remained out of public life, following local and international developments from his farmhouse, far removed from Mogadiscio, the civic, cultural and social nucleus of the nation, which he visited only occasionally. Very often he was seen in the normal queue in offices and market places to pay the account to cashier. However, he would assume a renewed place in the political life of the nation in the 1980s, as one of a group of mediators who tried to redeem its fate from the brink, playing the role of elder statesman, which stemmed as much from his age as the reputation he had acquired in his years in public office.

# SECTION 1

# PART 7

# SECTION ONE, PART SEVEN

# BIDDING ABDULLAHI ISSA FAREWELL (1922-1988)

## Bidding Abdullahi Issa farewell (1922-1988)

Under the military government, the right to association and assembly were suspended. Indeed, many prominent Somalis who had been detained without trial for over a decade were released only to find that they were placed under travel restrictions. Apart from the official government ceremonies, there were therefore few opportunities for congregation and mixing. A rare example, however, was the state burial of the first Somali Prime Minister (1956-60), Abdullahi Issa Mohamud in early 1988.

Born in Afgoye in 1922, soon after the death of his father, Abdullahi Issa moved with his mother to Mogadiscio where he enrolled in Quranic schools and later the government ones. He entered government service at the age of sixteen, assigned to the Post Office in Merka, before returning to the capital, serving in the Economic Affairs and Finance Directorate, before transferring to Bulo Burti in 1939. He started some business ventures in 1942 in Belet Uen. Two years later, he joined the Somali Youth Club (later the Somali Youth League),

When Yassin Haji Osman Sharmarke fell ill, it was his wish that Abdullahi Issa replace him, which happened after his death in June 1947. It was in this capacity that Abdullahi Issa's name became a houshould one not only in the south but in all the Somali areas in the Horn of Africa in the late 1940s when he represented the Somali Youth League before the United Nations during the deliberations over the future of the former Italian colonies.

When the initial Somali internal government was introduced in 1956, he was appointed Prime Minister. After independence in 1960, he served as Minister of Foreign Affairs under Abdirashid's government (1960-1964). In Abdirizak's Cabinet (1964-7), he served as Minister of Health, Veterinary e and Labour and Minister of Industry and Commerce, and again in May -October 1969 he held up the same Ministry under Egal's last government.

When Abdirashid was assassinated, Abdullahi Issa had been in Italy for a medical check-up. When he heard the news, he rushed back to participate in the funeral rites and soon afterwards, found himself detained with the other politicians. While in detention, he – like a few others – assumed a neutral attitude towards the military government. After their release in 1973, he was appointed Somali Ambassador to Sweden. He remained in this post until 1986. He quietly returned from public life, resigning from the position and settling in Rome, where he died in March 1988. He was flown to Somalia, where he was accorded a state funeral and was buried in the National Cemetery in Mogadiscio. Aden Abdulla, Abdullahi Issa's friend and long-time colleague, joined President Mohamed Siad Barre at the graveside in performing the final rites.

Amidst the outpouring of grief, for several days, people gave tribute to the nationalist leader. At the sitting held at the Abdullahi Issa family home in Mogadishu, a poem was performed by Abdi Bashiir, known as "Indhabuur", which had the refrain *Godka cara la'aan jiif, Jannada Caadil kuu garaye.* [Sleep easily, for all worries you are now free / Heaven, the Most High the final abode will make for thee]. It was a rare occasion in which the old generation of political leaders were given prominence of place. Among those saying a few words about Abdullahi Issa included Abdurahman Haji Mumin Mohamud, Yusuf Osman Samatar "Bardacad". Others from that generation who could be seen in the crowd included Sheikh Mohamed Iman Adan. Some of those present even indulged in a bout of nostalgia for earlier days – some typically not appreciated by the military government – including "Bardacad" who made a plea for people to conduct research and write about that period and Salad Osman Roble, the chairman of the Somali youth organisation, who referred to Abdullahi Issa as a beaming star in the golden era [*Taariikhda ummadda Soomaaliyeed xiddig mar soo maray ka mid ahaa – waqtiga waqtiyada ugu mudnaa*].

Previously, the military government had typically swept aside the generation of politicians it overthrew, even devoting more significance to the date of the 1969 military coup (21 October) which was given two days of public holiday while 1 July – Independence Day in 1960 – only one. A short film to commemorate his life was also filmed at the old SYL headquarters in the capital in April 1988, featuring Mohamud Yusuf Aden "Muro", Ali Shiddo Abdi, Mohamed Salah Ladane, Mohamed Ahmed Elmi "Ottavio" and Mohamud Mohamed Gaagaale. Others from the activist era who were also filmed in different locations included Hassan Ali Badal, Mohamed Farah Osman (known as "Mussolini"), Moallim Isaaq Hussein and Haji Abdullahi Fiqow.

## On the brink

A sense of unease shrouded the country in the 1980s. Unlawful arrests became routine, including against the government's own ministers and officers. When the Italian representative of the Vatican Bishop Salvatore Colombo was killed in Mogadiscio in 1989, many were under arrest, mainly Islamic religious leaders like Sheikh Abdirashid Sheikh Ali "Sufi". However, the lawyer Ismail Jimale Ossoble and Eng. Abdulkadir Aden Abdulla, were among them. Abdulkadir Aden and Jimale would be released months later in October. Abdulkadir had been familiar with the killed Bishop since the early 1950s, when Monsignor Colombo was head of the Catholic Mission in Belet Uen. Monsignor Colombo had been in Somalia for more than forty years and over the years had established good relations with many Somalis, including pious, devout Muslims, owing to his commitment to social welfare.

Wishing to see the country saved from its slump in fortune, a diverse group of prominent Somalis came together and penned an open letter to the President, calling it Manifesto I, and its signatories became known as the Manifesto Group (or *Maanifeesto* in Somali). Identifying themselves as 'the elders who took part in the national struggle for independence', they felt driven by a sense of necessity, writing that 'We...strongly and unanimously feel that we can no longer remain passive spectators nor ignore the duties and responsibilities that we owe to our people and our country, both from Somali and Islamic points of view' and moved by the 'sufferings, the bloodshed and the incalculable loss of life and property that our people have suffered for so long'.

Detailing the deep malaise that had beset the country—politically, economically, physically, morally—they concluded that 'only a replacement of the present regime by a caretaker government will get us out of the present mess', proposing a National Reconciliation and Salvation Conference (NRSC), of the most popular political, tribal, religious and business leaders from all regions of Somalia who would convene on neutral ground as soon as possible, mentioning a few potential countries. The letter was signed by political leaders from the civilian period, including Aden Abdulla Osman (the first signatory); Sheikh Mukhtar Mohamed Hussein (President of the National Assembly, 1966-69), Haji Mussa Bogor, Haji Osman Ahmed Roble and others. Unsettled by this development, the military government responded by detaining many of them. However, well-intentioned this initiative was, it resulted not enough to save the country from perdition that lay in its path and it would all descend into clan-based fratricide, leading to the destruction of property and a beautiful city and most tragically of all, the untold loss of innocent lives.

Many reconciliation conferences would subsequently be called. The first of these was called in Djibouti in early 1991. Aden Abdulla chaired the conference and was assisted by two former Prime Ministers from the 1960s, Abdirizak Haji Hussein and Mohamed Haji Ibrahim Egal. The meeting and the several few which followed were not as effective as was hoped. In his mid-eighties, Aden Abdulla suffered a mild stroke while in Djibouti and was admitted to hospital. After his treatment, he returned to his farm in Jenaale. Throughout his own career, Aden Abdulla had been able to rise to the highest position in the land and was never affected by tribalism and sectarism. A new, unhelpful logic had set in. Things had irreversibly changed.

# SECTION 2

# THEMATIC ESSAYS

# SECTION TWO – THEMATIC ESSAYS

## Essay One – The President as diarist

Aden Abdulla was inaugurated as the first president on July 1, 1960 and ended on June 30, 1967. He wrote his first diary entry in January 1958, at a time when he was serving concurrently as Leader of the majority party, the SYL, and President of the Legislative Assembly. No other president has thought to do such a thing. During this the two years preceding the independence the diaries cover a number of crucial pre-independence developments, notably the transfer of full power from the administering power (Afis) to the future independent Somali government, and the long and delicate process of drafting the Constitution. The President emphasizes his disagreements with the ruling party and the government on certain political and legal questions which, at times, reached near breaking point. The role played by the United Nations to assist solving the disagreements with the ruling party fellow members is highlighted. Mention is given to the process leading to the union between the two territories of former British Protectorate of Somaliland and the former Trust territory of Somalia. The early diary entries consisted of few lines covering limited domestic events, but from 1960 entries became expanded, with rare gaps, usually a page written in a clear hand with few portions crossed out.

The diaries also shed quite a bit of light on his frequent clashes with the leadership of the Central Committee of the party on number of political issues.

A particular example is in the late 1950s, when he publicly blamed certain members of the SYL Central Committee for believing that they were unconditionally supporting the Abdullahi Issa government. In this, he felt they were supporting the government solely for their personal interest and out of clan considerations.

Again Aden Abdulla clashed with the Central Committee of the ruling party when, following the political elections in 1959, he brought forward a proposal to call a Party Congress in order to give a voice to local branch secretaries from across the country in important issues including who the party might endorse for the positions of Prime Minister and President of the Legislative Assembly. Certain members, who together represented a majority on the Central Committee at the time, were able to put down the proposal. In this, he felt they were supporting the government solely for their personal interest and out clan considerations.

He vehemently clashed with Haji Mohamed Hussein, leader of the party, over the latter's extreme left-leaning views, which were far outside the mainstream attitudes of society. Aden Abdulla's disagreements with his fellows, when he was part of the party leadership, were frequent and concerned all manner of things. He condemned and disassociated himself from members of the party, who used the party platform to promote narrow tribal interests. On both occasions, these disagreements led to his resignation from the party leadership. In general, he deplored the corruption of certain politicians and wished that candidates for parliamentary seats had responsible aims, instead of wanting only to win by hook or crook too much "election for the spoil".

The diaries chronicle such activities as visitors, meetings, social activities, public ceremonies and travel. Whether he was in his Villa Somalia residence or aboard, each night before retiring to bed, the President wrote about the events of his day. He followed closely the political turbulences taking place in various parties of the world, in particular events taking place in Africa and Middle East, areas plagued by frequent military coups and counter coups. His handwritten diaries recorded his innermost thoughts and observations on the the routine day-to-day occurrences of his presidency. But the diaries also record the smaller, everyday occurrences of Abdulla's life, events that would otherwise have gone unrecorded such as weather fluctuation, temperature, wind speed, rain falls and meteorological oddities. Day after day, week after week, he recounted in his unedited diaries his experiences with the hosts of political crises the country had gone through his time in office as Head of the State and Leader of the party. The diaries can provide answers to key questions such as whom a president meets with and talks to; what are the activities he regularly is involved in.

In this, one gets an insight into differing perspectives of that generation of Somali leaders. For instance, Abdirizak Haji Hussein wrote in his memoir that in early 1951, he decided that "I would die liberating my country by eliminating a powerful Italian official". He settled on Mr Benerdelli, the Director of the Political Department of AFIS, who he believed was "the most venomous and the most heinous man in Mogadiscio", who was known for his anti-SYL attitudes and ultimately responsible for "[a]nything of a political nature that took place in any region of the country", concluding that "The SYL hated him more than any man the Italian Administration". Although Abdirizak's plan did not succeed, it seems that Aden Abdulla had a different view of Gualtiero Bernardelli. Receiving Benardelli in his office in the presidential mansion, who had since become the Italian ambassador based in Sana'a (Yemen), recalled that he had been a colonial official in Somalia for decades before becoming Head of the Internal Affairs Directorate with AFIS. "In this last period of the Trust Administration", he observed, "he [Bernardelli] had always shown himself to be one of the least nasty and obtuse officials towards the SYL, which was anti-Italian and an independence movement" before adding, however, that he "of course had to have been influenced by his colonial past and by other less level-headed colleagues" [*In questo'ultimo periodo di Amministrazione Fiduciara, si era sempre dimostrato uno dei meno cattivi e ottusi funzionari verso la Lega dei Giovani Somali, ani-italiana e indipendentista, ma naturalmente doveva essere influenzato dal suo passato coloniale e dagli altri colleghi meno equiliberati*].[272]

Diaries covering all seven years of what we now regard as the Aden Abdulla era, a crowded hour in the nation's history that included, among other things, the declaration of independence and the union between the two parts of Somalia, the promulgation of the provisional constitution and the aborted coup d'etat in 1961, the clashes with the National Assembly, vetoing draft legislations passed by the Deputies and much more. A passage that reveals the President's frustration with the MPs, when they approved a draft legislation providing for the increase of their salaries described the bill as "immoral", (*Diary November 30 November, 1963*). Other epithets favorite included "irresponsible," His anger appeared to return in 1965 and in the years thereafter with complaints about the rejection of non-controversial legislative decrees introduced by the government. The President referred to those MPs who, in the secret ballot, voted in a manner different from the way they voted publicly, as "cowards" and 'franchi tiratori", an expression widely used in Italian political jargon to define a Member of Parliament who votes against his party in a secret ballot. *(Diary June 24, 1966*)

As much as this diary tells us about the presidency, it tells us even more about the man who occupied the office. Here is a man who revered the office of the president, but didn't personally care for re-election when his first term came to end. He considered that 7 years term of office were enough time for incumbent and a new person should be given the chance to lead the country.

The President was fully aware of the weaknesses of the post-colonial political and administrative systems, further exacerbated by the Somali inexperience in management of the state affairs. He publicly denounced the system calling for its review. As leader of the party he called to reform the electoral system in favour of fairer and acceptable one. In 1956 and 1959, for instance, he spearheaded a campaign for the formation of a coalition government in which, in addition to the members of the ruling party, members of the opposition parties too would be represented in the Cabinet, an innovative idea that fell short of being accepted by his fellow party members.

The diaries reflect his vision on the areas of foreign policy, good governance and economic management. He always pursued genuine principles and firm policy objectives: anti-Communism, military rule, moralization of the public administration. He was convinced that the poor economic conditions of the country in general, and the chronic budget deficit, in particular, could have been addressed had the government forgone some unnecessary expenditure in order to reduce/eliminate the budget deficit. He considered the annual foreign contribution to the national ordinary budget as an element undermining the prestige of the country. In the diary entry of February, 1, 1961, he wrote: "It is inconsistent with the self-respect and dignity of independent people to rely any longer than is necessary on the generosity of foreigners for covering ordinary budget deficit and for providing fund for development projects." (*Diary February 1, 1961*). He encouraged the government to take measure aimed at reducing the nation's debt and place its finances on sound footing.

He believed in multiparty system, not too many parties, of course. A single party system gives too much temptation for the development of a man-on-horse who might want to become a dictator. In an interview with E.A. Bayne, he is reported as saying: "This dictator would never be Aden Abdulla, but it might be someone who comes after me". (*E.A. Bayne, page 114*) In 1967, He put the following entry in the diary "Military rule is some thing I would never wish on Somalia", (*Diary 10 June, 1967)* Still, the diaries do seem to confirm that Aden Abdulla had an ingrained principle of favouring strong diplomatic and economic cooperation with East and West on equal footing. In particular, with regards to the relations with the neighboring countries, Ethiopia and Kenya, he preferred a policy of quiet diplomacy as opposed to military confrontation. He often used his diaries to explain his polices: for example, the president explained why his "quiet diplomacy", approach to the irredentism scheme was preferable to the guerrilla activities preferred by his first Prime Minister. He records in the diaries how his policy was undermined by the Prime Minister who favoured, instead, a policy of encouraging guerrilla movements to carry out sabotage activities inside Ethiopia, a policy which triggered heavy air and land Ethiopian military retaliation targeting civilian population living along the border areas. Aden Abdulla saw the advantage of advocating the principle of self-determination for the Somali population under foreign domination, instead of advancing territorial claim in international arena. In fact, he writes in his diary: "To justify our policy and canvass large international support, it is necessary to reiterate that our difficulties with our neighbours are not based on territorial claims, but on the search for justice to the Somalis kept under force by those countries. (*Diaries March 24 and March 28, 1963*) Nothing could explain his vision on the missing territories better than the following diary entry on December 28, 1964 "What constantly preoccupies me is how to convince Ethiopia to comply with our wishes and agree with the Somalis to resolve all pending issues so to generate friendly ties between the two people. I wonder if it is worth going to Addis Abeba to meet again Haile Sellassie to talk to him with the heart on the sleeve, or to invite him here in Mogadiscio. Without a military might to be reckoned with, and popular uprising, comparable to the Algerian one, so powerful to influence the world opinion, we cannot hope to win unless Ethiopia accepts". (*Diary December 28, 1964)*

With regard to relationship with the Arab world, and in particular with Egypt, he was convinced that the idea of special relations with the Arabs enjoyed gained strong support in Somalia. In fact, in an interview in December 1965 he is cited as saying that "While we certainly do not wish to be seen as followers of Egypt, we do feel in our hearts that, in the last analysis, the friends of Somalia will be in the Arab world". He had not always agreed with the policies of Arab politicians. Nevertheless, he was convinced that "the Arab countries are the rock on which our outside friendships rest".

The president's main area of discretion, under the Constitution, was the choice of the personalities he would deal with directly in the every day running of the country. One of the most important elements of his discretion involved the designation of the Prime Minster. Two Prime Ministers served during his seven years long stint (1960-1967). In the first four years of Aden Abdulla's time of office the government was led by Abdirashid; and in the remaining three, the Premiership passed over to Abdirazak. A long and uneasy 'cohabitation' between the President and his first Prime Minister soon developed. The President thought that his Prime Minister was not very receptive of his suggestions aimed at moralizing the public administration and insuring democratic national unity transcending ethnic differences. However, despite this uneasy relation, the President decided not to exercise his constitutional power and dismiss the Prime Minister preferring instead to wait the right time to substitute him with a new Prime Minister. His diary entry for October 1, 1963 reads "I pray that God Almighty gives me the fortitude to be patient with him up to the election in March 1964". That time came in 1964 after the general elections held in that year.

Again and again, there is evident in his writings a note of despair and dissatisfaction about the political behavior displayed by many of his fellow politicians with whom he often clashed over moralization of the public administration and electoral fraud.

The politicians, among his old friends, he kept in high esteem included Abdirazak H. Hussein, Haji Bashir Ismail Yusuf, Abdullahi Issa Mohamud and Mohamed Ali Dhorre "Agaweyne". The senior Civil Servant breed he gave credit for the work they were doing included Ahmed Dahir (Magistrate of Account), Haji Yahya (the Accountant General) and Hussein Nour Elmi (Career Diplomat)

Family and religion were two subjects that received a great deal of President's attention. Whoever reads the diaries cannot remain without realizing that Aden Abdulla's marriage to Asha Elmi Mattan was the cornerstone of his family life. In 1934 Donna Asha met Aden Abdulla, then a civil servant, visiting Mogadiscio on mission from Shalambod. He proposed to her and she accepted, but her acceptance was conditional to her father's consent. They were married in November 1934. Aden Abdulla often wrote of his loneliness when his family was away. The president was first and foremost a family man. If the president's love for his wife and children fills the diaries, so does his affection to affect excursions to areas around Mogadiscio. But apparently, he was never happier than when he was riding at Shalambod and Jenale during week ends, places he was emotionally linked to. In scores of entries, the highlight of a day seems to be the visit he enjoyed with the family or, some times, with friends to visit these two places. This was Aden Abdulla's world, and revisiting it as frequently as he could obviously cheered and relaxed him.

Aden Abdulla's religion, in turn, comes across as important as one reasonably think, He was considered as the exemplar of a tolerant, open, democratic style of Muslim leadership, in contrast to the archetypes of the mad mullahs which dominate our contemporary view of the Muslim faith. The diaries indicate that he rarely missed the Friday collective prayer performed in various Mosques of the capital amid a large number of worshipers without being bothered by security concerns.

The diaries document Aden Abdulla's whole life, both public and personal, Over the course of his career, he would go on to serve the fledgling Somalia as, vice president of the Legislative Assembly, as a delegate to the first Islamic Conference in Karachi, Pakistan, as delegate to the Trusteeship Council of the United Nations, as legislator and, finally, as the country's first President.

All in all, these diaries offer a delightful look into the life of a man who sometimes seems to have gained more stature and recognition after his departure from the Villa Somalia than he was accorded when he lived in it. The diaries suggest that there was nothing to hide. After decades in the public eye as a leading politician, the public man and the private man were one. One strength manifest in these diaries is that Aden Abdulla, was an active and alert Head of State than his detractors care to admit.

The significance of the diaries as important primary source for researchers and historians cannot be overemphasized in a country where history is shared orally or through speech, usually handed down from generation to generation. Regrettably, however, the diaries are yet to be edited, translated into Somali language and published to give Somali public access to them. If edited and published, the diaries will provide a striking insight into one of this nation's most important presidencies and sheds new light on the character of a true Somali leader.. Love him or hate him, agree with his policies or not, it is difficult to put the diaries down without being impressed by Aden Abdulla's wit, his balanced perspective on life.

The diaries of President Aden Abdulla are in the custody of his elder son, Eng. Abdulkadir's house in Virginia, USA...

In the last two years of his tenure of office, one of the things that jump out with particular force was his public utterances not to seek re-election for1967. He gave two basic justifications, extensively reported in the diaries for this. Firstly, he felt he served enough time as head of State and that it was time for a new person to be tested. "I do not consider myself indispensable, my advice and ideas are not appreciated, therefore I feel useless as Head of State. Consequently, I do not see why I should prolong my stay at the Palace (Villa Somalia). Seven years are considerable amount of time to weigh up the pros and cons", his entry for July 1966 notes. Secondly, he loathed the endemic deplorable practice of greasing the palms of the parliamentarians or making them promises in return for their support. However, his indifference did not deter his close supporters (Osman A. Roble, Sheikh Ali Jimale and Abdullahi Issa, Mohamed Ali Dorre, among others) from applying persistent pressure on him not to withdraw from the race. He was constantly encouraged to meet all parliamentarians and solicit/canvass their vote in the same manner as his contending rival was doing. But he was unreceptive to such a suggestion, for he knew that most of the Deputies would not support a candidate without money is paid or a promise for future cabinet positions is made. To all the MPs who approached him to enquiry about his intention he exhorted to give their vote to the candidate they believed would better serve the country. After long hesitations and sleepless nights, the President eventually accepted his many supporter's offer in order "not to disappoint my friends" (*Diary April, 1967*).

## Essay Two – The Presidential ideal

One of the major issues debated by drafters of modern constitutions involves the system of government at the national level. Two primary models have emerged: those of the presidential and the parliamentary systems. We try first, to explain, in simple manner, the key differences between these models and secondly, shed light on erroneous application/interpretation of the provisions set out in the constitution regarding the responsibilities and functions of the President of the Federal Republic of Somalia.

A primary difference between the two systems is, in the presidential system, the Head of State, is elected directly by the people, and as such, exercises wide range of executive powers, whilst in the parliamentary system , the Head of State is elected by the Parliament; he has no executive power. The executive power is vested in the government.

The framers of the Somali Provisional Constitution of 2012, labored through innumerable years to create a document that would more adequately suit the needs of the fledgling Federal Somali State. They were mindful of the negative legacy of the accumulation of powers in the hands of one person which had characterized the authoritarian military leadership (1969-1990). The final text they have come up in 2012 follows closely the Constitution of 1960, in particular with regard to the division of powers between the Parliament, the Government and the President of the Republic. However, the balance of power that the fathers of the Somali constitution had thought about and enshrined in the Constitution appears now to have eroded and undermined by a serious flaw reflected in the article 89 (8) of the provisional Constitution itself.

The problem with Article 89 (8) of the Provisional Constitution

A telling illustration of the flaw of the current provisional constitution is found in article 89 (8) which stipulate: "Every presidential candidate has to declare his candidacy to the House of Federal Parliament and shall present his election programme to the Federal Parliament"

The wordings reflected in paragraph 8 as referred to above, are unfortunate. They have created confusion in the mind of the legislators and the public, at large, with the lamentable consequence that this may eventually lead (as it indeed did in the recent past) to the wrong conclusion that the President of the Republic of Somalia wields executive powers.

Jurists know very well that, in a Parliamentary State, hopeful presidential candidates should not, and must not be expected, for their election, to present a programme of their own to the Parliament. The powers the constitution endows on the President of the Federal Republic of Somalia are clear; they do not include executive functions. The framers of the provisional Constitution were careful not to put too much power in the hands of the Head of State. By contrast, in a presidential system of government, the prospective candidates for presidency are expected, for their election, to present their political programme to the people of the country at large. The president, in a presidential system of government, is an individual elected by the citizens to be head of government and state..

Under the current provisional Somali Constitution, the Government, and not the President of the Republic, is responsible for deciding how the country is run and for managing things, day to day. The Prime Minister and the Council of Ministers, not the President of the Republic, are responsible to the Federal Parliament for the acts of the government, even though they are signed and promulgated by the President.

Form of Presidential Acts

The power to appoint the senior government officials is vested in the government, as the constitutional organ holding the executive power (article 97 Federal Constitution). However, this choice has to be transposed into an act of the President of the Republic.

The President must follow the government indications and promulgate the decree unless he has to raise objections concerning the legality of the government decision.

The expression "appoint", appearing 5 times in article 90 of the provisional Constitution has led to the wrong understanding that the President has the authority to appoint senior government officials without first receiving proposals from the Government. This is a misleading notion which has already created confusion in the mind of those not well familiar with the letter and spirit of the Constitution.

To promulgate is to officially put a law into effect. The word promulgate comes from the Latin word promulgatus, meaning 'make publicly known.' After the promulgation, the decree is inserted in the Official Gazette (Bollettino Ufficiale).

All presidential acts are issued in the form of decrees; they bear the denomination of Presidential Decree followed by the date, the year and the serial number of the decree. The form of the Presidential acts is therefore always the same whatever their contents.

All acts issued by the President in the form of presidential decree shall be signed by the Prime Minister and the Minister responsible for the matter to which the presidential decree relates. In fact, a presidential decree is valid only if it is countersigned by the Prime Minster and the competent Minister.

In a parliamentary system of government, the President of the Republic cannot take proprio motu (of his volition) administrative decisions without a formal request from the Council of Ministers. Of course, The President is not a Public Notary notarizing or authenticating the acts of the government. He is consulted in every measure political issues the government introduces. But he has no the initiative of those measures.

# ENDNOTES

## SECTION ONE, PART ONE
## ITALIAN PENETRATION INTO SOMALIA................*Notes to page* 3-37

1 Luigi Robecchi Brichetti, *Dal Benadir, lettere illustrate alla Societa'Antischiaivistica* d'Italia. La Poligrafica Milano, 1904, p, 48.

2 R. Hess, *Italian Colonialism in Somalia* (University of Chicago Press, 1966), p. 58.

3 Decree n. 161, April 5, 1905. Nuredin Hagi Scikei, Somalia un' invenzione Italiana, Africana, Miscellanea di Studi Extraeuropei, Associazione di Studi Extraeuropei ESA, 2001, pp, 95-108.

4 Its topography is similar to Huddur further south. Cf. L. V. Bertarelli, *Possedimenti e Colonie: Isole Egee, Triplitania, Cirenaica, Eritrea, Somalia* (1929), pp. 784, 786; Salah Mohamed Ali, *Huddur & the history of Southern Somalia* (Cairo: Al-Nahda Bookshop, 2005), p. 26.

5 Giuseppe Stefanini, Nello Puccioni, Enrico Cerulli, Alberto Baldini, Riccardo Riccardi and Fabrizio Cortesi, "Somalia" in *Enciclopedia italiana* (1936).

6 Personal notes, memoir, c.1957.

7 Kenneth Cecil Gandar Dower, *Askaris at war in Abyssinia* (1944), 27.

8 For instance, Aden Abdulle writes, "Quando emigrammo dalla zona di Belet Uen, che allora conoscevo per Hiiraan, i miei zii, e probabilmente quasi interamente la gente della mia cabila, erano già passata alla Somalia Italiana, e più precisamente, sis ono stabiliti a Baidoa e dintorni".

9 Sheekh Jaamac Cumar Ciise, *Diiwaanka Gabayadii Sayid Muxammad Cabdulle Xasan, 1856-1921*, 2nd ed. (Oslo: n.p., 1999), p. 18, 109.

10 For recent images of the area and retellings of the history of this period, see: 'Maxamuud Macalin "Cagadhiig (sic) iyo qalcada Aamin 1913,' Sollas Media, 19 Dec. 2013, **https://www.youtube.com/watch?v=n88am2BHBtQ**; "Goobaha Caanka ah ee Baladweyne" RTN Somali TV, 11 Aug. 2018, **https://**

**www.youtube.com/watch?v=MxYyu3YkdY8**; Maxaad ka taqanaa micnaha iyo meesha uu ka yimid magaca Gobalka Hiiraan?," RTN Somali TV, 7 Aug. 2018, **https://www.youtube.com/watch?v=ULdLuGsseT0**; "DAAWO: Sheeko Ku saabsan Taariikhda Magaalada Beledweyne Iyo Sharaxaad Qoto dheer.", Hansare Media Group, 16 Sept. 2020, **https://www.youtube.com/watch?v=gTH3Lu8KO2E**.

11 Said Sheikh Samatar, Oral Poetry and Somali Nationalism: The Case of Sayyid Mahammad 'Abdille Hasan (Cambridge: Cambridge University, 1982), p. 133.

12 Sheekh Jaamac Cumar Ciise, *Diiwaanka Gabayadii Sayid Muxammad Cabdulle Xasan, 1856-1921*, 2nd ed. (Oslo: n.p., 1999), 107-109, 184, 231 and *passim*.

13 Salah Mohamed Ali, *Huddur & the history of Southern Somalia* (Cairo: Al-Nahda Bookshop, 2005), p. 27.

14 Relazione sulla Somalia Italiana del Governatore Nobile Giacomo De Martino, Senator del Regno, per gli anni 1911 e 1912 (Articolo 22 della legge 5 aprile 1908, n. 161) – Presentata dal Ministro delle Colonie (Bertolini) nella tornata del 4 dicembre 1912 (Roma: Tipografia della Camera dei Deputati, 1912). p. 7.

15 Mohamed Haji Mukhtar, Historical Dictionary of Somalia, p. 107.

16 Salah Mohamed Ali, *Huddur,* 54-55.

17 Somalia: dalle origini al 1914, pp. 174-5.

18 The word may originally have come from the Somali word for 'he who lays out the carpet' which in military parlance might be rendered vanguard or advance guard.

19 L. V. Bertarelli, Possedimenti e Colonie: Isole Egee, Triplitania, Cirenaica, Eritrea, Somalia (1929), p. 746.

20 Mukhtar, Historical Dictionary, 107-8.

21 "PRC-aided water project completed in Somalia", OW251446 Beijing XINHUA in English 1220 GMT 25 Jul 79 OW, *Daily Report: People's Republic of China, Issues 139-148* (Springfield, VA: U.S. Department of Commerce, National Technical Information Service), p. 11.

22 Abdi M. Kusow, "The Somali Origin: Myth or Reality" in The Invention of Somalia (1995), 81-106 at p. 94.

23 Il Corriere della Somalia, July 1, 1960.

24 Robert L. Hess, *Italian Colonialism in Somalia* (Chicago: University of Chicago Press, 1966), pp. 111-12.

25 "Prima Question: Organizzazione e Funzionamento del Servizio Sanitario nelle Spedizioni Coloniali – Relatore: La Competenza del Esercito, Tenente Colonnello Medico Ugo Reitano" / First Question: The Organization and Function of the Medical Services in Colonial Expeditions – Reporting on Italy by Ugo Reitano" in Official Reports. Tenth International Congress of Military Medicine and Pharmacy, Washington, D.C., 7-15 May 1939, Vol. I (Washington, D.C.: Government Printing Office, 1939), 3-45 at p. 30.

26 Jacqueline Andalib & Derek Duncan, *Italian Colonialism: Legacy and memory* (Bern: Peter Lang, 2005), p. 66.

27 TNA FO 371/125691, confidential report from British Embassy in Addis Abeba, August 29, 1950.

28 UN Doc. T/484. March 2, 1950.

29 Del Boca, 2001.

30 Proclamation No. 4 of 1948.

31 Hess, R, op, cit, p, 186.

32 Report of the Four Power Commission of Investigation for Former Italian Colonies, vol. III, pp. 7- 40.

33 See SYL Chairman, Haji Mohamed response to Mr. Utter, the US member of the Four Power Commission, on January 20, 1948.

34 I.M. Lewis, op, cit, p, 112.

35 Diary June 27, 1961.

**SECTION ONE, PART TWO**
**ENTRY INTO FULL-TIME POLITICS** ......................... *Notes to page* **37-71**

36 Ioan M. Lewis, *The Modern History of Somaliland, from Nation to State* (New York: Frederick A. Prager, 1965), p. 122.

37 Vide: Diary, January 17, 1963.

38 Lake Success is a village and a capital of the Great Neck School District in Nassau County, New York in the United States, which was the temporary home of the United Nations from 1946 to 1951.

39 Interview with Mohamoud Yusuf Aden "Muro" by the author in Belgium, 2009.

40 *Somalia Courier*, April 16, 1947.

41 Il Popolo, December 14, 1947 reported in A. Bullotta, "La Somalia Sotto Due Bandiere", Garzanti, pp 244-45, 1949.

42 Mesfin Wolde Mariam "The Background of the Ethio-Somalian

Boundary Dispute" The Journal of Modern African Studies Vol. 2, n, 2 July 1964. [insert page number].

43 UN Doc A/64, 15 September 1948.

44 Resolution 289 (IV) of 21 November 1949.

45 UN Doc. A//C.1/ 522, Nov. 1, 1949.

46 Art. 3 of the Trusteeship Agreement of the Territory of Somaliland under Italian Administration, adopted by the Trusteeship Council on January 27, 1950.

47 A.A. Castagno, 1964. [insert page number].

48 A.A. Castagno, 1964. [insert page number].

49 Article 5 (3) of the Trusteeship Agreement in conjunction with Article 87 of the Charter of the United Nations.

50 TNA, CO 537/3641.

51 TNA, FO 371/73797, telegram from Gamble to FO, Nov. 1949.

52 TNA FO 371 /73797, telegram from Gamble to FO, November 1949.

53 Interview with Mohamoud Aden Yousuf "Muro" on August 9, 2009 at Louvien, Belgium.

54 TNA C O 537/5938 Bimonthly intelligence report for month ending February 1950.

55 UN Trusteeship Council Official Records, seventh session, Vol.1, 1950. [insert page number].

56 Decree N. 2357 of December 2, 1952, was issued by the President of Republic of Italy, soon after the Trusteeship Administration came into being.

57 Corriere della Somalia, 1 Aprile, 1950 [insert page number].

58 Del Boca, 2001. [full reference and page number required].

59 "Costituzione del Consiglio Territoriale della Somalia", Ordinanza n.144, Dec. 1950 reported in *Bollettino Ufficiale* (Mogadiscio: 2 gennaio 1951).

60 Angelo Del Boca, Gli italiani in Africa Orientale: Nostalgia delle colonie (Roma-Bari: Laterza, 1976), p. 235.

61 The Somali leader's remarks were made in an interview reported on the weekly Italian magazine, *Epoca*, in March 1954.

62 ASCM "Brusasca 81/ONU Memorandum to GA from the Somali delegation, Lake Success, N.Y. October, 1950.

63 TNA FO 371/80887, letter to the Administrator, July 25, 1950.

64 TNA FO 1015/553 Report on the Transfer of Administration in Somalia from the United Kingdom to Italian trusteeship, 1950.

65 A. Del Boca, 2001. [full reference and page number required].

66 Angelo Del Boca, Gli italiani in Africa Orientale: Nostalgia delle colonie (Roma-Bari: Laterza, 1976), p. 224.

67 TNA FO 371/1025691. report from the British Consulate in Mogadiscio to FO, November 21, 1954.

68 Abdirazak, 2017, p. 100. [full reference and page number required].

69 TNA FO 371/108101. Report from the British Consulate in Mogadiscio to FO, March 18, 1954.

70 Ordinance no. 6 of March, 1955.

71 ASMAE, AFIS, box 9, file 9, 'Breve cronostoria di come si è giunti alla tenuta degli 'scir' per l'elezione dei capi (istituzione dei consigli distrettuali) e per l'elezione del Consiglio Territoriale, p. 4.

72 ASMAE, AFIS, box 9, file 9, 'Breve cronostoria di come si è giunti alla tenuta degli 'scir' per l'elezione dei capi (istituzione dei consigli distrettuali) e per l'elezione del Consiglio Territoriale, p. 5.

73 Corriere della Somalia Maggio 2, 1956.

74 Law No. 1 of May 5, 1956.

75 UN Doc. T 1311, April 22, 1957, par. 106, p. 45.

76 Legge n° 10 December 30, 1956, 'Rilevazione demografica delle popolazioni extra-municipali', Bollettino Ufficiale, ottobre 1, 1956.

77 UN Doc. T 1311, April 22, 1957, par. 106, pp. 45-46.

78 UN Doc. T 1311, April 22, 1957, par. 77, p, 29.

79 UN Doc. T1311, April 22, 1957.

80 UN Doc. T 1311, April 22, 1957.

81 International Cooperation Administration. DC, July 1958.

82 G.F. Malagodi, 'Linee programmatiche per lo sviluppo della Somalia', Roma 1953.

83 Malagodi, 1953.

84 Abdirazak 2017, p, 123.

85 UN Doc.T/1372, April 12, 1958 page 2.

86 ASMAE, AFIS, box 9, file 2, Letter no. 22092, from Anzilotti to Abdullahi Issa, Febbraio 7, 1958.

87 Telegram from British Consulate Mogadishu to FO, London, February 6, 1958.

88 Diary, January 19, 1958.

89 Diary, January 19, 1958.

90 TNA FO 371/131463 confidential report dated April 1, 1958 from

British Consulate Mogadiscio to FO.

91 Diary May 8, 1958.

92 Corriere della Somalia, maggio 26, 1958.

93 ASMAE, AFIS, box 9, file 2, resolution adopted by the Central Committee of the Lega dei Giovani Somali.

94 Corriere della Somalia, giugno [June] 9, 1958 ASMAE, AFIS, box 9, file 2.

95 Diary, June 12, 1958.

96 ASMAE, Afis, Cassa, busta 2. Mogadiscio June, 1958.

97 Article 9 of Law n. 26 of December 1958.

98 Diary March 11, 1959.

99 ASMAE, AFIS Box 4, file 9, Ruling of the Regional Judge of Upper Juba, April 9, 1959.

100 Diary March 24, 1959.

101 Diary April 3, 1959.

102 Corriere della Somalia, Aprile 25, 1959, p. 2.

103 Diary May 22, 1959.

104 Corriere della Somalia May 27, 1959.

105 Corriere della Somalia May 27, 1959.

106 Cf. David D. Laitin, *Politics, Language and Thought: The Somali Experience* (London: The University of Chicago Press, 1977), 95.

107 Diary April 11, 1959.

108 Diary July 9, 1959.

109 Diary June 13, 1959.

110 Diary June 27, 1959.

111 Abdirazak Haji Hussein, My Role in the Foundation of the Somali Nation-State, A Political Memoir". Edited by Abdisalam Isse-Salwe, Africa World Press, Trenton, New Jersey 2017, p, 127.

112 Corriere della Somalia, July 23, 1959.

113 Abdirazak Haji Hussein op cit, p, 129.

114 TNA FO 371/138390, Confidential telegram from the UKDEL, New York, to FO, August 10, 1959.

115 TNA FO 371/138390 Confidential telegram from the UKDEL, New York, to FO, August 10, 1959.

116 Costanzo, op. cit., p. 9.

117 Decreto No. 140 of September 6, 1957.

118 Law n. 6 of January 8, 1960.

119 D'Antonio, op. cit., p. 4, quoting Records of the Constituent Assembly, no. 6, April 6, 1960, pp 5-6.

120 GA Resolution 1415 (XV).

121 Costanzo 1962.

122 Corriere della Somalia, May 23, 1960.

123 Paolo Contini, The Somali Republic: An experiment of legal integration (London: F. Cass & Co., 1969), p. 3.

124 [Haji] N. A. Noor Muhammad, *The Legal System of the Somali Democratic Republic* (Charlottesville, VA: The Michie Company, 1972), 129.

## SECTION ONE, PART THREE
## INDEPENDENCE COMES AT MIDNIGHT............*Notes to page* 71-119

125 A/4402, 11 July 1960.

126 UN Doc. UNOR, A/R. 418 (XIV), December 5, 1959.

127 Del Boca, 2001.

128 Michele Pirone, "Appunti di Storia d'Africa, 1961.

129 Angelo Del Boca, Gli italiani in Africa orientale: Nostalgia delle colonie (Roma: Editori Laterza, 1984), 292.

130 Corriere della Somalia, July 1, 1960.

131 The New York Times, July 1, 1960.

132 Del Boca, Gli italiani in Africa orientale: Nostalgia delle colonie (1984), 292.

133 The New York Times, July 1, 1960.

134 Article 77, 1960 Constitution.

135 Decreto Amministrativo n. 2 del 22 Luglio 1960. Bollettino Ufficiale, suppl. N. 3 al n. 1. 30 Luglio 1960.

136 Renato Angeloni, Diritto Costituzionale Somalo, Milano, Giuffre', 1964, p, 277.

137 Article 70 of the 1960 Constitution.

138 Articles 77 and 83 of 1960 Constitution.

139 Abdirazak Haji Hussein, My Role in the foundation of the Somali Nation-State, A Political Memoir Edited by Abdisalam Issa-Salwe. The Red Sea Press, 2017, p. 145.

140 Ibid.

141 Diary July 4, 1961.

142 La nuova Italia d'oltremare: L'opera del Fascismo nelle colonie italiane

– Notizie, dati, documenti raccolti d'ordine di S. E. Emilio de Bono, Ministro delle Colonie, e coordinate a testo, con riferimenti d'indole generale, da Angelo Piccioli, con prefazione di Benito Mussolini (Casa Editrice A. Mondadori, 1933), 996.

143 Austin Hubert Wightwick Haywood and Frederick Arthur Stanley Clarke, The History of the Royal West African Frontier Force (1964), 339; Ralph Jerome Holmes, A Reconnaissance Survey of the Mineral Deposits o Somalia (former Italian Somaliland): A Report of Technical Assistance Mission (T.A. 45-125) (World Mining Consultants, 1954), 14.

144 "Aden Abdullah President again", *Somali News,* 7 July 1961, p. 2.

145 "Aden Abdullah President again", *Somali News,* July 7, 1961, p. 2.

146 "Aden Abdullah President again", *Somali News* July7, 1961, p. 2.

147 Diary, July 6, 1961.

148 A.A. Castagno, Somali Republic 547-548.

149 Somali News July 14, 1961.

150 Diary July 27, 1961.

151 Diary July 27 1961.

152 "Ali Ismail deplores revolt by youths", Hargeisa Domestic Service, 11 December 1961 in *DAILY REPORT. Foreign Radio Broadcasts (FBIS-FRB-61-239) – SOMALIA, AFRICA, Excerpts,* p. I9-I11.

153 Diary January 6, 1962.

154 Diary, October 25, 1962.

155 "Dissident deputies again quit Parliament", Mogadiscio Somalia Domestic Service, 30 October 1962 printed in *DAILY REPORT. Foreign Radio Broadcasts (FBIS-FRB-62-213), 31 October 1962, SOMALIA, AFRICA, Summary,* p. I8-I9.

156 Diary, 10 and 24 September 1962.

157 Ioan M. Lewis, The Modern History of Somaliland, from Nation to State (New York: Praeger, 1965), 176.

158 "President addresses people of North", Mogadiscio Somalia Domestic Service, 24 September 1962 printed in *DAILY REPORT. Foreign Radio Broadcasts (FBIS-FRB-62-189), 27 September 1962, ETHIOPIA & SOMALIA, AFRICA, Excerpts,* p. I7-I9.

159 Diary June 10, 1962.

160 Diary October 3, 1963.

161 Diary October 17, 1963.

162 Diary November 7, 1963.

163 Diary October 24, 1963; Diary November 25, 1963.

164 John Gordon Stewart Drysdale, *The Somali Dispute* (London: Pall Mall Press, 1964), 145.

165 Government Activities from Independence until today (July 1, 1960 to December 31, 1963) (Mogadiscio: Presidency of the Council of Ministers, 1964), p. 84.

166 Diary September 12, 1963.

167 Diary, 24 October 1963.

168 Diary October 23, 1963.

169 "X. Law no. 4 of 22 January 1964: Political Elections" in *The Electoral Legislation of Somalia, 1953*-1969, ed. Maarten Halff, pp. 166-188.

170 Diary January 6, 1964.

171 Diary January 7, 1964.

172 Diary January 30, 1964.

173 Article 70(3): "On assuming his functions, the President of the Republic shall take the following oath of loyalty to the State before the National Assembly: «In the name of God I swear that I will discharge faithfully all my duties as President of the Republic and defend the Constitution with all my strength in the interest of the Country and the Nation»."

174 Diary June 7, 1964.

175 Diary March 13, 1964.

176 "Parliament: New Deputies take oath – Pledge to serve the people", *Somali News,* 29 May 1964, p. 5.

177 "Supreme Court's ruling brings N.A. to full strength, *Somali News,* 10 July 1964, pp. 2, 4, 5.

178 "The N.A.'s New President", *Somali News,* 29 May 1964, pp. 1 and "Parliament – New Deputies take oath: Pledge to serve the people", *Somali News,* 29 May 1964, p. 5.

179 "Il nuovo Presidente dell'Assemblea Nazionale", *Il Corriere della Somalia*, 27 maggio 1964, p. 2.

180 Diary, April, 30, 1964.

181 "Parliament: New Deputies take oath – Pledge to serve the people", *Somali News,* 29 May 1964, p. 5.

182 "Abdirizak Hagi Hussein named new Premier", Mogadiscio Somalia Domestic Service, 8 June 1964 published in *DAILY REPORT. Foreign Radio Broadcasts (FBIS-FRB-64-112),* 9 June 1964, SOMALIA, Africa, Summary, Page I6.

183 Diary May 1, 1964.

184 Diary April 17, 1964.

185 Diary November 12, 1963.

186 Jeanne Contini, "The Somali Republic: Politics with a Difference", *Africa Report,* 1 November 1964, 3-8 at p. 6.

187 'Abdirazak accepts "Government to Deserve Confidence of Whole Nation"', *Somali News,* June 12, 1964, p. 1.

188 Jeanne Contini, "The Somali Republic: Politics with a Difference", *Africa Report,* 1 November 1964, 3-8 at p. 6.

189 "Abdirazak briefs new Ministers: Government change-over complete", *Somali News,* 19 June 1964, p. 1.

190 "Presidential consultations reopen as Government falls", *Somali News,* July 17, 1964, p. 1.

191 Jeanne Contini, "The Somali Republic: Politics with a Difference", *Africa Report,* 1 November 1964, 3-8 at pp. 6-7.

192 Diary, 7 August 1964.

193 Diary August 7, 1964.

194 "L'On. Abdirizak reincaricato della formazione del nuovo Governo", *Corriere della Somalia*,8 agosto 1964, p. 1.

195 "Country needs firm leadership – President tells New Government", *Somali News,* September 4, 1964, p. 1.

196 Michael Roemer, "Economic Development in Africa: Performance since Independence, and a Strategy for the Future", *Daedalus,* Vol. 111, No. 2, Black Africa: A Generation after Independence (Spring, 1982), pp. 125-148 at p. 125.

197 "Life expectancy at birth, total (years) – Sub-Saharan Africa". Sources based on: (1) United Nations Population Division. World Population Prospects: 2019 Revision, or derived from male and female life expectancy at birth from sources such as: (2) Census reports and other statistical publications from national statistical offices, (3) Eurostat: Demographic Statistics, (4) United Nations Statistical Division. Population and Vital Statistics Reprot ( various years ), (5) U.S. Census Bureau: International Database, and (6) Secretariat of the Pacific Community: Statistics and Demography Programme. Hyperlink: https://data.worldbank.org/indicator/SP.DYN.LE00.IN.

198 Diary February 1, 1961.

199 Diary October 31, 1961.

200 Somali News, May 14, 1965.

201 Diary November 5, 1961.

202 Diary August 31, 1966.

203 Article 61 of the Constitution.

204 Diary November 30, 1961.

205 Diary, 10 December 1961.

206 "Parliament – Bill rejected", *Somali News,* 28 May 1965, p. 5.

207 "In Parliament, by a Special Correspondent", Dalka, No. 1, Vol. I (1 July 1965) in Dalka ['The Homeland']: Documents from a free Somalia Press, Facsimile Edition, Vol. 1 (1965), ed. Yousuf Duhul (London: HAAN Publishing, 1997), pp. 12-13.

208 "Our Foreign Policy Incoherence Unlimited", Dalka, No. 1, Vol. I (1 July 1965) in Dalka ['The Homeland']: Documents from a free Somalia Press, Facsimile Edition, Vol. 1 (1965), ed. Yousuf Duhul (London: HAAN Publishing, 1997), pp. 14-15.

209 "Parliament – Bill rejected", *Somali News*, May 28, 1965, p. 5.

210 "Parliament – Debates Rejected Bills", *Somali News,* 30 December 1966, p. 7.

211 "Parliament – More Money for Deputies", *Somali News,* 30 December 1966, p. 9.

212 For a discussion of the bill and the wider issues at stake, see: "Somalisation of the jobs in the private sector", *Somali News,* 6 January 1967, p. 7.

213 "Parliament – More Money for Deputies", *Somali News,* 30 December 1966, p. 9.

214 Diary January 17, 1967.

215 "Respinto dall'Assemblea il disegno di legge sulla delega al Governo ad emanare i Codici – Con 51 voti contrary e 38 favorevoli", *Corriere della Somalia,* 23 giugno 1966, pp. 1, 4.

216 Diary June 23, 1966.

217 Diary June 24, 1966.

218 Diary June 24, 1966.

219 "Somali—Government Resigns", Africa Research Bulletin: Economic, Financial and Technical Series, Vol. 3, No. 3 ( p. 554.

220 "Prime Minister Agrees to Remain in Office", Mogadiscio Somalia Domestic Service, 28 June 1966 published in *DAILY REPORT. Foreign Radio Broadcasts (FBIS-FRB-66-125), 29 June 1966, Somalia, Africa,* p. I5.

221 *The Annual Register: World Events in 1966, Vol. 208*, eds. Ivison S. Macadam, Margaret Usborne and Ann Boas (London: Longmans, Green and Co., 1967), p. 350.

222 Mohamed Trunji, *Somalia: The untold history, 1941-1969* (Leicester: Looh Press, 2015), pp. 486-489.

223 Abdirazak Haji Hussein, *My role in the foundation of the Somali nation-state, a political memoir*, ed. Abdisalam Issa-Salwe (Trenton, NJ: The Red Sea Press, 2017), pp. 256.

224 *The Annual Register: World Events in 1966, Vol. 208*, eds. Ivison S. Macadam, Margaret Usborne and Ann Boas (London: Longmans, Green and Co., 1967), p. 350.

225 "Iniziato il 7° anno d'indipendenza con un importante parata e gaie manifestazioni popolari", *Corriere della Somalia,* 2 luglio 1966, pp. 1, 8.

226 Radio Mogadishu (12/4/1966) reported in "Foreign Aid", *The Anglo-Somali Society Newsletter*, No. 22, ed. F. J. Chambers (April 1966), p. 5.

227 Abdirazak Haji Hussein, *My role in the foundation of the Somali nation-state, a political memoir*, ed. Abdisalam Issa-Salwe (Trenton, NJ: The Red Sea Press, 2017), pp. 207-8.

228 Abdirazak Haji Hussein, *My role in the foundation of the Somali nation-state, a political memoir*, ed. Abdisalam Issa-Salwe (Trenton, NJ: The Red Sea Press, 2017), pp. 208-9.

229 "Il Partito di maggioranza riconferma la fiducia al Governo Abdirizak – Al termine di una serie di riunioni nella sede dell'SYL", *Corriere della Somalia*, 9 luglio 1966, p. 1.

230 "Presentata all'Assemblea Nazionale la mozione di fiducia del Governo – Aderendo alla richiesta del Capo dello Stato", *Corriere della Somalia,* 12 luglio 1966, p. 1.

231 "Riconfermata con schiacciante maggioranza la fiducia al Governo Abdirizak – 74 voti favorevoli, 21 contrari e 13 astenuti", *Corriere della Somalia*, 13 luglio 1966, pp. 1, 4.

## SECTION ONE, PART FOUR
## 1967 PRESIDENTIAL ELECTION............................ *Notes to page* **119-137**

232 Abdirazak Haji Hussein, *My role in the foundation of the Somali nation-state, a political memoir*, ed. Abdisalam Issa-Salwe (Trenton, NJ: The Red Sea Press, 2017), pp. 251-2.

233 Diary March 6, 1967.

234 Diary May 20, 1967.

235 Abdirazak Haji Hussein, *My role in the foundation of the Somali nation-state, a political memoir*, ed. Abdisalam Issa-Salwe (Trenton, NJ: The Red Sea Press, 2017), p. 252.

236 Diary May 1, 1967.

237 Diary May 25, 1967.

238 Diary July 8, 1966.

239 November 7, 1966.

240 Abdirazak Haji Hussein, *My role in the foundation of the Somali nation-state, a political memoir*, ed. Abdisalam Issa-Salwe (Trenton, NJ: The Red Sea Press, 2017), p. 255.

241 Diary May 30, 1967. "SYL backs Aden", *Somali News,* 2 June 1967, p. 1.

242 Diary June 1, 1967. "SYL backs Aden", *Somali News,* 2 June 1967, p. 1.

243 Diary, June 1, 1967.

244 "La decisione del partito non è la Vittorio di un individuo o di un gruppo – Lo ha affermato il Segretario Generale della SYL", *Corriere della Somalia,* 4 giugno 1967, pp. 1, 4.

245 "Necessaria la disciplina del partito", *Corriere della Somalia,* 4 giugno 1967, pp. 1, 3.

246 "SNC changes name", Mogadiscio Somalia Domestic 21 April 1965 published in *DAILY REPOR T. Foreign Radio Broadcasts (FBIS-FRB-65-077), 22 April 1965.*

247 "SNC to support Aden interview with Jumale", *Somali News,* 5 May 1967, p. 2. Abdirizak Haji Hussein however believed that other members of the SNC party voted for Abdirashid Ali Sharmarke, on promise of ministerial posts, which is plausible since some of them rejoined the SYL and were appointed to such positions. Hussein, *My role in the formation of the Somali nation-state,* p. 262.

248 "HDAS Party backs Aden", *Somali News,* 12 May 1967, p. 1.

249 "Party", *Somali News,* 5 May 1967, p. 2.

250 Abdirazak Haji Hussein, *My role in the foundation of the Somali nation-state, a political memoir*, ed. Abdisalam Issa-Salwe (Trenton, NJ: The Red Sea Press, 2017), pp. 252-253.

251 Diary June 6, 1967.

252 "Somalia to send Troods (sic) to war", *Somali News,* 9 June 1967, p. 1.

253 "Seduta di emergenza dell'Assemblea Nazionel – Per discutere la situazione nel Medio Oriente", *Corriere della Somalia,* 7 giugno 1967, p. 1.

254 "Somalia to send Troods (sic) to war", *Somali News,* 9 June 1967, p. 1.

255 "Chiesta per gli aerei militari somali il sorvolo dell'Etiopia", *Corriere della Somalia,* 8 giugno 1967, p. 1.

256 "Votata per acclamazione la mozione governativa, auspicante la pace nel diritto e nella libertà – Ieri all'Assemblea Legislativa", *Corriere della Somalia,* 3 novembre 1956, pp. 1, 4.

257 'Costituto il "Comitato della Somalia per il soccorso ai martiri dell'Egitto" – Significativo successo delle sottoscrizioni", *Corriere della Somalia,* 4 dicembre 1956, p. 2.

258 TNA FO 371/125676.

259 "Gli aiuti per Port Said – Ringrazimento del Console egiziano", *Corriere della Somalia*, 22 giugno 1957, p. 2.

260 "Aden promises help for all Arab states", *Somali News,* 9 June 1967, p. 1.

261 "Messaggio dell'Emiro del Kuwait al Presidente della Repubblica – In risposta al messaggio inviato precedentemente", *Corriere della Somalia,* 10 giugno 1967, p. 1.

262 Diary April 2, 1967. The lawyer consulted by Scek Mukhtar, the President of the National Assembly, was Avv. Gaetano Chapron, the Assembly's legal advisor.

263 "Abdirashid chosen", *Somali News,* 16 June 1967, p. 1.

264 Martin Meredith, *The State of Africa: A History of the Continent since Independence* (London: Simon & Schuster, 2011), insert page number.

## SECTION ONE, PART FIVE
## OUT OF PUBLIC OF OFFICE........................................ *Notes to page* 137-155

265 "Riunito il Comitato Centrale della Lega dei Giovani Somali", *Corriere della Somalia,* 19 dicembre 1967, p. 4.

266 "L'ex Presidente Aden Abdulla Osman primo Vice Presidente del Congresso Islamico – Un riconoscimento per la Somalia", *Corriere della Somalia,* 27 settembre 1967, p. 1.

267 "Somalia welcomes Motamar – President Aden will open Sixth World Muslim Conference on Sunday", *Somali News,* 25 December 1963,

p. 1; "Conferenza Mondiale Islamica inizierà domani i suoi lavori – Molte delegazioni sono giunte", *Corriere della Somalia,* 26 dicembre 1964, p. 1.

268 Diary, 30 June 1968.

## SECTION ONE, PART SIX
## THE PRESIDENT ASSASSINATED........................... *Notes to page* **155-165**

269 La Somalia non e' un isola (2010), p. 57.

270 Diary, 23 October 1969; Abdirizak Haji Hussein, *My role,* pp. 301-302.

271 Diary, 23 October 1969.

## SECTION ONE, PART SEVEN
## BIDDING ABDULLAHI ISSA FAREWELL
## (1922-1988)........................................................................*Note to page* **173**

272 Diary, 12 October 1966.

# APPENDIX 1: LIST OF SYL CENTRAL COMMITTEE

On 31 March, 1947, the party Congress has elected the members of the SYL Central Committee (Somalia Courier, 16 April, 1947)

| | | |
|---|---|---|
| 1. | Hagi Mohamed Hussein, | President |
| 2. | Ali Sciddo Abdi (called Dorre), | Vice President |
| 3. | Yassin Hagi Osman, | Secretary-General |
| 4. | Abdullahi Issa, | Assistant Secretary-General |
| 5. | Scek Issa Mohamed, | Cashier Generale |
| 6. | Mohamed Hagi Osman, | School Superintendant |
| 7. | Ali Osman, | Cash Verifier |
| 8. | Osman Scek Mao, | Cash Verifier |
| 9. | Mohamed Ahmed Elmi "Ottavio", | Interior Inspector |
| 10. | Sheik Mohamoud "Malingour", | Interior Inspector |
| 11. | Sugulle Mohamed Mohamoud, | Member |
| 12. | Abdulkadir Mohamed "Zoppo", | Member |
| 13. | Yassin Osman Yousuf, | Membr |
| 14. | Ahmed Scire Egal "Lawaha", | Member |
| 15. | Ali Moallim Mohamed, | Member |

## 1948 SYL Central Committee members (PRO, "FO" 1015/51)

| | | |
|---|---|---|
| 1. | Hagi Mohamed Hussein, | President |
| 2. | Ahmed Scire Addaue, | Vice President |
| 3. | Abdullahi Issa, | Secretary-General |
| 4. | Osman Mohamoud, | Assistant Secretary-General |
| 5. | Sceikh Issa Mohamed, | Cashier |
| 6. | Mohamed Auale Liban, | member |
| 7. | Abdirascid Ali Sciarmarche, | member |

| | |
|---|---|
| 8. Ali Moallim Mohamoud, | member |
| 9. Osman Sceikh Mao, | member |
| 10. Dahir Hagi Osman, | member |
| 11. Ali Hersi Farah, | member |
| 12. Sceikh Mohamed Osman, | member |
| 13. Mohamed Ahmed Elmi "Ottavio", | member |
| 14. Sceikh Mohamoud "Malingour", | member |

## 1949 SYL Central Committee Members (ASMAE, Box 9, File 11)

| | |
|---|---|
| 1. Hagi Mohamed Hussein, | President |
| 2. Ahmed Scire Addaue, | Vice President |
| 3. Abdullahi Issa, | Secretary-General |
| 4. Scek Issa Mohamed, | Cashier |
| 5. Mohamed Ahmed "Ottavio", | Inspector |
| 6. Scekh Mohamoud "Malingour", | Inspector |
| 7. Sceikh Mohamed "Occhiali", | member |
| 8. Mohamed Auale Liban, | member |
| 9. Abdirascis Ali Scermarche, | member |
| 10. Dahir Hagi Osman, | member |
| 11. Osman Sceikh Mao, | member |
| 12. Ali Moallim, | member |
| 13. Ali Herzi, | member |

## 1950 SYL Central Committee Members (Il Corriere della Somalia, no.37 of May 15, 1950)

| | |
|---|---|
| 1. Hagi Mohamed Hussen, | President |
| 2. Ahmed Addaue Hassan, | Vice President |
| 3. Abdullahi Issa, | Secretay-General |
| 4. Hagi Farah, | Vice Secretary-General |
| 5. Scek Issa Mohamoud, | Cashier |
| 6. Ali Hersi Farah, | member |
| 7. Scek Mohamoud Malingour, | member |

| | |
|---|---|
| 8. Ali Moallim Mohamed, | member |
| 9. Mohamed Yousuf Aden "Muro", | member |
| 10. Mohamed Ossoble Adde, | member |
| 11. Hussein Scek Hassan, | member |
| 12. Mohamed Ahmed Elmi "Ottavio", | member |
| 13. Osman Scek Mao, | member |
| 14. Dahir Hagi Osman, | member |
| 15. Hagi Omar Scego, | member |

## 1952 SYL Central Committee members (ASMAE, AFIS, Box 4, File 16)

| | |
|---|---|
| 1. Hagi Farah Ali Omar, | President |
| 2. Mohamed Osman Barba, | Vice President |
| 3. Abdullahi Issa, | General-Secretary |
| 4. Abdirascid Ali, | Vice General Secretary |
| 5. Sceikh Issa Mohamed, | Treasurer |
| 6. Mohamoud Yousuf "Muro", | member |
| 7. Ali Hersi Farah, | member |
| 8. Sceikh Mohamoud "Malingour", | member |
| 9. Mohamed Ahmed "Ottavio", | member |
| 10. Osman Sceikh Mao, | member |
| 11. Osman Ahmed Roble, | member |
| 12. Omar Banafunzi, | member |
| 13. Ali Moallim Mohamed, | member |
| 14. Abdi Hagi Mohamed, | member |
| 15. Mohamed Farah Kid, | member |
| 16. Hagi Mohamoud "Borracco", | member |
| 17. Hagi Mohamed Abdulle "Qurmone", | member |
| 18. Hagi Moussa Bogor, | member |
| 19. Mohamed Auale Liban, | member |

## 1953 SYL Central Committee members (PRO "FO" 371/108101).

| | |
|---|---|
| 1. Aden Abdulla Osman, | President |
| 2. Hagi Farah Ali Omar, | Vice President |
| 3. Abdullahi Issa, | Secretary-General |
| 4. Mohamoud Yousuf "Muro", | Assistant Secretary-General |
| 5. Sceikh Issa Mohamedd, | Cashier |
| 6. Hagi Mohamoud "Borracco", | member |
| 7. Abdi Hagi Mohamed, | member |
| 8. Hassan Barre Toho, | member |
| 9. Ali Moallim Mohamed, | member |
| 10. Ali Raghe Afrah, | member |
| 11. Osman Ahmed Roble, | member |
| 12. Osman Sceikh Mao, | member |
| 13. Ahmed Mohamed Ali "Allora", | member |
| 14. Sceikh Mohamoud "Malingour", | member |
| 15. Salad Aden Hassan "Yanyuro", | member |
| 16. Mohamed Ahmed Elmi "Ottavio", | member |
| 17. Omar Hagi Ali Banafunzi, | member |
| 18. Mohamed Sceikh Hassan Aden, | member |
| 19. Mohamed Ossoble Adde, | member |

## 1956 SYL Central Committee members (FO 371/118675)

| | |
|---|---|
| 1. Abdirazak Hagi Hussein, | President |
| 2. Abdi Mire Nour "Termus", | Vice President |
| 3. Mohamoud Yousuf Aden "Muro", | Secretary-General |
| 4. Scek Issa Mohamoud, | Treasurer |
| 5. Salad Aden Hassan, | member |
| 6. Mohamed Abdulla Farah, | member |
| 7. Dere Hagi Dere, | member |
| 8. Mohamed Ossoble Adde, | member |
| 9. Mohamoud Ahmed "Kutabahor", | member |
| 10. Hussen Auale Uehelie, | member |
| 11. Giama Khalaf Farah, | member |

| | |
|---|---|
| 12. Mohamed Sobrie Odasughe, | member |
| 13. Abdulkadir Issa Abdi, | member |
| 14. Ibrahim Moallim Ali Ade, | member |
| 15. Abdi Ali Mohamed, | member |
| 16. Mohamed Scek Aboukar Scek Ahmed, | member |

## 1957 Central Committee Members (Diario Aden Abdulla, 1958).

| | |
|---|---|
| 1. Hagi Mohamed Hussein, | President |
| 2. Aden Abdulla, | Vice President |
| 3. Bascir Scekh Hussen, | Secretary-General |
| 4. Scekh Issa Mohamed, | Cashier |
| 5. Mohamed Ossoble, | member |
| 6. Giumale Barre Toho, | member |
| 7. Hassan Barre Toho, | member |
| 8. Osman Ahmed Roble, | member |
| 9. Ali Moallim, | member |
| 10. Abdi Namous, | member |
| 11. Ahmed Ali "Allora", | member |
| 12. Hussein Abdi Abdulle "Farmacia", | member |
| 13. Mohamed Ahmed Elmi "Ottavio" | member |
| 14. Mohamed Ali "Sciandile", | member |
| 15. Ahmed Mohamed Hassan Darman | member |
| 16. Gouled Dini, | member |
| 17. Hagi Yousuf Egal, | member |
| 18. Ahmed Hagi Soliman, | member |
| 19. Osman Sceikh Mao, | member |

## 1958 SYL Central Committee Members (Diario Aden Abdulla, 1958).

| | |
|---|---|
| 1. Aden Abdulla Osman, | President |
| 2. Ali Hersi Farah, | Vice President |
| 3. Mohamed Hagi Sobrie, | General-Secretary |

| | |
|---|---|
| 4. Scekh Issa, | Treasurer |
| 5. Abdirazak Hagi, | member |
| 6. Sceikh Mohamoud "Malingour", | member |
| 7. Hussein Abdi Abdulle "Farmacia", | member |
| 8. Mohamed Ahmed Elmi "Ottavio", | member |
| 9. Hassan Barre Toho, | member |
| 10. Giumale Barre Toho, | member |
| 11. Ali Moallim Mohamed, | member |
| 12. Osman Ahmed Roble, | member |
| 13. Osman Scekh Mao, | member |
| 14. Hagi Abdisamad Mohamed, | member |
| 15. Mohamed Ossoble Ualaio, | member |
| 16. Abdinour Mohamed Hussen, | member |
| 17. Ali Afrah Iare, member | member |
| 18. Ahmadei Mohamed Nour, | member |
| 19. Mohamoud Mohamed "Kutuba-hor" | |

## 1959 SYL Central Committee Members (ASMAE, AFIS. 1959).

| | |
|---|---|
| 1. Sceikh Issa Mohamed, | President |
| 2. Nour Hasci Alas, | Vice President |
| 3. Mohamed Hagi Sobrie, | Secretary-General |
| 4. Scerif Mukhtar Ibrahim, | Cashier |
| 5. Ali Hersi Farah, | member |
| 6. Mohamed Ossoble "Ualaio", | member |
| 7. Abdi Dahir Farah, | member |
| 8. Abdurahman Hagi Moumin, | member |
| 9. Abdirazak Hagi Hussen, | member |
| 10. Mohamed Ahmed Elmi "Ottavio", | member |
| 11. Scekh Mohamed Issak, | member |
| 12. Osman Scekh Mao, | member |
| 13. Ali Moallim Mohamed, | member |
| 14. Abdurahman Omar, | member |
| 15. Hassan Barre Toho, | member |
| 16. Mohamed Aboukar Ibrahim, | member |

| | |
|---|---|
| 17. Hagi Abdisamed Mohamed, | member |
| 18. Mohamed Hagi Bile, | member |
| 19. Hersi Kheire Issak, | member |

## 1960 SYL Central Committee Members

| | |
|---|---|
| 1. Sheikh Mohamoud Mohamed Farah, | Secretary-General |
| 2. Abdurahman Hagi Mumin, | Vice Secretary-General |
| 3. Mohamed Abdi Kheire, | Administrative Secretary |
| 4. Mohamed Sheikh Dahir, | Cashier |
| 5. Bascir Ali Hagi Issa, | Inspector |
| 6. Hussein Abdi Abdulle "Farmacia", | Ispector |
| 7. Yusuf Mussa Abukar, | member |
| 8. Sherif Mukhtar Ibrahim, | member |
| 9. Abdi Dahir Farah, | member |
| 10. Mohamed Gianacow Giumale, | member |
| 11. Hagi Abdissamad Mohamed, | member |
| 12. Salad Elmi Mohamoud "Durua", | member |
| 13. Sheihk Mohamoud Mohamed Fighi,"Farur", | member |
| 14. Omar Hussein Abdi Alim, | member |
| 15. Osman Hagi Mohamed Afrah, | member |
| 16. Hagi Abdulkadir bin Aboubaker, | member |
| 17. Ahmed Egag Aboukar, | member |
| 18. Mrs Raha Egal | member |

19. Omar Hussein "Starlin" (Corriere della Somalia August 30, 1960)

## 1962 SYL Central Committee Members 1962 (Corriere dlla Somalia, Maggio, 12 1962)

| | |
|---|---|
| 1. Sheikh Mohamoud Mohamed Farah, | Secretary-General |
| 2. Abdurahman Haji Moumin, | Vice Secretary-General |
| 3. Mohamed Abdi Kheyre, | Administrative Secretary |
| 4. Sherif Muqtar Ibrahim, | Cashier General |
| 5. Hassano' Alio' Mursal, | Controller |
| 6. Abdi Dahir Farah, | Controller |

| | |
|---|---|
| 7. Mohamoud Abdinour "Juju", | member |
| 8. Sheikh Muctar Mohamed, | member |
| 9. Nour Hashi Alas, | member |
| 10. Haji Abdisamad Mohamed Matan, | member |
| 11. Abdullahi Haji Mohamoud "Insania", | member |
| 12. Osman Haji Mohamed Afrah, | member |
| 13. Hassan Ali Abdi, | member |
| 14. Ali Ga'al Afrah, | member |
| 15. Ahmed Mohamed Elmi "Ottavio", | member |
| 16. Haji Mohamed Nour Sheikh Hussein, | member |
| 17. Bashir Haji Ali, | member |
| 18. Hassan Barre Toho, | member |
| 19. Mohamed said Iyow "Gentleman" | Member |
| 20. Omar Hassan "Stalin", | member |
| 21. Omar Hussein Abdi Calin "Gurei" | Member |

## 1963 SYL Central Committee Members 1963 (Corriere della Somalia Luglio 30, 1963)

| | |
|---|---|
| 1. Yassin Nour Hassan: | Secretary-General |
| 2. Dere Hagi Dere, | Member |
| 3. Sheikh Mukhtar Mohamed, | Member |
| 4. Ali Sheikh Gess Mohallim, | Member |
| 5. Bascir Ali Hagi, | Member |
| 6. Sheikh Mohamoud Mohamed Farah, | Member |
| 7. Abdurahman Hagi Mumin, | Member |
| 8. Abdi Gis, | Member |
| 9. Mohamed Ali Dorre, | Member |
| 10. Osman Hussein Qorei, | Member |
| 11. Mohamed Sheikh gabio, | Member |
| 12. Aden Osman Impero, | Member |
| 13. Osman Mohamed Afrah, | Member |
| 14. Abdi Hasan Boni, | Member |
| 15. Omar Starlin, | Member |
| 16. Mohamed Ahmed Elmi "Ottavio", | Member |
| 17. Sheikh Mohamud Mohamed Farah, | Member |

| | |
|---|---|
| 18. Mohamed Aboukar Yero, | Member |
| 19. Mohamed Sheikh Mohamed Tahir, | Member |
| 20. Mohamwed Gianoco Giumale, | Member |
| 21. Dahir Nour Egal, | Member |
| 22. Abdinour Mohamed Hussein, | Member |
| 23. Mohamed Abdi Amalo, | Member |

## 1964 SYL Central Committee members 1964 (Somali News November 27, 1964)

| | |
|---|---|
| 1. Abdirazak Haji Hussein: | Secretary-General |
| 2. Mohamed Jama Badmah: | Vice Secretary-General |
| 3. Ali Mohamed Hirave: | Administrative Secretary |
| 4. Mohamed Hassan Nour "Jasti": | Treasurer |
| 5. Mohamed Sheikh Gabio, | Member |
| 6. Salad Abdi Mohamoud, | Member |
| 7. Omar Osman Yabe, | Member |
| 8. Ugas Yassin Abdurahman, | Member |
| 9. Mohamed Ahmed Elmi "Ottavio", | Member |
| 10. Abdi Bulle Aden, | Member |
| 11. Aden Osman "Impero", | Member |
| 12. Dahir Nour Egal, | Member |
| 13. Nour Mohamed Hussein "Afkoro", | member |
| 14. Sheikh Mohamoud Mohamed Fighi, "Farur", | Member |
| 15. Ahmed Hassan Ali "Giudicino" | Member |
| 16. Ali Garad Giama, | Member |
| 17. Muqtar Ibrahim Hussein, | Member |
| 18. Rashid Sultan Abdillahi, | Member |
| 19. Sheikh Omar Qorei, | Member |
| 20. Omar Hassan "Istalin", | Member |
| 21. Hussein Abdi Abdulla "Farmacia", | Member |
| 22. Mohamed Aboukar "Yarow", | Member |
| 23. Hussein Hire Abdi, | Member |

## 1967 SYL Central Committee members 1967 (Corriere della Somalia, Luglio 30, 1967)

| | |
|---|---|
| 1. Abdirazak H. Hussein: | Secretary-General |
| 2. Mohamed Jamac Badmah | Assistant Secretary-General |
| 3. Haji Ibrahim O. Fod,"Basbas", | Member |
| 4. Ali Garad Jama, | Member |
| 5. Jama Nour, | Member |
| 6. Salad Abdi Mohamoud, | Member |
| 7. Ugas Yassin Abdirahman, | Member |
| 8. Hussein Hire, | Membr |
| 9. Ahmed Ali Hassan "Giudicino", | Membr |
| 10. Abdi Bulle Aden, | Member |
| 11. Mohamed Aboukar "Yero", | Member |
| 12. Mohamed Hassan Nour "Jasti", | Member |
| 13. Nour Mohamed Hussein "Afkoro", | Member |
| 14. Haji Ali Ghedi Shador, | Member |
| 15. Sheikh Mohamed Mohamoud "Farur", | Member |
| 16. Hussein Abdi Abdulle "Farmacia", | Member |
| 17. Muqtar Ibrahim Hussein, | Member |
| 18. Mohamed Sheikh Gabio, | Member |
| 19. Omar Hassan "Stalin", | Member |
| 20. Mohamed Ahmed Elmi "Ottavio", | Member |
| 21. Abdi Dahir Farah | Member |
| 22. Omar Hussein "Qorei", | Member |

## 1968 SYL Central Committee Members 1968 (Somali News March 8, 1968)

| | |
|---|---|
| 1. Mohamed Haji I. Egal: | Party Leader |
| 2. Ali Mohamed Hirave: | Secretary-General |
| 3. Mohamed Jama Badmah | Assistant Secretary-General |
| 4. Ahmed Gure Mamun | Administrative Secretary |
| 5. Salad Abdi Mohamoud | Treasurer General |
| 6. Hussein Ali Ebrow Talasso | Controler |
| 7. Ahmed Hassan Ali "Giudicino" | Controller |

| | |
|---|---|
| 8. Ahmed Qumane Roble, | Member |
| 9. Haji Mussa Boqor Osman, | Member |
| 10. Haji Abdurahman Mohamed Hassan, | Member |
| 11. Haji Yousuf Egal, | Member |
| 12. Mohamed Hassan Nour "Jasti", | Member |
| 13. Garad Ali Garad Jama, | Member |
| 14. Abdurahman Haji Moumin, | Member |
| 15. Islaw Osman Nour Amir, | Member |
| 16. Hassan Aden Haji Mohamed, | Member |
| 17. Sheikh Omar Sheikh Hassan, | Member |
| 18. Hussein Omar Hassan, | Member |
| 19. Ahmed Mohamed Ali "Allora", | Member |
| 20. Haji Ali Aden, | Member |
| 21. Yousuf Shire Barre, | Member |
| 22. Haji Ali Ghedi Shador, | Member |
| 23. Mohamed Ahmed Elmi "Ottavio" | Member |
| 24. Ali Sheikh Jes Moallim "Sciopero", | Member |

# APPENDIX 2: FAREWELL SPEECH

## FAREWELL SPEECH FROM PRESIDENT ADEN ABDULLA OSMAN TO THE SOMALI PEOPLE

In the last months of his presidency, the President felt he needed to give his country one last measure of himself. He composed his Farewell Address to the Somali people, which urged his fellow citizens to cherish the Union and avoid discord. He said:

People of Somalia,

After seven years in the highest post of the State, I am handing over the reins to my successor who has democratically been elected by our representatives in the Parliament. It is normal and right these sons of our Country should avail themselves in this way of their responsibilities as representatives of the people

From six o'clock on the evening of 30th of this month, I shall be serving you in another capacity, that of Deputy, in the National Assembly according to the provision of the Constitution. I have faith in the future of our Country which is in the hands of men who have emerged and who will emerge from this new situation. These men had served the Nation in the past and will not fail to give the best of themselves, each one in his own capacity, strong in experience and with the support of those of us who wish to put the interest of our Country above everything and everybody.

I offer my most sincere gratitude for the high honor which has been accorded me, and the trust that has been put in me over the last seven years by every one of you People of Somalia, by your representatives in the Parliament, by the government that have borne the burdens of State, by the Judiciary, by the Armed Forces and those other bodies, organized in the same way, and the Civil Service, from the highest officials to the humblest soldier, and constable and doorman.

Since independence and up to the present day our Country has known many difficult moments, but it has always been able to emerge from these ever stronger, thanks God, to our democratic system and to the self-sacrifice of all men and women of good will, and I am certain that it will be able to overcome every adversity if we, its children, can remain always united rejecting once and for all every prejudice and personal resentments. To encourage these would be a serious crime and most hurtful to the Country.

I am grateful, and I thank you, my brothers, for that maturity in democratic institutions which you have shown the world distinguishing yourselves notably among the newly emerged Nations, and I exhort you to continue in the same path paying particular attention to the sector of economic production in our Country, success in which, can go a long way towards the providing solutions to our most difficult problems of every kind. Without battering our economy through the combined efforts of all, government and People alike, we cannot resolve any of our most important problems.

Nor we must neglect or forget respect and preservation for our Faith and Islamic culture and customs. Our culture cannot be considered apart from our religion. Consider that, if we Muslims leave our Islamic culture we shall lose our piety and we shall experience a social dissolution and disintegration. It is vital, therefore, to defend our Islamic Society against the influx of anti-Muslim sentiments, and especially against atheistic materialism.

Finally, as well as you, citizens of the Republic, my greetings go out to our brothers still suffering under a foreign domination , and I promise them that all Somalis, and all free Somalis, have not forgotten them. We believe in the justice of their cause and, in the mercy of Allah, their aspirations to liberty, are sacrosanct.

My brothers,

I offer my fraternal greetings to all. May God protect Somalia. Long live Somalia!

# APPENDIX 3: IMAGES

# 1. GENERAL IMAGES - OFFICIALS & DIGNITARIES

**Figure 1:** Aden Abdulla, Avv. G. Chapron and Ambassador Mario Di Stefano. Di Stefano was the fourth and last Administrator of Somalia (1958-1960).

**Figure 2:** Mogadiscio. His Excellency Ambassador Giovanni Fornari receiving military honours in Viale Cristoforo Colombo, popularly known as "Secondo Lido"

**Figure 3:** Ambassador Giovanni Fornari, the first Administrator of Somalia (1950-1953) reviewing army unit (Corpo di Sicurezza) stationed in Belet Uen.

**Figure 4:** Ambassador Enrico Martino, the second Administrator of Somalia (1953-1955) welcoming a group of Somali Police Officers after completing training course in Italy.

**Figure 5:** Ambassador Enrico Anzilotti, third Administrator of Somalia, accompanied by Minister Hagi Moussa Bogor and Dr. Piero Franca, Secretary General of the Trusteeship Administration.

**Figure 6:** Ambassador Enrico Anzilotti and his spouse returning to Mogadiscio by sea from Italy.

**Figure 7:** Abdullahi Issa Mohamoud, a veteran politician.

**Figure 8:** President Aden Abdulla with Emperor Haile Sellassie of Ethiopia.

Il Ministro degli Esteri Fanfani e il «Premier» Eg
l'Ospite è appena giunto in Somalia per la sua visita ufficia
di quattro giorni. L'accoglienza si è già rivelata calorosa, a
dirittura commovente. Il Ministro Fanfani sosta ad ammira
lo spettacolo della folla plaudente. Poi suonano gli inni italia
no e somalo. I due uomini di Governo li ascoltano sull'attent

L'arrivo del Ministro degli Esteri d'Italia ricevuto dal Primo Ministro Egal

**Figure 9:** 1968. The Italian Foreign Minister Amintore Fanfani was welcomed at Mogadiscio airport by Premier Mohamed Ibrahim Egal and General Mohamed Siad Barre, the Commander in Chief of the Somali National Army

**Figure 10:** 1967 Hon. Sheikh Ali Giumale, a prominent politician elected from Belet Uen Constituency and Leader of the opposition SNC Party,

**Figure 11:** Dr. Haji NA Noor Muhammad, a learned Judge from India, served as Vice President of the Supreme Court and Legal Advisor to the Prime Minister of Somalia.

**Figure 12:** General Umberto Ripa di Meana, Chief of the Somali Police Force (1951-1956).

# 2. BELET UEN IMAGES

**Figure 13:** Aden Abdulla's old house in Belet Uen.

**Figure 14: Image 1/2:** School girls in Belet Uen with Signora Lucia De Menna, the teacher.

**Figure 15:**

Mogadiscio 1929. Nurses at Giacomo De Martino Hospital. Aden Abdulla is number 21 in the photo group.

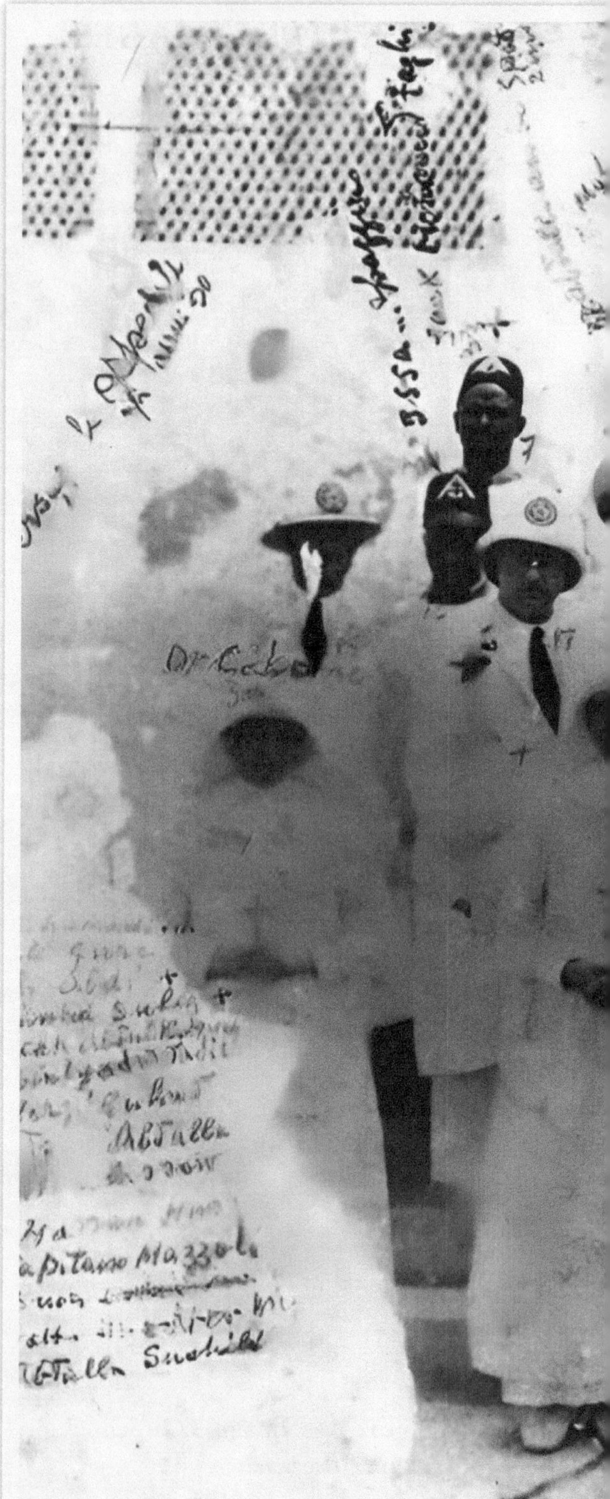

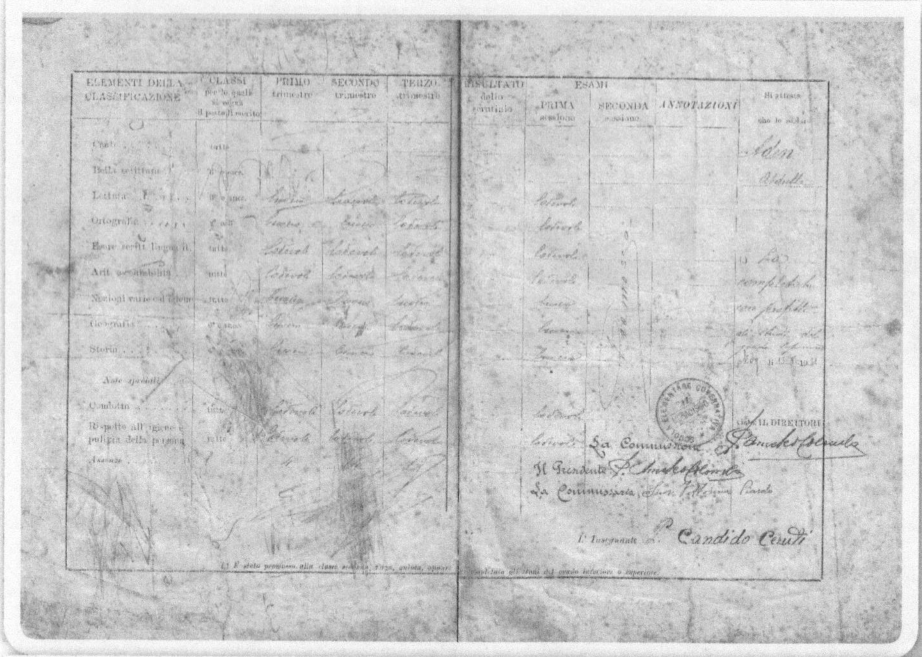

ELEMENTI DELLA CLASSIFICAZIONE | CLASSI | PRIMO trimestre | SECONDO trimestre | TERZO trimestre | RISULTATO dello scrutinio | ESAMI PRIMA sessione | SECONDA sessione | ANNOTAZIONI

Canto; Bella scrittura; Lettura; Ortografia; Esercizi scritti lingua it.; Aritmetica e contabilità; Nozioni varie e elementi; Geografia; Storia; Note speciali; Condotta; Rispetto all'igiene e pulizia della persona; Assenze

Aden Abdulla

IL DIRETTORE

La Commissione

Il Presidente

L'Insegnante Candido Ceruti

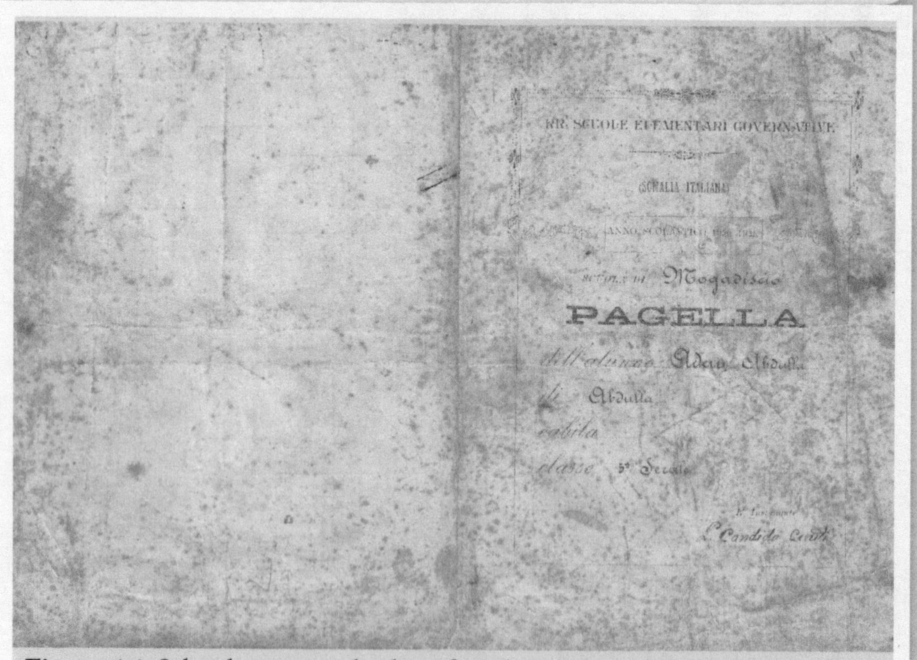

RR. SCUOLE ELEMENTARI GOVERNATIVE

(SOMALIA ITALIANA)

ANNO SCOLASTICO

Mogadiscio

PAGELLA

dell'alunno Adan Abdulla

di Abdulla

cabila

classe 5ª Serale

L'Insegnante Candido Ceruti

**Figure 16:** School report with a list of student Aden Abdulla's grades in the subjects studied at the elementary school level in 1933.

**Figure 17:** The swinging bridge (Liqliqato) over the Shabeelle River

**Figure 18:** Large gathering of local authorities and other people to mark the Independence Day, 1st July 1960, in Belet Uen. The presence of Padre Salvatore Colombo among the public is striking.

**Figure 19:** Belet Uen Ark. Erected to immortalize the date of 1 July 1960.

**Figure 20:** This is the Ark erected in Belet Uen on the occasion of 1st July, 1960. The photo shows, among others, the Governor of Hiran at the time, Hussein Nour Elmi and the District Commissioner of Belet Uen, Osman Moallim Abdulla.

**Figure 21:** Rare photo of Aden Abdulla's family members.